EUREKA!

Also by Peter Jones

Vote for Caesar

*Learn Latin: The Book of the
Daily Telegraph QED series*

Veni Vidi Vici

EUREKA!
EVERYTHING YOU EVER WANTED TO KNOW ABOUT THE
ANCIENT GREEKS
BUT WERE AFRAID TO ASK

PETER JONES

Atlantic Books
London

First published in hardback in Great Britain in 2014 by Atlantic Books,
an imprint of Atlantic Books Ltd.

1 2 3 4 5 6 7 8 9

A CIP catalogue record for this book is available from the British Library.

Hardback ISBN: 978-1-78239-514-0
E-book ISBN: 978-1-78239-515-7
Paperback ISBN: 978-1-78239-516-4

Designed by Carrdesignstudio.com
Printed and bound by CPI Group (UK) Ltd, Croydon, CR0 4YY

Atlantic Books
An Imprint of Atlantic Books Ltd
Ormond House
26–27 Boswell Street
London
WC1N 3JZ
www.atlantic-books.co.uk

CONTENTS

Maps   vii

Introduction   xiii

I   2000–800 BC

From Bronze Age to Dark Age   3

II   800–725 BC

Competing for glory

Olympics and the Olympian gods   31

III   725–700 BC

From Homeric hero to Hesiod's peasants   47

IV   c. 700–593 BC

Tyranny, poetry and speculation   75

V   593–493 BC

Athens: from tyranny to democracy   109

VI   493–450 BC

From Persian empire to Athenian – tyranny?   143

VII   450–421 BC

Athens v. Sparta: the Peloponnesian War   181

VIII 421–399 BC
Athens capitulates: the execution of Socrates   229

IX 399–362 BC
City-states at war in Greece   255

X 360–336 BC
The rise of Macedon: Philip II takes over Greece   277

XI 336–322 BC
Alexander the Great and the end of democracy   293

XII 322–229 BC
After Alexander: the empire divided   313

XIII 229–146 BC
Macedon falls to Rome   339

XIV 146–27 BC
The end of Alexander's empire   347

Epilogue: the survival of Greek literature   360
Reading list   373
Index   377
A note on the author   384

MAPS

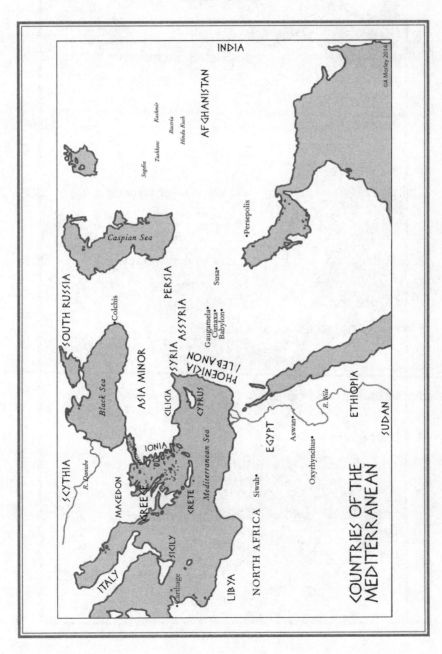

COUNTRIES OF THE
MEDITERRANEAN

INDIA

AFGHANISTAN

©A Morley 2014

Kashmir

Bactria

Tashkent

Hindu Kush

Sogdia

Caspian Sea

•Persepolis

SOUTH RUSSIA

PERSIA

Susa•

Colchis•

ASSYRIA

SYRIA

Gaugamela•
Cunaxa•
Babylon•

ASIA MINOR

CILICIA

PHOENICIA /
LEBANON

Black Sea

CYPRUS

SCYTHIA

R. Nile

ETHIOPIA

IONIA

R. Danube

SUDAN

MACEDON

EGYPT

Aswan•

GREECE

Oxyrhynchus•

CRETE

Mediterranean Sea

Siwah•

ITALY

SICILY

NORTH AFRICA

LIBYA

•Carthage

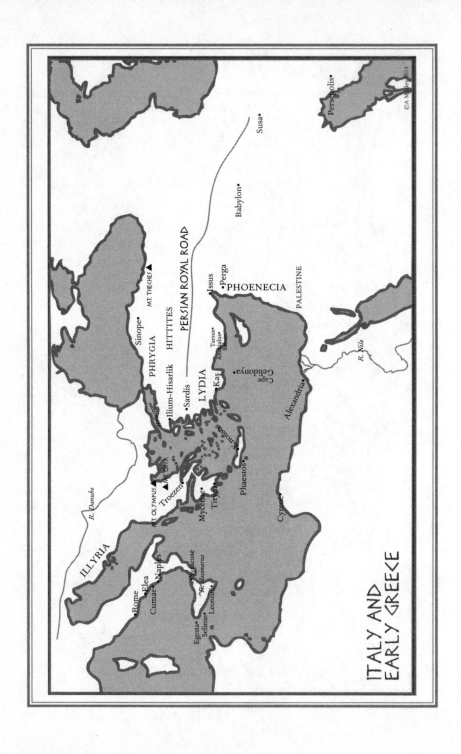

ITALY AND
EARLY GREECE

©A Mobley 2014

Persepolis•

Susa•

Babylon•

PERSIAN ROYAL ROAD

Issus• •Perga
PHOENECIA

Sinope• MT. THECHES▲
PHRYGIA HITTITES
Ilium-Hisarlik
•Sardis PALESTINE
LYDIA
Tarsus•
Anemalus•
Kas Soli•
Cape Gelidonya•
R. Nile
Alexandria•
Knossos•

MT. OSSA▲
MT. OLYMPUS▲
Troezen• Phaestos•
Mycenae• •Tiryns
R. Danube
Cyrene•

ILLYRIA

•Rome
•Elea
Cumae•Naples
Syracuse•
•Pithecusae
Egesta• Leontini•
Selinus•

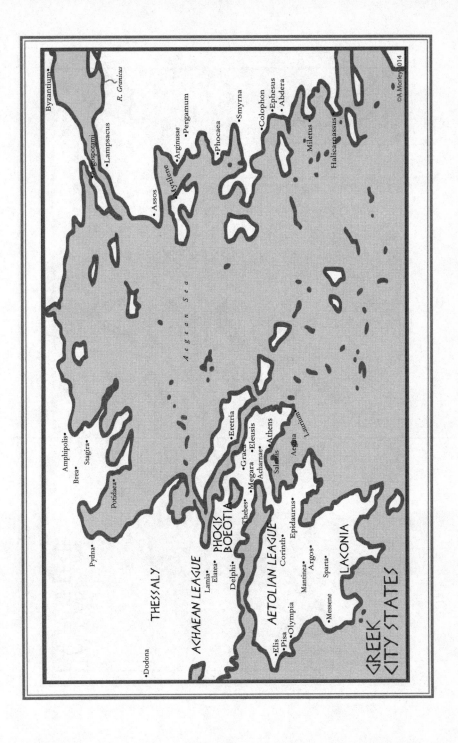

GREEK
CITY STATES

THESSALY

ACHAEAN LEAGUE

PHOCIS
BOEOTIA

AETOLIAN LEAGUE

LACONIA

Aegean Sea

R. Granicus

Byzantium•

•Lampsacus

Aegospotami•

•Assos

Mytilene•
•Arginusae
•Pergamum

•Phocaea

•Smyrna

Colophon•
•Ephesus
•Abdera

•Miletus

Halicarnassus•

•Amphipolis
Brea•

Stagira•

Potidaea•

Pydna•

•Dodona

Lamia•
Elatea•

Delphi•

Thebes•

•Eretria

•Graea
Megara• •Eleusis
Acharnae• •Athens
Salamis•
Aegina•
Laurium•

Corinth•
Epidaurus•

Mantinea• •Argos

Elis•
Pisa•
Olympia•

Sparta•

•Messene

©A Morley 014

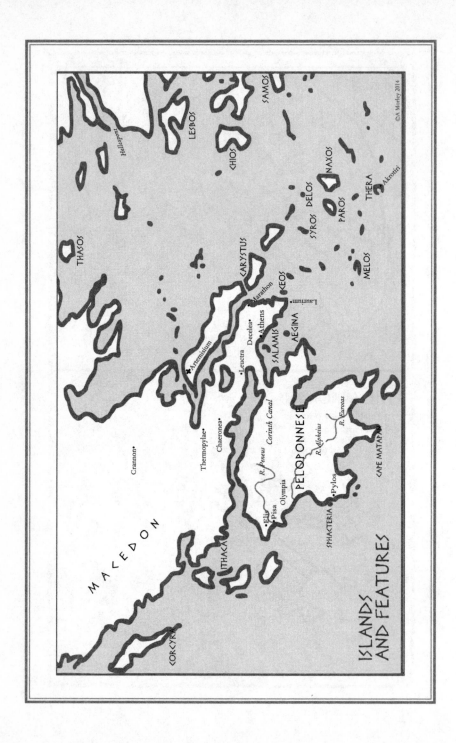

ISLANDS AND FEATURES

©A Morley 2014

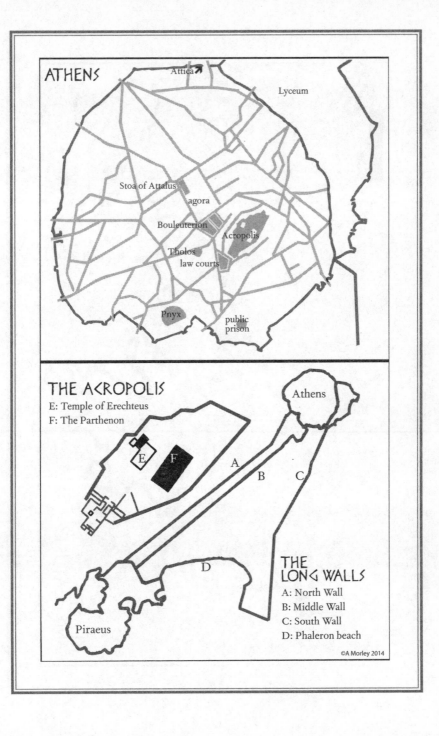

INTRODUCTION

I f the Greek philosopher Plato is to be believed, the story of this
book goes back 12,000 years – all the way to Atlantis. But he was
making that story up, so it goes back a mere 3,000 years or so, from
the Minotaur's Crete and the Trojan War to the Olympic Game (yes: it
all started with just the one), the invention of our alphabet, the West's
very first literature (the epics of the *Iliad* and *Odyssey*), the Persian
wars, the subsequent ferocious conflict for mastery of Greece between
Athens and Sparta, the emergence of Philip II of Macedon and his son
Alexander the Great, Alexander's conquest of the East as far as India,
and the gradual collapse of that 'empire' before the unstoppable march
of that new power to the West – Rome. It ends in 27 BC, when the last
piece of Greek territory receives a Roman governor.

Further along that sometimes inspiring, sometimes dispiriting way,
the immense influence of the ancient Greeks on our world will emerge.
At almost every point of Western thinking about politics, literature,
mathematics, art, architecture, drama, philosophy, education, war,
sex, medicine, cosmology, astronomy, biology, the body, the emotions,
ethics, linguistics, death, logic, race, slavery, history, quite apart from the
wonderful worlds of myths and oracles, the Greeks are somewhere there.

The book (for the title *Eureka!*, see p. 79) adopts the same format
as my *Veni Vidi Vici* (Atlantic Books, 2013). Each chapter begins with

a timeline and a broad summary of the chapter's contents, followed by a series of brief 'nuggets', some fleshing out the summary, others digressing into different areas of interest.

But the contrast with *Veni Vidi Vici* will soon become apparent. The history of Rome offers a coherent story of one highly influential city that, between 700 BC – AD 500, came to dominate much of Europe, North Africa and the Near East. But neither Athens nor Sparta nor any other Greek community ever dominated as Rome did.

As a result, the ancient Greek world lacks such intense focus. Consequently, while this account will be chronological, it will not tell a single story, but concentrate on the various differing big players as they emerge over the centuries, and over the Mediterranean too. For the Greeks, who mistrusted the sea, were still great adventurers, always on the lookout for the main chance and new experiences, and they established cities all over the Mediterranean and the Black Sea. That said, there will be a bias towards Athens, because for all its disappointments after its glory years in the fifth and fourth centuries BC, its achievements at that time still electrify the imagination.

Jeannie Cohen (she and I run the charity *Friends of Classics*) read the whole book in its various forms and made countless improvements. I am most grateful to Martin West for permission to use his superb translations of Hesiod (*Hesiod: Theogony, Works and Days*, Oxford, 1988) and the Greek lyric poets (*Greek Lyric Poetry*, Oxford, 1993) and, as ever, to Andrew Morley for the maps.

Peter Jones

Newcastle on Tyne

June 2014

NAMES AND NUMBERS

GREEK NAMES

Greek names in English have, by historical convention, been adapted from Latin. Sometimes they are virtually identical in the three languages: Greek *Periklês*, Latin *Pericles*, English Pericles. At other times, the Greek and Latin are similar, but the English different: Greek *Aristotelês*, Latin *Aristoteles*, but English Aristotle. Sometimes the Latin (and so the English) are very different from the Greek: *Thoukudidês*, *Thucydides*, Thucydides (pronounced 'Thewsiddiddees').

Note that the Greek long *ô* was pronounced 'or', and the Greek long *ê* was pronounced 'air'. So *Hellênes* was pronounced 'Hellairness', *arkhôn* 'arkhorn'. On this convention, see my *An Intelligent Person's Guide to the Classics* (Bloomsbury 1999, Appendix 1).

The long mark ^ is applied only to transliterated Greek words in italics, not to their English form. Thus *Periklês*, exactly representing the Greek, but Pericles in English. Observe that the Greek *k* becomes the English c (*drakhma*: drachma), and the Greek *u* becomes the English y (*Olumpikos*: Olympic).

GREEK MONEY, WEIGHTS AND DISTANCES

Obol[os] is the lowest unit of money:

6 *oboloi* = 1 *drakhma*, lit. 'handful'

100 *drakhmai* = 1 *m(i)na*

60 *m(i)nai* = 1 talent

These are related to the weight of the coins. On the Attic standard, an obol is about 0.72 grams, a drachma 4.31 grams, a mina 431 grams (about 1 lb), a talent 25.86 kg (about 60 lb). Other cities adopted different weight standards.

VALUE OF MONEY

As ever, there are no meaningful correspondences between ancient Greek money and ours. One calculation suggests that, for a family of four in Athens c. 400 BC, the cost of living varied from 2.5 to 6 obols a day (see p. 178-9 on pay for jury service and p. 247 on pay for attending the Assembly). The pay for a skilled craftsman varied from 6 to 9 obols (1 to 1.5 drachmas) a day.

DISTANCES

These are given in modern measurements, roughly equivalent to the Greek ones. Thus the 200 metres of the first Olympic game (p. 37) represent one *stadion* in Greek (whence 'stadium').

WHO WERE THE GREEKS?

When 'ancient Greeks' are being discussed, it is usually assumed that they are people who live in Greece. But Greeks did *not* think of themselves first and foremost in that way. What made them Greek, as the historian Herodotus tells us in the fifth century BC, was not their location but their shared stock, language, culture and gods (but not politics, interestingly). And Herodotus meant it, because Greeks established settlements all over the Mediterranean, 'like frogs around a pond' (as Plato put it), without compromising their Greekness.

So to talk of 'ancient Greece' and 'ancient Greeks', is not to imply a politically unified country and people as in, for instance, 'England' and 'the English', but people who spoke Greek and lived, in their own separate, autonomous Greek communities, not only on the Greek mainland but also (in time) in Asia Minor (roughly modern Turkey), the Black Sea, the Near East, parts of North Africa, southern Italy, Sicily and the coastal regions of southern France (Gaul) and Spain.
Nor did their common heritage mean they all lived in harmony. On the Greek mainland, in particular, these independent communities – Athenians, Spartans, Thebans, Corinthians and so on – were regularly at each other's throats.

Hint: every time you come across a place-name, find it on the map. That will make the point most forcefully that not all Greeks lived in

Greece, let alone in Athens. Greeks lived and worked all over the place. Indeed, Greeks living on the west coast of Asia Minor (Turkey) were, arguably, the originators of 'the Greek miracle'.

Finally, and rather surprisingly, Greeks did not call themselves 'Greeks': they called themselves *Hellênes* and their country *Hellas* (see p. 46), and still do. Why, then, do we call them 'Greeks' and say they lived in 'Greece'? Because of the Romans, as usual, who were captivated by Greek language and culture and transmitted so much of it to us. They called the people *Graeci* ('Gr-eye-kee') and the country *Graecia*, and we anglicized the Roman forms into 'Greeks' and 'Greece'.

And why did the Romans call them that? We do not know, but see p. 79 for two possible guesses.

I

2000–800 BC

TIMELINE

2000–1600 BC	Minoan Crete – the golden age
c. 1600 BC	The explosion of Minoan Thera
1600–1150 BC	Late Bronze Age; the rise and fall of 'Mycenaean' Greeks
1450 BC	Mycenaeans move into Knossos
1400 BC	(Greek) Linear B writing
1350 BC	Knossos destroyed
c. 1200 BC	Mycenaean attack on Hisarlik?
c. 1150–800 BC	End of Bronze Age society and culture; the Dark Ages

FROM
BRONZE AGE
TO DARK AGE

This is a much debated period of history because we have virtually no written sources for it. Two peoples and one site will dominate the greatly simplified story of the Bronze Age world presented here: Minoan Cretans; Mycenaean Greeks; and Hisarlik, a site of major importance in what is now north-west Turkey (Asia Minor) at the entrance to the Dardanelles.

Crete at this period is called 'Minoan' merely because Minos was a famous mythical king of Crete and Knossos' excavator Sir Arthur Evans decided to call it that; but – this is important – Crete at this time was not inhabited by Greeks. Who the inhabitants were, we do not know.

From about 2100 to 1700 BC the Minoans developed the building of impressive courtyard-centred 'palaces' on Near Eastern models. Those at Knossos and Phaestos are especially notable. The wealth required to do this came from their fleets trading all round the eastern Mediterranean, especially to get copper and tin (Crete lacked any metal deposits). There is evidence of Minoan 'colonies' along the coast of Asia

Minor set up, among other things, to get a foothold in the trade routes and inland resources.

These palaces were seats of political, administrative and ceremonial power rather than urban concentrations. They were held by a chieftain, many of whose acolytes lived in nearby 'mansions'. They stored and redistributed goods: grain, especially drought-resistant barley, olive oil, wine (the Mediterranean's staple foods), spices like saffron, coriander and woollen products. The script Linear A, so called by Evans and as yet undeciphered, was used to administer the system. Knossos could serve (it has been roughly calculated) around 15,000 people.

The island of Thera exploded in a massive volcanic eruption *c.* 1600 BC. This may have had some effect on Minoan power; it certainly did on nearby islands. The major change to Minoan power came around 1450 BC. This was when people who were Greeks from mainland Greece attacked Crete or took it over. We call these 'Mycenaean' Greeks. The epithet 'Mycenaean' is, like Minoan Crete, a modern invention to denote 'Bronze Age Greeks'. Mycenae itself is simply an impressive Bronze Age palace site on the Greek mainland, rich in gold (to judge from its graves). Many Minoan palace sites were destroyed or abandoned at this time.

Mycenaean Greeks were warriors and traders .Their trade expanded widely after Crete was taken over, possibly because the Minoan navy no longer controlled the seas. When the Mycenaeans moved into Crete, they converted the signs of Linear A to create both in Crete and in Greece a new, Greek script, Linear B, for purposes of administration. The palace of Knossos was finally destroyed – why, we do not know – around 1350 BC. Further, around 1200 BC, Mycenaean Greeks may have been involved in the demise of the important site of

Hisarlik, on the Turkish coast near the entrance to the Dardanelles.

But around 1200 BC this Bronze Age culture was beginning to collapse in the Greek, Egyptian and Hittite worlds: sites were being destroyed or abandoned, for reasons that still remain mysterious, and skills (including writing) were being lost. Many Greeks began to leave the mainland and make their way east to the coast of Asia Minor (western Turkey). The Iron Age had begun, and the Dark Ages were about to close in.

THE BRONZE AGE

The Bronze Age is so called because bronze was the standard metal in use. This metal is a combination of tin and copper. Our word 'copper' derives from Greek *Kupros*, 'Cyprus', which was well known for its copper mines (copper is a chemical element with the symbol *Cu*, from Latin *cuprum*, via the Greek). Tin is assumed not to have been available around the Mediterranean and was perhaps brought in mainly from the East, or even from Cornwall.

BEFORE THE WRITTEN WORD

'Pre-history' is defined as a period of time from which we have no written records.

The Greek world of the second millennium BC does not quite count because written clay tablets, called 'Linear B', survive from this time (see p. 12). But since these are simply economic accounts for one year, they give us no help with establishing a sequence of events. So we rely primarily on archaeology, though written accounts from Hittites (in central Turkey), for instance, and Egyptians also come into play.

DATING THE UNWRITTEN WORLD

Archaeology does not tell a story. But it can reveal processes of change over time, for instance a settlement's population expanding or contracting, becoming more or less wealthy, forging trading connections, or new populations with different styles of goods coming in, and so on. Burial sites in particular often yield highly informative hauls, such as prestige goods and precious metals from distant lands.

Dates are very cautiously attached to the period – as far as they can be – mainly by the following methods:

(i)   Tracing the changes in style of decoration on pots. Because some of this pottery is found in dateable locations abroad (e.g. Egypt, where a dating system survives), scholars have been able to draw up a system of rough-and-ready dating by changing pottery style.

(ii) Radiocarbon dating of objects and dendrochronology (tree-ring analysis). These techniques are used to firm up the results, though they often suggest earlier dates than the pottery analysis.

THERA THEORY

The middle of the ancient island of Thera, modern Santorini, just south of Crete, blew up some time around 1600 BC. It did so because it was and still is a volcanic island, which will one day blow up again as the volcanic core slowly rebuilds itself in the middle of the roughly circular caldera, the 'cauldron'-like shape left by the explosion. The explosion is calculated to have been one of the largest ever, punching about 24 cubic *miles* of material (15 billion tons) into the air, many times larger than the

1883 eruption of Krakatoa. The fallout and accompanying tsunamis must have caused widespread devastation, though scholars still argue over the details and the precise dating. Some think that memories of this explosion influenced Plato's story of Atlantis some 1200 years later (see p. 9).

Incidentally, the name 'Santorini' derives from Santa Irene ('Holy Peace'). This was the name of a local church, given to it in the thirteenth century AD when it was part of a short-lived 'Latin' empire. Its official name in modern Greek is Thira.

AKROTIRI

The town on Santorini known today as Akrotiri was a Bronze Age settlement. It was buried Pompeii-like by the explosion, and since 1967 it has been excavated. Houses were rectangular, with flat roofs, two, sometimes three, stories high; the main door opened onto wide streets or squares. Storerooms and workrooms were on the ground floor. They provide evidence of businesses in farming, fishing, woodwork, textiles and metalwork; jars from Lebanon, stone vases from Egypt, ivory work and ostrich eggshells testify to flourishing trade abroad. Living accommodation was on the upper floor or floors. Each private house (of those so far excavated) has a fresco, often visible from outside via a large window. Santorini is typical of many Aegean islands in having strong connections with Minoan Crete: its wonderful frescoes are thoroughly Minoan in style – landscapes in exotic locations, featuring monkeys, leopards and antelopes – and Linear A writing was found there. There is a cache of clay impressions from seal-stones, all of them common in Crete but not made of clay from Thera – clear evidence of flourishing trade connections.

SECURITY-SEALS

Seal-stones are gems or stones, engraved with depictions and/or writing. They are miraculous works of miniature art in themselves: about an inch long, exquisitely engraved with a whole range of images, from ceremonials to wild animals (craftsmen engraving them were helped by miniature 'magnifying glasses' that survive naturally in rock crystal).

Worn round the neck or wrist, these seal-stones had a practical use. To seal a document or lid in the Minoan world, one tied it up, pressed clay around the knotted fastening, and then 'sealed' the clay by impressing it with your own seal-stone, which could indicate personal ownership or controlling authority. That 'seal' should be unbroken when the item was delivered.

This was all part of the Minoan system of the control and distribution of goods and produce. In Phaestos, there is an archive of 6,500 clay seal impressions, indicating the vast scale of this operation. When the Mycenaeans arrived in Knossos, seals began to feature the Linear B script.

WHAT'S IN A NAME?

We do not know what the people of Crete called themselves. In Egypt, however, there are paintings in tombs of Cretan young men (one can tell by the clothing) called Keftiu. They are bringing gifts – evidence of Cretan trade. There is also a bull-leaping fresco in the Nile delta (see p. 15). The Syrians called Crete 'Kaptaru', the Bible 'Kaphtor'. So the letters 'K', 'p' or 'f' and 't' should feature in the name.

KNOSSOS AND LINEAR A

Knossos in Crete was the name of the fabled palace of the mythical Cretan king Minos. When coins bearing the name of that place emerged from the ground near modern Heraklion, Arthur Evans, keeper of the Ashmolean Museum in Oxford, decided to investigate. He had already become excited by the possibility that signs on seal-stones from Crete bought in Greek antique shops were a form of writing; here was a chance to prove it. In 1900 he bought up the location, convinced that Minoan Crete, as he called it, was history, not myth, and started to excavate. To his great excitement, he immediately started turning up seal-stones and clay tablets. The language on them turned out to be the language of Minoan Cretans, which Evans called Linear ('script written in lines') A. This language turned out not to be Greek (see p. 12). So whoever the Minoans were, Greek they were not.

KNOSSOS AND LINEAR B

At the same time, Evans also began turning up evidence of a different script, which he called Linear B, clearly related to the script of Linear A but significantly different from it. He found great quantities of this script in continuous lines of writing, inscribed on clay tablets (around 1,800 in all), bunched together like files or dossiers of some sort, datable to around 1400 BC. Even more exciting, in 1939–40 Carl Blegen, leading an American expedition excavating near Navarino bay in south-west Greece, was excavating a palace which we know to be Pylos (mentioned in Homer), and he too uncovered a great cache of writing on clay tablets (636 of them), exactly like the Linear B from Minoan Crete, datable to around 1200 BC. What was this script doing in Greece? Had the

Minoans taken over Greece? In fact, as we know, it was the other way round. What language was it? We now have some 5,000 clay tablets inscribed with Linear B from Crete and the Greek mainland (including Mycenae, Tiryns and Thebes), all dated to *c.* 1450–1200 BC, and all from large settlements.

TAXING DOCUMENTS

In 1953 the Linear B puzzle was solved. Building on a great deal of earlier work and inspired by the Second World War code-crackers at Bletchley Park, the young architect Michael Ventris and the Cambridge Greek scholar Dr John Chadwick announced that Linear B was a form of ancient Greek. But far from being exquisite early poetry or accounts of battles between Greeks and Trojans, the Linear B clay tablets were not evidence for general literacy but the work of an official class of trained bureaucrats. The tablets describe a society labelled, inspected, rationed and controlled by an officialdom of a sort to make the heart of any EU bureaucrat beat that little bit faster. Records of economic activity, the tablets cover four main types of transaction: taxation (on an annual basis, with recurrent formulas for assessment, payments and deficit, if any); agricultural production; maintenance of palace staff; and craft production (chariots, textiles, furniture, leather goods, etc.). Religious activity was also monitored, and records kept of offerings, land and allowances that were given to gods, workers (in return for services) and priests. Interestingly, nearly all the Greek Olympian gods feature – Zeus, Athena, Hermes, even Dionysus, who was once thought to be a late arrival in the Greek pantheon. The only exceptions are Aphrodite and Apollo. The palace bureaucrats clearly had no business plans for sex and the arts.

COMMAND ECONOMY

We must forget about markets and money. Minoan Crete was a command economy, under palace control. From the territory they controlled, officials drew foodstuff and raw materials. This was then given to workers in the palace and the region: food, so that they did not struggle to stay alive, and raw materials to be turned into manufactured goods to palace specifications. These included textiles, metalwork, furniture and perfumes, both for internal consumption and for bartering (how trade was carried on before money or its equivalent was invented).

RECORD SURVIVAL

There is a delicious paradox about these clay tablets. They were meant to be only temporary records, before the information was transferred to more 'permanent' materials such as skins. But when the palaces were burned down, the clay was fired hard and so preserved, whereas the 'permanent' materials were destroyed! We know the tablets were a temporary record because they refer to just one year's economic activity, mentioning only 'this year's' flocks (etc.), and occasionally 'last year's' (for comparative purposes).

TAXING DETAILS

The details of the records give us some idea of the enthusiasm of the civil servants. Stocks of spare chariot wheels are recorded: 'one pair of wheels, bound with silver'; 'one pair of cypress-wood with borders, and one single wheel'; 'six pairs, unfit for use'. Among much else we also learn:

- what the acreage of Alektryon's estate is and how much he should pay in annual tax, as well as to the gods Poseidon and Diwieus (Zeus);
- that in one Cretan village two nurses, one girl and one boy are being employed;
- that Dynios owes to the palace 2,220 litres of barley, 526 litres of olives, 468 litres of wine, fifteen rams, eight yearlings, one ewe, thirteen he-goats, twelve pigs, one fat hog, one cow and two bulls;
- who is looking after Thalamatas' cattle;
- the amount of tax to be paid in linen by the town of Rhion (with certain deductions for a certain class of workmen);
- the wheat and fig rations for thirty-seven female bath attendants and twenty-eight children at Pylos;
- the number of hammers, brushes and fire-tongs to be found in a room in the palace; and
- the names of four oxen: Dusky, Dapple, Whitefoot and Noisy.

FLOCK STOCKS

By far the largest interest of the Minoan Linear B tablets is in sheep. Over 800 of the tablets, each dealing with a single flock, produce a total of around 100,000 sheep in Crete. They are identified by sex and categorized as 'old', 'young', 'this year's' and 'last year's'. The purpose of this was to ensure that flocks of castrated rams, which produced the wool, were kept up to strength. Target figures for wool production (about 2 lb/0.9 kg per ram, 1 lb/0.45 kg per breeding ewe) and actual figures were recorded: they had targets and league tables even then. Presumably each sheep was marked with a baa-code. Then on to textile production: we can follow the process from the wool being ordered; collected; spun and carded; woven and finished; and finally turned into everything from headbands to heavy rugs. Every step of the way, restless officialdom wielded its stern recording clipboard. Incidentally, since the Linear B tablets consist largely of lists of objects, very few verbs are used.

DANGEROUS SPORTS, CRETAN STYLE

Seal-stones and frescoes from Crete provide hundreds of depictions of men leaping over bulls. In one type, it appears that a man grasps the bull's horns and, as it tosses its head, levers himself up over the bull in a backward somersault. Another type depicts a man diving head-first over the horns and using his hands to somersault backwards off the bull's back. Young women may also have had a role – though it is hard to be certain – as they seem to be depicted standing in front of and behind the bull. Since in many Mediterranean countries bulls were venerated – they were the largest and most dangerous animals on Crete – this may well have been part of a religious ceremonial. But it could equally be some sort of spectacular involving man and beast. Bull-leaping can still be seen in parts of Spain and south-west France.

MYTHS OF KNOSSOS (I): MINI-MINOS

When King Minos, the myth went, broke his promise to sacrifice an especially fine bull to the sea-god Poseidon, Poseidon made his wife Pasiphae (sister of the witch Circe) fall in love with it. This created a technical problem; but fortunately for her, the great craftsman Daedalus was a prisoner in the palace at the time. So, she invited him to turn his mighty brain to the solution. He constructed a cow-frame on wheels and covered it with the skin of a cow he had killed. He then inserted Pasiphae into it and pulled it into the meadow where the bull grazed. The bull was duly Pasiphaed, and the result was the birth of the bull-headed man, the Minotaur (literally, 'Minos-bull'). Minos, less than impressed, imprisoned it in the maze-like labyrinth which Daedalus built, on Minos' orders, to keep it hidden from sight (of which maze, in 1914, a Cambridge academic said the swastika was the model; see p. 68).

Incidentally, Pasiphae grew tired of Minos' various love affairs and, using her witchcraft, caused him to ejaculate snakes, scorpions and millipedes. These killed his lovers, but she sensibly took precautions, nullifying their effects on herself.

MYTHS OF KNOSSOS (II): INTO THE LABYRINTH

Aegeus, king of Athens, while passing through Troezen, had a brief fling with Aethra, daughter of the local king. Aegeus left a sword and a pair of sandals under a heavy stone and told Aethra that, if she bore a son strong enough to move the stone, she should send him, with the gear, to Athens. Aethra called her son Theseus. When he grew up, Theseus retrieved the gear and made his way to Athens by a route that required him to deal with a varied assortment of monsters (a sort of alternative labours of Heracles). Aegeus recognized him as his son and enlisted him to deal with a dreadful promise the Athenians had made to King Minos: to send him, every nine years, a tribute of seven girls and seven boys to provide food for the Minotaur. The third tribute was about to be paid, and lots to be drawn to select the youths. Theseus volunteered, and Aegeus instructed him, if he killed the Minotaur, to hoist white sails on the ship when he returned.   When Theseus arrived in Knossos, Ariadne, daughter of Minos, fell in love with him and begged Daedalus (himself an Athenian) to help her. Daedalus told her to give Theseus a ball of thread to attach at the entrance to the maze. He should spool it out behind him as he searched for the Minotaur, and follow it back after he had done the deed. Theseus duly did so, beating the Minotaur to death with his fists. Theseus, Ariadne and the others fought their way back to the ship and set sail for Athens. On the island of Naxos, the two lovers fell out, and Ariadne was abandoned. Theseus sailed on, but forgot to change the sails. The watching Aegeus hurled himself into the sea (hence the 'Aegean' Sea), and Theseus was both joyfully and sorrowfully welcomed back and made king.

THE ATHENIAN CONNECTION

Athens did not have much in the way of great heroes, but after all that Heracles-style giant-killing on top of the Minotaur episode, Theseus seemed to fit the bill. The Minos story was one way of fitting him into Athenian 'history' with an Athenian adventure all of his own, even though he was the son of a woman from Troezen, and not Athenian-born (see p. 45). The fact that he did not have many sanctuaries in Attica suggests he was a 'late arrival' in Athens's story of its own history; he subsequently featured in a number of major Athenian festivals.

WAR AND PEACE

There is a striking difference between Minoan and Mycenaean palaces. Minoan palaces were not fortified, and their magnificent frescoes show scenes not of warfare, typical elsewhere, but of plant and animal life (birds, monkeys, cats), processions and ceremonies, goddesses and (often bare-breasted) women (compare, in this respect, Akrotiri, p. 9 above).

Many of the Mycenaean palaces were heavily fortified. Mycenae's walls were up to 40 feet (12.5 metres) high and 25 feet (7 metres) thick. The stones used are up to 120 tons in weight, e.g. the lintel across the door-posts of the beehive tomb misnamed the 'Treasury of Mycenae'. (Such vast stones were cut to shape by huge saws suspended from pendulums, swung back and forth by workers.) No wonder the walls were later called Cyclopean, as if made by the Cyclopses (see p. 42). Mycenae's rich graves were full of arms and armour. Mycenaean frescoes imitated Minoan ones to some extent, but also featured notable scenes of warfare, such as horses, chariots, warriors, death in battle, and huntsmen closing in for the kill.

KNOSSOS AS PARIS

One of the problems we have with Knossos today is that Evans reconstructed it in accordance with his own theories about its 'meaning'. He registered Knossos' absence of defensive walls, saw the many images of goddesses and bull-worship, made links with the myth of the Minotaur and became convinced that there was some truth to the story of Theseus and Ariadne. So, in accordance with the fashions of the day, he concluded that Knossos was a pacifist, matriarchal kingdom, full of goddess-worshippers. The bare-breasted ladies (see above) suggested to others a hippie society enjoying 'a free and well-balanced sex-life', where in all likelihood 'drugs were sometimes taken to encourage a sense of revelation, possession and trance'. It was all in strong contrast with those horrid, unbalanced, undoped Mycenaeans.

The first fresco Evans uncovered was at once proclaimed to be Ariadne (it was in fact male); as soon as the room with a decorated gypsum chair was revealed, it was a 'throne room'; the nearby bath was 'Ariadne's bath'. Evans compared Minoan civilization to Medici Florence, the Renaissance and baroque Europe. One of the restored frescoes of a woman's face was entitled (daringly) 'La Parisienne' – the height of French sophistication. Evans was determined to prove that Minoan civilization 'was at once the starting point and the earliest stage in the highway of European civilisation' and King Minos 'a beneficent ruler, patron of the arts, founder of palaces, stablisher of civilised dominion'. How, then, to explain the Minotaur and labyrinth? Evans argued that they were the result of Athenian propaganda, designed 'so to exaggerate the tyrannical side of the early sea-dominion as to convert the Palace of a long series of great rulers into an ogre's den'.

KNOSSOS AS VOGUE

Evans hired the Swiss artist and restorer Émile Gilliéron, later to be joined by his son, to get to work restoring the fragments of frescoes and artefacts. They turned them into precisely what Evans wanted to see. In 1929 Evelyn Waugh visited Knossos and commented that it was not easy to judge the merits of Minoan painting since 'only a few square inches of the vast area exposed to our consideration are earlier than the last twenty years, and it is impossible to disregard the suspicion that their painters have tempered their zeal for accurate reconstruction with a somewhat inappropriate predilection for the covers of *Vogue*'.

Evans's restorers were indeed very keen to confirm their master's prejudices. The fresco of a monkey gathering saffron was restored by them as a 'Blue Boy'; a fresco of a complete procession of ladies appeared from a row of ankles; from a heap of fresco fragments emerged 'a crowd of spectators... overlooking an orgiastic dance'. Evans said of Gilliéron's son, 'I had at hand not only a competent artist, but one whose admirable studies of Minoan Art in all its branches had thoroughly imbued him with its spirit.' Evans really meant his own spirit.

FAKING IT UP

The finds at Knossos were not just enormously romantic in themselves, but were also actively romanticized by Evans in line with his theories. Forgers flourish under such conditions, and they were quick to provide punters – and Evans – with what they wanted. Evans was well aware of the problem; indeed, he visited the home of a forger betrayed to the police. One of the most famous examples of what is almost certainly a fake is a gold and ivory ('chryselephantine') snake goddess, 6½ inches/16.1 centimetres high. She sports impressive bare breasts (one nipple the tip of a golden nail) and both hands hold snakes that, twined round her arms, stretch outwards, tongues flickering. The forger whom Evans visited had everything that was needed to construct such an image: ivory, gold, acid baths to give the ageing effect, and so on. Such statuettes in gold, ivory and stone poured out of Knossos into the hands of museums and collectors, all eager to have them. It is suspected that the Gilliérons were at the centre of this, producing many fakes like the chryselephantine snake goddess.

LOST IN THE RAIN

Linear B consists of pictorial representations of people and objects (some very recognizable, e.g. sword, horse, pig), symbols, and about ninety signs for vowels (*a, e, i, o, u,* etc.) and syllables (e.g. *da, de, di, do, du, ka, ke, ki, ko, ku,* etc.). The relation between pictures and syllables was a vital aid to deciphering the language. For example, our word 'tripod' derives from the Greek stem *tripod-*. When the Linear B tablets were deciphered, the depiction of three-legged objects was found to be accompanied by the syllables *ti-ri-po-de*. But while the script of Linear B is clearly derived from Linear A, applying the syllabic values of Linear B to similar signs in Linear A produced linguistic nonsense. That is what makes it highly likely that Linear A is a different language entirely, perhaps a branch of Semitic. But we need to find a lot more before we can begin to make a guess at what language it might be; only then can we apply appropriate values to the various signs to see if they produce results.

IT ALL ADDS UP

Economics entails counting, and counting entails numbers. The Linear B number system was cracked early on. | signified a unit; — signified tens; ○ signified hundreds; and ⊕ signified thousands. So ⊕○○ — — | = 1,221. We know it is a decimal system because no symbol appears more than nine times in any one number.

MYCENAEAN COOK-OUTS

Cooks are among the groups of workers mentioned in the Linear B tablets, and rectangular clay pans for cooking kebabs (souvlaki) have been excavated. These have indentations on the raised sides, across which metal rods were placed with chunks of meat skewered on them. Charcoal was then heaped into the bottom of the pan to cook the kebabs above. Such trays were portable and would be ideal for outdoor picnics, though the Linear B for 'picnic' is not currently known. Incidentally, Mycenaeans drank their wine flavoured with pine resin. Retsina has a long history.

MYCENAEAN SHIPWRECK (1)

In 1954 a shipwreck dated around 1200 BC was indentified at Cape Gelidonya off the southern coast of Turkey and excavated six years later. The main cargo was a ton of metal, most of it nearly pure copper from Cyprus. There was a lot of scrap bronze as well for melting and recasting, and a white material (with the 'consistency of toothpaste') that turned out to be tin oxide. Also on board were pan-scales with weights set to Near Eastern standards, so this ship probably came from northern Israel or southern Lebanon (the same region as the Uluburun wreck; see below). Interestingly, later excavations with a metal detector revealed a trail of material on the sea-bed leading to the very rock on which the ship foundered.

MYCENAEAN SHIPWRECK (2)

In 1982 the world's oldest-known shipwreck was discovered at Uluburun, a few miles along the coast from the town of Kaş in southern Turkey. Carbon dating and items from the cargo suggest it sank around 1315 BC. Its journey is thought to have begun from a port in what is now northern Israel or southern Lebanon because a major item of cargo was 150 clay jars of a type known to have come from that region. Some of the jars contained olives and one contained beads, but most contained terebinth, a turpentine-like substance used as a base for perfumes and medicines, from around the Dead Sea in Israel. There were also copper and tin ingots – the tin from southern central Turkey and around Afghanistan, analysis suggests – which together would make about 11 tons of bronze; 175 glass ingots of cobalt blue, turquoise and lavender; logs of blackwood from Africa (a hard, heavy wood, used for carving luxury ornaments); ivory tusks, hippos' teeth, tortoise-shells, three ostrich eggshells (one intact), semi-precious stones, jewellery, gold and silver items, weapons (arrows, spearheads, maces, daggers) and food (almonds, pine-nuts, figs, grapes, pomegranates). There was a wooden 'diptych' inside – a double writing tablet – on the waxed surface of which could be kept a running record of details of the cargo, in and out; and pan-scales, some for precision-weighing of precious objects, some for heavier duty. The presence – to judge from the finds – of two Mycenaeans on board suggests that some of the precious cargo was bound for Greece, and they were there to ensure safe delivery. In all, 18,000 items were catalogued from places as far apart as Mycenaean Greece, Syria-Palestine, Cyprus, Egypt, Babylon, Assyria and northern Sudan. Such was international trade in the late Bronze Age – though perhaps Copper and Tin Age would be more accurate.

MASTERS OF EVERY ART

The skill level of Bronze Age craftsmen in Greece, Crete and the Near East was remarkable. Fire is a powerful tool but needs careful controlling. Bronze Age Greeks had open fires, which could be enclosed, and bellows, but no other control mechanisms, let alone thermometers. They simply tested as they went along. Though the failure rate was doubtless high, they were masters of metal-working – smelting and gold- and silver-work involving fusing and soldering. Ceramics, including faience (a form of high-gloss, multicoloured vitreous ceramic) and glass, which also required careful heat control, were mostly imported from Egypt and elsewhere. Frescoes of great sophistication decorated plaster-lined rooms, with pigments from soils (though blue was artificial) and colours freely combined. Stone-work is everywhere, ranging from the massive walls of Mycenae to stone jars, seal-stones and jewellery. So too decorative ivory, bone and shells, often inlaid, often combined into elegant figurines, and so too woodworking, perfume and textile manufacture.

HISARLIK: GROWTH TO POWER

Hisarlik was an extremely important site for ancient Greeks. Located in an earthquake-prone area in what is now north-western Turkey, it was inhabited from about 3000 BC and consisted of a small central citadel and, as was discovered in 1993, a lower area for the local population. Its interest is that it may have had very significant dealings with Mycenaean Greeks. The town's wealth must surely be connected to its location, controlling the entrance to the Dardanelles and therefore lucrative trade links between the Aegean and the Black Sea. Archaeologists identify nine phases (Hisarlik I, starting around 3000 BC, II, III, etc.), differentiated by changes in such things as pottery styles, imports, or degrees of grandeur and therefore wealth. There is no doubt that it was very wealthy. Gold items have been found there from around 2400 BC.

HISARLIK: THE FINAL YEARS

Hisarlik VI (around 1700 BC) represented the town at its most splendid, far larger and better constructed than any of its predecessors. It was notable for its monumental architecture – huge stone walls, gateways and towers – and a water-supply system via shafts and tunnels tapping into aquifers. The citadel was surrounded by a large settlement, encircled by a defensive ditch. Horses were kept there (Hisarlik was a main entry point for the horse into western Europe). But the town was partially destroyed around 1270 BC, by earthquake or war. Hisarlik VIIA was patched up and partly rebuilt by survivors before it too was destroyed by fire and perhaps war around 1190 BC. Hisarlik VIIB, further patched up, lasted into the Iron Age till around 950 BC, when it was again destroyed by fire. That marks the end of Hisarlik as a place of economic and political significance. The site was then (perhaps) abandoned till about 700 BC, when Greek colonists settled there.

HISARLIK: THE HITTITE CONNECTION

Whatever the archaeologists tell us about Hisarlik, the evidence from the powerful kingdom of the Hittites, in central Turkey, adds to the possibilities. Stored on clay tablets in the public state archives are copies of letters sent by Hittite kings in the thirteenth century BC which mention:

(i)   a powerful area in north-western Turkey called Wilusa, under the general control of the Hittite king;

(ii) a king of Wilusa called Alaksandu; and

(iii) dealings between the Hittite king and an overseas power called Ahhiyawa. At this time, it appears, Ahhiyawa is

extending its influence on the Turkish coast, and the Hittite
king does not like it much.

Since there was only one powerful city in north-western Turkey,
ancient Wilusa was surely modern Hisarlik. Further, 'Ahhiyawa' looks
linguistically close enough to the Greek word *Akhaioi*, 'Achaeans' –
Greeks living in southern Greece. So were Mycenaean Greeks causing
trouble in that part of the world? Were they responsible for an actual
attack on King Alaksandu of Wilusa? It is possible, though there is no
archaeological evidence of an attack by Greeks.

That summarizes the state of our hard knowledge about Hisarlik.
Until, that is, half a millennium later when, quite out of the blue, the first
poet of the western world hurled a gigantic spanner into the ointment...
To him, or her, we shall turn in chapter 3.

THE END OF THE MYCENAEANS

The archaeological record is clear: from around 1200 BC, major sites
including Mycenae, Tiryns, Pylos, Thebes and many smaller ones
across Greece were destroyed by fire and/or abandoned. Many were
not reoccupied for centuries. Where there was rebuilding, it was not on
anything like the earlier scale, nor were new buildings put up. Linear
B, seal-stones, frescoes and all the rest disappear. So do palaces, kings
and royal families. Unstable population movements seem to have been
the order of the day. There is no uniform pattern of collapse – Crete,
for instance, comes off better than mainland Greece – but the relatively
stable and prosperous world of the Bronze Age is gone.

Three explanations have been offered: warfare, internal or external
(Greek myth tells of Dorian Greeks, 'sons of Heracles', living outside

the Mycenaean world, causing mayhem and finally settling in the Peloponnese; Egyptian documents talk of raiding 'sea peoples'); natural disaster (earthquake? famine? disease?); or some sort of economic collapse. That said, this was an environmentally fragile and uncertain world. It would not be surprising if men were drawn to plunder those parts of it that had enjoyed such notable economic success. One consequence of this breakdown was a movement of Greeks from the mainland across the Aegean to resettle on the coast of Turkey and its nearby islands – the first of a number of Greek migrations.

THE END IS NIGH?

Linear B tablets in Thebes at the time of its destruction were burned while the clay was still wet. This might suggest a sudden, quite unexpected attack, catching the scribes wholly unawares. A set of tablets from Pylos is even more suggestive. One mentions the establishment of a coastguard operation – 800 men (one every 220 yards/201 metres) along the coast; another mentions movement of troops; another 600 rowers; another requisitions scrap bronze 'for points for javelins and spears'; another demands unnaturally large payments of gold from local governors; and another, written in great haste, refers to gifts (gold cups) and 'victims' for the gods – human sacrifice as a last desperate measure to stave off disaster? But it must also be said that these tablets may be entirely innocent records of regular deployments and requisitions in the Pylos region. Romance is – or may be – dead.

INTO THE DARK AGES

The end of the Mycenaean–Minoan world was so final that when the Greek world emerged into some sort of daylight in the eighth century BC, it bore very little relationship to what had gone before. To generalize from the archaeology: there were no more big, palatial buildings; no more graves filled with rich goods; little contact with the wider world. Given that the whole palace system, and with it the leadership it entailed, had collapsed, we can assume that people were thrown back on their own resources. That spelled trouble for craftsmen, who relied on the community to buy their goods. To produce bronze required access to markets abroad – that surely hastened the use of locally available iron. However, some features lived on:

- the Greek language; thanks to Linear B, it now has a continuous history for some 3000 years and provides our language with words from drama, skeleton, squirrel and butter to rhinoceros, pterodactyl, hypocrite and helicopter;
- the Olympian gods, though not the rituals typical of Mycenaean culture;
- the myths associated with the gods;
- memories of a heroic past.

900–750 BC: LIGHT DAWNS?

The concurrent collapse of Near Eastern civilizations at the same time at least meant that Greece was free from foreign invasion. As a result, the scattered communities, now deprived of centralized control, were left to work out their own salvation with whatever resources they had. It is perhaps this feature that resulted in the emergence of the independent, autonomous communities called *poleis* that were to characterize classical Greece (see p. 69). What leadership such communities had is hard to assess. In Athens there was a traditional belief that kings had given way to three *arkhôn*s ('rulers' or 'officials'), two elected and one appointed, with tenure for life, later changed to ten years; and then nine *arkhôn*s each for one year (from 683 BC, it was claimed). If these positions were dominated by powerful families, it would not be surprising, especially as later developments point strongly to the desire of people to have some sort of political say in their communities, against the wishes of the elite.

II

800–725 BC

TIMELINE

776 BC   The Olympic Game

750 BC   Greek alphabet invented

            Hesiod on the gods

COMPETING FOR GLORY

Olympics and the Olympian gods

The Dark Ages seem to come to an end with a sudden, dazzling burst of light: the Olympic Game (*sic*), the invention of alphabetic writing, and the epics of Homer and Hesiod (see chapter 3). But had we had written records from 1000–700 BC, we would have been able to trace a much more gradual process. For example, epics had been sung for hundreds of years before Homer and Hesiod; those two mighty oral composers had a long history of epic song behind them on which to draw. But to us they seem to burst onto the scene. In other words, Western literature, of which Homer and Hesiod are the very first examples, was not invented at this time. It emerged – because writing emerged too.

The eighth century BC prepares us for some of the most important characteristics of the Greek world during its classical period. The Olympic Game (776 BC) in honour of Zeus, god of Olympus, illustrated the Greek passion for competition – as long as you won – and the status that went with it. Little was more shaming for an ancient Greek male in any sphere of life than to be seen as a loser. The Olympic Game would soon become the enormously popular Olympic Games and expand in number of events and spread of competitors till they became a pan-Greek celebration. So after some 200 years of Dark Age, Greeks were growing in confidence again, travelling, interacting and rediscovering their communal identity.

Hesiod's account of the birth of the gods reinforced the obsession with competition and winning. Hesiod saw the cosmos (physical world and gods) brought to birth by a process of sexual activity between primal powers of Earth and Sky and such like; but Zeus fought his way to become top god, no holds barred, a position which he ultimately maintained by brute force. At the same time, the gods were constructed as a family. Some family!

FINGERS IN PIES

It is now known that almost all European languages, Iranian (Persian) and the Indian language Sanskrit – in all about half of the 439 known languages and dialects – have descended from a single ancestor, many thousands of years ago. We call it 'Proto-Indo-European', or PIE. When and where the speakers of that ancestral language lived, however, is much disputed.

Greek is one of these PIE languages. A few examples of linguistic family likenesses (there are thousands more) will demonstrate the reason for this conclusion. Note that Latin, Greek, Sanskrit and German do not derive *from each other*; each derives *separately* from PIE. English, however, derives directly from German.

PROTO-INDO-EUROPEAN

LATIN	GREEK	SANSKRIT	GERMAN →	ENGLISH
pater	patêr	pitar	Vater →	father
mâter	mêtêr	mâtar	Mutter →	mother
três	treis	trayas	drei	three
septem	hepta	sapta	sieben	seven

ALPHA, BETA, GAMMA...

Until the Phoenicians (modern Lebanon) realized that a language could be represented by around twenty-five signs, each consisting of a few simple strokes, writing systems had been enormously complex, involving hundreds of signs with many functions (to that extent Linear B with about ninety signs was quite an advance). This Phoenician alphabet was the source from which Greeks developed their own, c. 750 BC. The very word 'alphabet' derives from *alpha*, *beta* – our 'a', 'b', the first two letters of the twenty-four-letter Greek version. But Greeks made one important improvement. Phoenician was a consonantal script, omitting vowels; but Greeks wanted to represent vowels, and took Phoenician signs to do so.

The alphabet was Greece's most influential export: within forty years it had spread throughout the Greek world and made literacy for everyone a real possibility. So, laws, for example, could now be written down and displayed in the public domain. The time when aristocrats could make it up as they went along would soon be over (see p. 91).

UNPROSAIC EARLY WRITING

The earliest writing we have consists of metrical inscriptions, especially on pottery:

> I am the cup of Nestor, a pleasure to drink from.
> Whoever drinks this cup, desire for beautiful-crowned
> Aphrodite [i.e. sex]
> Will seize him straightaway. (c. 725 BC)

On Thera we find early graffiti:

> Barbax dances well, and he's given me pleasure.

This may be connected with homosexual rituals at a nearby shrine. Another graffito there pulled no punches:

> Pheidippides got fucked; Timagoras, Empheres and I – we got fucked too.

The world of drinking parties, dancing, poetry and sex were all in good shape.

It is remarkable that early literature is all poetry – even the early philosophers (i.e. natural scientists). Perhaps, in an oral society, poetry, being a special form of utterance, was thought to bestow a prospect of immortality.

Writing in prose (bar public edicts, laws, etc.) emerged some 200 years after writing was invented. Pherecydes (c. 550 BC) from the island of Syros is said to have been the first to use it. The first Greek prose work to survive is Herodotus' history of the Persian wars (see p. 119).

THE OLYMPIC GAME

We always think in terms of the Olympic Games (plural), but when they started in 776 BC, there was only one: the 200 metres. Another, the 400 metres, was added in 724 BC, and a third, the 4,800 metres, in 720 BC. In 708 BC the pentathlon and wrestling were added, followed by boxing (688 BC), chariot-racing (680 BC), horse-racing and all-in fighting (*pankration*) (648 BC), and various boys' events (200 metres, wrestling, boxing) up to 616 BC; then there is a big gap until the race in armour (520 BC). After that time, only seven new events were introduced (mostly involving mules and mares). The most popular by far was the boys' *pankration* introduced in 200 BC.

Such Panhellenic games gave the rich and powerful a stage on which to show off what they could do. Greeks loved competing, and even more winning. This sense of needing to come out on top, whatever the cost, is a typical feature of the ancient Greek world. (For later developments in the Olympic Games, see p. 114.)

CULT OF OLYMPIAN ZEUS

The Olympic Games may have been played in honour of Zeus, god of Mount Olympus, but they were not actually on, or even near, Mount Olympus. The competition took place at a cult centre to *Zeus Olumpios* in Olympia. This was a backwater of southern Greece in the territory of Elis, 140 miles south-west of Mount Olympus. Religious ritual, a public activity in honour of Zeus, had been going on there for some 300 years, and the games were simply an addition to it (gods, of course, loved competition, having come to power that way; see p. 42). Nor was there much in the way of buildings: just the precinct of Zeus, a shrine to

Pelops (see below) and a few altars. Indeed, Olympia never developed into a community at all; it remained a sacred precinct and nothing else.

THEY'RE OFF (I): PELOPS THE CHEAT

The Greeks told two stories about how the Olympic Games started. The first featured Oinomaus, king of nearby Pisa. He challenged any suitor for his daughter Hippodameia's hand in marriage to a chariot-race – the challenger to forfeit his life if he lost. Pelops fancied his chances, but just to make sure he persuaded the stable boy Myrtilos to replace the linchpins of Oinomaus' chariot with wax. As the wheels speeded up, the pins softened and melted; the wheels flew off, hurling Oinomaus to his death. Pelops won the girl and became king, and in the process gave the name 'Peloponnese' – the island (*nêsos*) of Pelops – to the whole of southern Greece. This was (apparently) the first Olympic game. It makes well the point about the Greek desire to win, at any cost. The Olympics have not cleaned up a great deal since.

THEY'RE OFF (II): HERACLES AND THE FLIES

The second story featured Heracles (Latin: Hercules), son of Zeus and the mortal woman Alcmena. He was one of the very few mortals to become a god because of his extraordinary feats of strength. Heracles had to carry out twelve labours, one of which was to clean the stables of Augeas, king of Elis. Heracles did this by diverting the rivers Alpheius and Peneius through them, but was not given his reward. So he drummed up an army, defeated Augeas and celebrated his victory in honour of his father Zeus with the very first games, which involved (quite unhistorically) chariot-races, foot-races, boxing, wrestling and the *pankration*: an obvious example of myths being invented to explain what were in fact *later* features of the Greek world.

Incidentally, in founding the games Heracles became fed up with the flies by which he was constantly plagued, and so sacrificed to Zeus *Apomuios* – Zeus, averter of flies – who kindly shooed them away across the river. From then on, at every Olympic Games a sacrifice was made to Zeus Fly-averter.

TRAINING AND NUDITY

For the first 150 years or so, athletes were essentially self-taught: gymnasiums and trainers were later developments. But they still experimented. We are told that Charmis, winner of the 200 metres in 668 BC, trained on a diet of dried figs (no comment). It is not certain when or why athletes competed naked. One source says it was due to Orsippus of Megara, whose loincloth fell off during the 200 metres in 720 BC; another says it was a Spartan; the historian Thucydides (*c.* 420 BC) says it was a Spartan too, but that the custom began 'not long ago'.

SPREADING THE GAMES

Elis, where Olympia was situated, was located in the north-west of the Peloponnese, an area over which Sparta's influence was strong (see p. 79). The winners of the first event ever came from Elis, and the first winners of the new events subsequently introduced (see above) came from Elis, Sparta, Sparta and Sparta. But of the next four new events down to 648 BC, the first winners came from Smyrna (in Asia Minor), Thebes, Thessaly and Syracuse (in Sicily). From being a basically local event, the games were starting to develop a pan-Greek reach. This says a lot about the post-Dark Age 'opening up' of the Greek world. The fact that during the seventh century BC most victors came from Athens and Sparta points up their increasing power, while in the sixth century BC it was the turn of the Greeks in Sicily and south Italy to come to the fore.

A FARMER ON THE BIRTH OF THE GODS

It is important to emphasize that there were absolutely no priests and no definitive 'sacred' books to sanction Greek accounts of their gods and their origins. Hesiod was a farmer-poet and the account he gives in his epic *Theogony* ('Birth of the gods') is a *secular* one: it does not consist of articles of faith. Many other versions were available, all of them equally secular and on many points contradictory.

This is a highly distinctive feature of Greek culture. Priests conducted traditional rituals; they did not control thought. So Greeks were used to alternative versions of their myths and therefore of their past, and were thoroughly accustomed to arguing over them. The idea that differing accounts of the world and of the past were to be welcomed and challenged is very characteristically Greek.

THE BEGINNING OF THE WORLD

Hesiod thought of the beginning of the world in terms of procreation – logical enough when one observes nature. So the gods and our world can be reconstructed in the form of a family tree. But how did it all start?

(i)   Hesiod begins with Khaos (our 'chaos'), which meant 'gaping void', 'emptiness' or 'chasm'. We might call it 'space'. In this space are created – we are not told how –

Gaia (Earth) and Eros (Desire). Eros is needed now because without desire copulation does not usually happen. Logical, the Greeks.

(ii) Gaia produces some offspring by herself, including Ouranos (Uranus, Sky). Together Gaia and Ouranos produced Mountains, Nymphs (associated with fertility), and Ocean (the great river thought to encircle the earth), and the physical world as we know it begins to take shape.

(iii) Soon all these are hard at it producing assorted minor gods, goddesses, Titans, Giants, Cyclopses, and so on, who carry on the good work – about 300 deities in all.

(iv) The key moment comes when Ouranos takes against the monsters he has engendered and forces them back into Gaia. So Gaia arms her son Cronus with a sickle, and when Ouranos comes down at night to lie with Gaia, Cronus lops off his genitals. The genitals drop into the sea and produce Aphrodite, who floats across the sea and comes ashore in Cyprus. But where are Zeus and the other Olympian gods? They are yet to come: they were not there in the beginning.

(v) Cronus and his sister Rhea produce six children (including future top Olympian gods Poseidon, Demeter, Hera, Hades and Hestia). But when Cronus hears that one of them will succeed him as top god, he swallows them one by one as they pop out. Rhea rather takes against this, and when she bears Zeus, she gives Cronus a stone to swallow instead and hides Zeus in a cave in Crete. When Zeus grows up, he defeats Cronus, forces him to regurgitate the children and releases

the Cyclopses, who in gratitude make Zeus' thunder and
lightning (often called thunderbolts) for him. After an epic
battle against assorted monsters, Zeus is installed as king of
the gods. By various means he produces more Olympian
gods, including Athena, Apollo, Artemis, the nine Muses,
Ares, Hermes and Dionysus, and ends up by marrying his
sister Hera.

The gods, then, far from being external to the world, were all made by
the world; and Zeus and the Olympian gods were relative late-comers.
Zeus initially fought his way to the top by force, but when the battles
were over, he was appointed top god with the agreement of the other
Olympians. And he stayed head of the family of gods – by force when
necessary. It would turn out to be a pretty quarrelsome, competitive
family as well. There is at this time little sign that these are gods of love
or justice, let alone peace, harmony and forgiveness.

ABSTRACTIONS

Gods were not just physical presences: they were abstractions too.
Night, for example, proceeded to give birth to the following largely
gloomy – but when you think about it, quite logical – list of deities: Day,
Doom, Fate, Death, Misery, Resentment, Deceit, Old Age and Strife,
alongside Sleep, Dreams and Intimacy.

THIS MORTAL CLAY

How humans were created is not at all clear. One suggestion (at which
Hesiod hints) was that they were moulded out of clay by the Titan
Prometheus (Forethought). But one thing is clear: man was an artificial,

manufactured product – not part of the same genealogy as produced gods and the world.

SACRIFICES FOR MANKIND

Prometheus was a great supporter of mankind, and Hesiod explains how he tricked Zeus out of the best part of the sacrifices which men were duty-bound to make in order to keep the gods sweet. He carved up the corpse of a bull into two packages, one of the edible flesh, the other (much bigger) of bones and fat, and asked Zeus to choose. Zeus naturally chose the bigger package, and from then on that was what Zeus got from a sacrifice, while humans got the meat. So sacrifice was an act shared between men and gods, but one achieved by trickery. Greeks always admired a weaker party turning the tables on the stronger by cunning.

Incidentally, it was only after a big, public sacrifice that most Greeks would have the pleasure of eating meat (it was specially parcelled up for distribution).

THE GIFT OF FIRE

Zeus did not thrill to Prometheus' trick. He therefore kept fire from men, so that they could not keep warm or cook food. Prometheus retaliated by delivering fire to men hidden inside a fennel stalk. The furious Zeus had Prometheus nailed up on a rock in the Caucasus and sent an eagle to peck out his liver by day. This would regrow by night, and the eagle repeated the trick in the morning. Many generations later, Heracles released him. The gods, in other words, did not appreciate being made fools of. They would exact revenge. All very Greek.

WOMAN(UN)KIND

Men would not get off scot-free in another sense: Zeus gave them – woman. He instructed Hephaestus, the blacksmith god, to construct a stunningly beautiful specimen out of clay, called Pandora ('All-gifts'), superbly dressed, 'with the mind of a bitch... and lies and specious words and sly ways... to be the ruin of man and their business'.

PANDORA'S JAR

Prometheus had warned his forgetful brother Epimetheus (Afterthought) never to accept any gift from Zeus; but Zeus, in his desire to punish Prometheus and men still further, knew that Epimetheus could never refuse anything as dazzlingly tempting as Pandora. So, Hesiod tells us, Zeus gave her to Epimetheus, together with a jar (not in fact a box), presumably with strict orders that Pandora should not pull out the stopper. Of course she did, and all the evils of the world immediately flew out of it. At once Pandora thrust the stopper back, trapping only Hope inside.

Together, these stories of Prometheus contain much of the Greek understanding of man's lot. All the responsibilities and problems of life as *males* understood them were introduced – women, marriage, work, property and succession, old age, and sickness. This is the human condition.

GOD OF JUSTICE?

Once Zeus was firmly in power, he married Mêtis (Resourceful Intelligence), producing Athena (from his head!), and then Themis (Right and Proper), who bore him *Eunomia* (Lawfulness), *Dikê* (Justice) and *Eirênê* (Peace), together with the Fates, 'who give mortals both good and ill'. Zeus thus became associated with these qualities: justice could not exist until Zeus had the power to impose it.

FIGURES OF MYTHTERY

Towards the end of the *Theogony*, Hesiod lists gods who bedded mortals, producing mortal offspring; and at this point, a sort of early Greek 'history' emerges – a golden age, when men and gods dined together, as Hesiod says. Among these heroes were Heracles, Memnon, king of the Ethiopians (who fought at Troy); Jason of the Golden Fleece; Dionysus who married Ariadne, daughter of the Cretan king Minos (p. 17); Thetis who married the mortal Peleus, producing Achilles (p. 59); and Aphrodite who bedded the mortal Anchises, producing the Trojan hero Aeneas... and seamlessly we are among heroes of the Trojan War.

EARLY GREEK 'HISTORY'

Later Greeks could not resist taking all these figures and inventing an historical framework, complete with dates, into which to put them! Here are four examples – there are many, many more:

- Cecrops became the first king of Athens in (Greeks decided) 1582 BC, when Prometheus was active in the world. Cecrops was half man, half serpent, which Greeks thought demonstrated that he was born from the Athenian earth, i.e. not an immigrant. This remained the Athenian boast: Athenians had never existed anywhere else but Athens (i.e. they were 'autochthonous'), giving them (as they saw it) exclusive rights to their territory.

- Another source says that Actaeus was the first king, followed by Cecrops, to explain how Athens' territory came to be known as Attica.

- About this date too, Poseidon, god of the sea, disputed the ownership of Athens with Athena. He struck a rock on the Acropolis to produce a stream of water; Athena caused an olive tree to spring up. The gods adjudged Athena the winner, and the city was named 'Athens' after her.

(Incidentally, 'Athens' is a plural form in Greek, meaning 'Athenas', possibly because in Attica there were many local villages all called 'Athena' which were united into the city.)

In 1529 BC Deucalion, a son of Prometheus, survived the Great Flood sent by Zeus to punish mortals, and his son Hellen gave his name to the Greeks ('Hellênes', see p. 79). His descendants gave their names to the four different linguistic branches of the Greek people: Dorus (the Dorians, i.e. mainly Spartans); Aeolus (the Aeolians); Ion (the Ionians, associated with the Athenians); and Achaeus (the Achaeans – one of Homer's names for Greeks). Note that 'Ionia' refers to that part of the central western coast of Asia Minor inhabited by those who spoke in the Ionian dialect.

And so on. All this became real, dated history for Greeks, on the strength of which the origin of many contemporary aspects of Greek life could be historically explained. Securing their past in this way was an important activity for Athenians from the third century BC, when Athens' glory days were over (see p. 318).

III

725–700 BC

TIMELINE

c. 725 BC   Homer's epics, *Iliad* and *Odyssey*

c. 700 BC   Hesiod on the peasant life

              The emergence of the *polis*

FROM HOMERIC HERO TO HESIOD'S PEASANTS

From the heights of Olympus, Homer's sensational epics – the *Iliad* and the *Odyssey* – bring the gods down to the human plane. The heroes of the *Iliad* – Greeks against Trojans, and all for Helen, the most beautiful woman in the world – take us into a world of two-edged greatness: the hero as soldier, close to gods both supportive and hostile; one capable of extraordinary feats of bravery on the battlefield, but also of egotistical anger, cruelty and violence when he sees his status in the eyes of others – his honour – threatened. At the same time, this hero is all too human, longing to return home from war to family, security and peace. Death is for losers.

So much for life lived on the front line, on the edge of death every day. The *Odyssey* follows the Greek hero Odysseus on his ten-year journey home from Troy, a world far from soldiering: life on the seas, challenges from different peoples and cultures – from one-eyed giants to dangerous witches – and finally home, where suitors for the hand of his wife threaten everything Odysseus had built up over the years.

Homer's picture of human and divine activity was hugely influential in shaping Greek values.

But heroism is one thing, everyday life in the real world quite another. Or perhaps not. In the daily struggle for survival, the ordinary peasants in the *polis* still needed to placate gods when it came to ensuring one's crops would grow, and one's status in society (however lowly) still had to be fought for – friends had to be helped, personal enemies defeated, and the family protected, however squabbling a unit.

THE BIG ONE

Arguably the biggest moment of the Greek past was the Trojan War. This was provided with various dates by ancient Greeks – all meaningless: 1334 BC, 1250 BC, 1218 BC and 1184 BC (see pp. 45, 319). Homer's version of it, composed around 700 BC, became accepted as the definitive historical account. More importantly, his *Iliad* and *Odyssey* became the focal point of Greek literary, cultural, social and political reference for a thousand years, and marked the moment for Greeks after which history became seriously *human* history: there might still be divine interventions, but it was no longer a time (as Hesiod had put it) when men actually dined with gods.

THE TROJAN WAR: HOW IT STARTED

The full story of the Trojan War, of which Homer in his *Iliad* only tells a small part, goes as follows. Zeus fell in love with the goddess Thetis, but was told that any son she bore would be greater than her father. Zeus therefore married her off to the mortal Peleus. At the wedding, all the gods were invited except for Eris (Strife). Infuriated, she threw a golden apple among the guests inscribed with the words 'To the most beautiful'. Hera, Athena and Aphrodite immediately quarrelled over it, and finally asked Zeus to be the judge. He wisely refused and suggested that the handsome Paris (also called Alexandros), son of Priam, king of Troy, should take on the task. The goddesses duly submitted. Hera offered Paris power; Athena offered him wisdom; and Aphrodite offered him sex, in the shape of the most beautiful woman in the world – Helen, wife of Menelaus, king of Argos. No contest: Paris gave the golden apple to Aphrodite, paid a visit to Menelaus, and seduced Helen back to Troy.

(Warning: I shall call the site of the Trojan War 'Troy'. Why the inverted commas? Because it is not what the only person who described it, the epic poet Homer, called it. He called it something quite different. The clue is in the title of Homer's epic: not the *Troiad* but the *Iliad*. See p. 53 to find out why.)

THE TROJAN WAR: HOW IT ENDED

Menelaus called on his brother Agamemnon to raise an army to sail to Troy and get back Helen – 'the face that launched a thousand ships', as Marlowe described her in his *Faust* (to be pedantic, it is 1,186 ships in Homer). For ten years the Greeks laid siege to Troy, taking the city eventually not by martial valour but by a trick: the wooden horse, devised by the cunning Greek hero Odysseus. This horse was filled with soldiers and left outside the city gates, while the Greeks pretended to give up the siege and leave. The Trojans, tricked into believing the horse was a lucky omen, foolishly dragged it into the city, celebrated the Greek departure...

and woke up in the small hours to find the gates flung open, the town full of Greeks and their world in flames. Retelling part of this story 700 years later, the Roman epic poet Virgil makes the Trojan priest Laocoon, suspiciously viewing the horse outside the walls, comment: 'I fear the Greeks, even when they bring gifts'.

AFTER THE TROJAN WAR

The war over, the heroes returned home. Two return stories stand out. The first of them is the return of Odysseus, which took ten years and encompassed many adventures with alien creatures, including the Cyclops, the Lotus Eaters, and Scylla and Charybdis, before he landed on the island of the demi-god Calypso. She kept him there for seven years until the gods ordered his release. When he arrived home, he found his household besieged by suitors for the hand of his faithful wife Penelope, to her despair and that of their young son Telemachus. Disguised by Athena as an old beggar, Odysseus checked out the palace before taking revenge on the suitors and killing them all. Homer told this story in his *Odyssey*.

The other influential story was the return of Agamemnon, leader of the expedition. To raise the wind for Troy, he had sacrificed his daughter Iphigeneia at Aulis, the departure point for Troy. When he returned home, his wife Clytemnestra, in league with her lover Aegisthus, slaughtered him and his mistress (the Trojan prophetess Cassandra). Agamemnon's son Orestes, however, returned to take revenge and kill his mother. The Furies pursued him to Athens, where he stood trial but was found innocent and released. The tragedian Aeschylus turned this into the magnificent trilogy *Oresteia* in 458 BC (see p. 179).

TROY AND THE TROJAN WAR: THE HISTORY

The big question is: was there really a Trojan war? The Greeks believed there was; and the site where they believed it happened was the place today called – Hisarlik! (See p. 24 above). This Greek belief, by itself, proves nothing. As we have already seen, archaeologists tell us that Hisarlik/Troy VI and VIIA were devastated by fire or earthquake (the site is located in an earthquake region), but there is no archaeological evidence *of any sort* to indicate that it was attacked at that time, let alone by Greeks. Indeed, it is only the epic poem of Homer *composed around 500 years later* that provides an account of any sort of war between Trojans and Greeks – and, as we have seen, Greeks were very keen to turn myths of the past into real, locatable history. So the Trojan War may, indeed, be nothing but an epic myth. But perhaps not...

THE CASE FOR A WAR (I): HITTITE HIT?

This is where the fun begins:

(i)   Homer's story of the Trojan War was called the *Iliad*. Why
      Iliad? Because *Iliad* meant 'story about *Ilios*', and *Ilios*
      or *Ilion* was the name Homer gave to the *town*, while he
      reserved *Troia* for the whole *region*. Further, in Homer's
      time, *Ilios* was actually *Wilios* (the Greek alphabet soon lost
      the 'w'). Now look back to Hisarlik on p. 25: could Wilusa
      be Homeric Wilios?

(ii) In Homer, Helen's lover Paris, son of the Trojan king
      Priam, has an alternative name: Alexandros. Look back to

Hisarlik and the Hittites on p. 25: any relation to the Trojan king Alaksandu, perhaps?

(iii)   And finally, 'Ahhiyawa' – the overseas power with which the Hittite king had been having dealings; see p. 25 – is linguistically relatable to one of Homer's names for the Greeks: *Akhaioi*, 'people of the Greek region of Achaea'. So did Mycenaean Greeks actually attack the city?

It may be, then, that in Wilusa/Ilios, Alaksandu/Alexandros and Ahhiyawa/Achaeans we have the actual historical names of people and places that were to feature in Homer's account.

THE CASE FOR A WAR (II): BRONZE TO IRON

Homer lived around 700 BC in an iron age. Yet in the *Iliad* he talks of his epic heroes as living in a *bronze* age: they all wield bronze weapons, wear bronze armour, etc. As we have seen, the Bronze Age had died out long ago. How on earth did he know about it?

Again, in Homer's day there were no grand palaces of the sort we have seen at Mycenae and Knossos. Yet his epic is full of talk of such palaces. He talks of Mycenae as 'rich in gold', which it certainly wasn't in Homer's day, but the archaeologist Schliemann uncovered plenty of it there (see p. 67).

Homer talks of warriors fighting from chariots, which Greeks did not do in Homer's day. He mentions soldiers wearing greaves, wielding huge shields, sporting boar's tusk helmets (one has been recovered) – none of them the case in Homer's day. He describes Tiryns as 'well-walled'; it was a wreck in Homer's day.

Finally, Homer's heroic world is one where farming meant predominantly cattle-raising, and heroes ate meat; in Homer's own time, arable farming was the norm (see p. 72).

THE CASE FOR A WAR (III): HOMER'S LANGUAGE

Homeric language is not an everyday spoken language but a special *poetic* language, designed purely for telling stories orally in a very complex verse; and that poetic language contains unique forms of words that go *right back 500 years to Linear B itself*. The conclusion is that oral poets were telling stories in 1200 BC, when a Trojan war, had there been one, might well have taken place.

THE CASE AGAINST A WAR (I): ARCHAEOLOGY AND LOGIC

The archaeological case for a Trojan war is non-existent: there is no evidence even for a battle between Greeks and Trojans, let alone a ten-year siege.

Second, Homer's heroes do not seem to be conducting a siege at all. They spend all their time fighting Trojans in the field of battle. What sort of siege is that? There is no indication that they did the sensible thing, i.e. cut off food and water supplies, sat about and waited. All this for a very good reason: what sort of exciting epic would consist of an army sitting around doing nothing for ten years?

Third, the Greek army in Homer is one of twenty-nine contingents led by forty-four commanders from 175 Greek localities in 1,186 ships containing (one may guess) 100,000 men: simply impossible in the Bronze Age world.

Finally, the ancient Greek historian Herodotus, writing in the fifth century BC, pointed out that no king in real life would allow his city to be sacked, his children to be killed and his people to be destroyed because his son, after a holiday jaunt abroad, had returned home with a foreign floozie.

THE CASE AGAINST A WAR (II): ORAL MORAL

Though Homer may have been able to write himself, he was composing in a tradition of oral poetry that was hundreds, if not thousands, of years old – because writing did not exist in the Greek world till Homer's day (as we have seen, Linear B was designed for stock-keeping; see p. 12).

Further, the poets were not historians or guardians of traditions. They were creative performers, working within a tradition that expected them to treat the tales handed down to them entirely as they pleased and as their audience demanded. We know the names of other oral poets (there must have been hundreds of them), though Homer was so vastly superior that little of their work has survived. But from what we have, it seems that they all told the story of 'Troy' very differently.

Then again, it is not surprising that Homer refers to a Bronze Age world and to Bronze Age ways of doing things. Oral poems were being sung half a millennium before Homer, and ways of saying things – phrases, clauses and whole sentences – that 'fitted the metre' of a highly complex verse became embedded in it. Since these repeated units were so useful for oral, on-the-spot composition, they were handed down the generations to succeeding oral poets, all learning the trade. Poets obviously welcomed them; Homer certainly did – his work is full of such repetitions. They gave their poems the patina of age, the sense of a remote and distant world of great heroes, heroes who mingled with the gods. But the poets *knew* nothing of this world: it was the story that counted.

That these poets knew nothing about that world is evident in the ways they handle it. For example, Homeric heroes have chariots, but they do not fight from chariots as Mycenaeans did. Instead, they use them as taxis to get to the site of the battle, jump off, fight, and then hail the driver to get back home again.

ƧO: WAƧ THERE A WAR AFTER ALL?

It is not *impossible* that Mycenaean Greeks fought a battle against the Wilusa (modern Hisarlik) that is mentioned in Hittite documents. But the *only* evidence for it is an oral poem composed half a millennium after the event, proposing an impossible military and political scenario.

It is true that Homer may well have known Hisarlik. He may well have based his picture of ancient Ilium on its remains at the time. He may well have used it as a sort of mental model for the ancient city. Further, there is much in the poem that locates the *Iliad* in that part of the world. But one thing is for sure: even if there was such a battle, it bore no relation whatsoever to Homer's version of it. All this raises the question: why did the *Iliad* ring so true with the Greeks? It is a good question, because kings run the show in Homer but, at the time Homer was composing, that monarchical world was disappearing in favour of the community-based *polis*. But to an extent all this is irrelevant: it is the poetry and sheer *human* interest of the *Iliad* and *Odyssey* that have placed them firmly among the world's masterpieces.

UNANSWERABLE HOMERIC QUESTIONS

1. Who was Homer?

Such was Homer's fame and importance that seven cities claimed he was born there: Smyrna, Chios, Colophon, Ithaca, Pylos, Argos and Athens. Since Homer's dialect and his descriptions of the area around Hisarlik all point to the coastal region of Turkey for his birthplace, only the first three are likely. Some Greeks thought Homer was blind, probably because the blind were thought to be especially inspired, as was Demodocus, the blind bard Homer depicts in the *Odyssey*. Homer was certainly not a woman, as Samuel Butler wanted him to be: oral poets were travelling entertainers, not a profession any woman could have taken up.

2. Who made up Homer's audience?

Our *Iliad* is 15,689 lines long, our *Odyssey* 12,110; they would have taken in the region of twenty to thirty hours to recite. Demodocus in the *Odyssey* sings his songs to the audience at dinner in the evening. Perhaps Homer developed his lengthy epics as a sort of serial, lasting many nights; or perhaps they were designed for recitation over the course of a festival.

3. Our version, Homer's version?

Since Homer was an oral poet, what relation does our version bear to his? Could he write? Did he dictate his text? Were his epics passed on by oral singers known as the *Homeridae* ('sons of Homer') and written down later? All we can be certain of is that the poems were known in a fixed form by the 550s BC, when they and other epics were recited 'in the proper order' at competitions for rhapsodes, who were professional reciters, not creative poets (see p. 125).

HOMER'S ILIAD – THE FIRST TRAGEDY

The first word of western literature is *mênin* – 'wrath': the wrath of Achilles, the greatest fighter of the Greeks, 'which brought endless agonies on – the Greeks!' Surely that should be 'Trojans'? No. Achilles, insulted and dishonoured by Agamemnon, leader of the expedition to Troy, stormed out of the fighting with his men and his close companion Patroclus; then (with the help of his divine mother Thetis) he won from Zeus the promise that Greeks – his own side! – would be slaughtered till they honoured him again and welcomed him back.

Refusing to return even when the Greeks came begging him to do so (with rich material compensation as well), he finally relented at the request of Patroclus when the Greeks were on the verge of defeat. But he did not enter battle himself. He agreed to allow Patroclus to return to the fighting to prevent the Trojans firing the Greeks' ships. Patroclus succeeded, but at the cost of his own life: he was killed by the Trojan hero Hector.

With all thought of revenge against Agamemnon turned now against Hector, Achilles returned to battle and, in an orgy of bloody slaughter, cornered Hector and killed him. Against all custom and honourable conduct, he refused to return the body but mutilated it. Only when the gods sent Hector's old father Priam, king of Troy, to beg for his return, did Achilles take pity and relent, and the *Iliad* end with Hector's funeral.

But, as every Greek knew – and Achilles knew too – his own death would come next. For his mother Thetis had warned him that, in slaughtering Hector, he would forfeit his own life. 'Then let me die at once!' was his uncompromising retort, 'since it was I that was responsible for Patroclus' death'. So the first epic of the west is also the first tragedy: a great hero, determined to assert his status in the face of insult, and taking exactly the right steps (in his view) to achieve that justifiable end, gets it wrong all the way down the line and instead brings death on himself and his dearest companion.

HOMER'S ODYSSEY – COMING HOME

Odysseus has spent ten years fighting at Troy and ten years facing challenges from men, gods and the elements to return home to Ithaca. The poet sets the story at the moment when Odysseus is about to return, and begins with the situation in Ithaca: Odysseus' despairing wife Penelope, and their son Telemachus, who is on the verge of manhood, trying to keep at bay 108 suitors set on forcing Penelope's hand in marriage. That scene established, Telemachus visits two heroes of the Trojan War – Menelaus and Nestor – to see if they have any news of his father, but gets only a mixed message.

The scene now changes to Odysseus; after three years of adventures at sea he is held captive on an island for seven years by the nymph Calypso. The gods order his release, and he sets out on the high seas, finally reaching Phaeacia. Here he is welcomed and entertained, and tells the story of his journey from Troy (including a visit to the Underworld) – the first flashback in history.

The Phaeacians see him safely home to Ithaca, where he is disguised as an old beggar by Athena, looked after by a faithful swine-herd Eumaeus and reunited with Telemachus. In this disguise he enters the palace, experiences the insults and assaults of the suitors and hears Penelope say it is time for her to remarry. In a night meeting with her – he is still disguised – he persuades her to marry the suitor who can string his bow (which he had not taken to Troy) and shoot it through some axes. Penelope agrees, the suitors fail the test, Odyseus gets his hand on the bow, easily strings and shoots it, and with the help of Telemachus and other faithful slaves slaughters the suitors and is reunited with his wife.

Odysseus is 'a man of high intelligence': faced with every sort of challenge to survival and return – from murderous monsters (Cyclops) to disloyal companions – he wins through by cunning, eloquence, capacity to endure and martial prowess. He has been seen as the loyal hero-husband, the eternal seeker after experience, the flexible, shifting anti-hero. His story is not an epic of massed combat but of the world in its infinite variety – the living and the dead, heroes of the past and seductive witches, young girls and aged slaves, faithful dogs and loyal swine-herds. The hero of this epic has to deal with them all – and win through to where he wishes most of all to be: home, a return denied to so many who (as Homer is always reminding us in the *Iliad*) never made it back from Troy.

ACHILLES AND PATROCLUS

Because Greek literature is full of same-sex love, it is assumed that Achilles and Patroclus were lovers. But this is to ignore what Homer tells us about them. When the Greek embassy begging Achilles (in vain) to return to battle finally leaves, Achilles beds down with Diomede, a girl he had taken in an attack on Lesbos, while Patroclus sleeps with well-girdled Iphis, whom Achilles had given him after sacking steep Scyros. Achilles' and Patroclus' closeness in the *Iliad* has nothing to do with same-sex love. Naturally, if vibrant modern authors with their fast-flowing biros wish to tell the story differently, it is up to them. But they must not call it Homer.

WOMEN IN HOMER

One of the most striking features of Homeric epic is the voice given to women in what seems to be a man's world: Andromache, wife of the Trojan hero Hector, Helen, Briseis (slave-girl of Achilles), Hecabe (wife of Priam, king of Troy), Penelope in the *Odyssey*, Eurycleia the faithful slave, Calypso, Nausicaa and so on. Far from being subjugated, they are protected by their menfolk. Their roles are complementary to that of men; valued for their beauty, skill and intelligence, they are never demeaned but admired for their work in the home and among their family, their personal sphere. Nor are they ever afraid to make their feelings known to the males around them. There is a deep respect for marriage and the mutual satisfaction of male and female needs within it. No wonder the heroes at Troy are all desperate to return home safe and sound to their *families*. See Hesiod for a contrasting view (p.73).

HEROES AND HONOUR

The Homeric word for 'honour' or 'respect' is *timê* ('tee-mair'). Literally, it meant 'price' or 'value' and was what a man was worth – in *other* men's eyes. This is one of the main motivations of the Homeric hero: to gain *timê* among his fellow men in the hope of winning a glorious, immortal reputation when he died. One's *timê* was physically demonstrated by the material wealth and social position one earned in amassing it: armour and booty from enemies you killed, fine lands and the best seat at feasts granted by your community, your success in returning home and reclaiming your inheritance.

Any slight to one's *timê* risked a ferocious response: hence Achilles' walking out on the army (see p. 59 above) even though the battlefield was his natural habitat, where he was most assured of winning the *timê* he craved. At the same time, the hero could not compromise another's *timê* in the search for his own; there was an obligation to co-operate alongside one's desire to compete.

These values remained pretty constant in the ancient world – some would say in the modern world, too.

RUSTIC AT HEART

Homeric society was, like the rest of the ancient world, agricultural, and the world of heroes Homer describes was no less so. Heroes pastured herds (Achilles killed some of Priam's sons as they did this); raised horses (Andromache personally fed her husband Hector's); Priam accused his sons of being sheep- and cattle-thieves and himself rolled in the dung of the courtyard when he heard of Hector's death. Values were assessed in worth of oxen, and the fighting was constantly being likened to farmers defending their livestock against wild animals.

SANDCASTLES IN THE AIR

Homer's *Iliad* took its listeners back to a heroic age of the deep past, mythical to us but historical to his audience. To make that past world real to his listening audience, Homer deployed similes – some 300 in the *Iliad* alone – which liken some heroic action to something familiar to the listening, largely farm-working audience. In particular, he uses weather and other natural phenomena (e.g. storms, floods, fires); hunting and herding (e.g. wild animals versus man or domestic animals); and human technology (e.g. carpentry, weaving, threshing). Lions occur forty times, the most common simile image; worms, trumpets and rainbows occur once. Two examples: when the god Apollo smashes down the wall defending the Greek camp, Homer likens him to a small boy kicking over a sandcastle on the beach; when Patroclus comes up to Achilles, weeping and demanding his attention, Achilles likens him to a young girl running after her mother, begging to be picked up, tugging at her dress, stopping her as she tries to hurry on, and tearfully looking up to her until she finally picks her up. These wonderfully human moments suddenly lift us into a different world of peace, far from the battlefield.

ALL AT SEA

Perhaps Homer's most famous phrase is (as translated by Andrew Lang, late nineteenth century) 'the wine-dark sea'. But the Greek word translated as 'wine-dark' is in its dictionary form *oinops*, which combines *oinos* 'wine' with *ops* 'face': so it means literally 'wine-faced/surfaced'. All very well, but Homer also used it to describe bulls, and in Linear B tablets it is used as the name for a bull! Not surprisingly, the ancients had no idea what it meant either.

THE INTERNATIONAL WORLD OF MYTH

Many Greek myths clearly have connections with Near Eastern cultures (Phoenician, Babylonian and others), with which Greeks were in contact from the second millennium. For example, in both the Babylonian epic of Gilgamesh (*c.* 1700 BC) and the *Iliad*, the main heroes Achilles and Gilgamesh are sons of goddesses, with mortal fathers; both are helped by their mothers, who use more powerful gods to support their cause; both heroes are obstinate and passionate, prone to snap decisions; both lose their dearest companions; both are devastated by their loss and take extreme action to try to compensate for it; and so on.

NO NORTH YORKSHIRE CYCLOPS

Whatever links we may find between Greek and Near Eastern myths, Greek myths were adapted to and specifically reflected Greek values, customs, interests and concerns. Take, for example, the myth of the one-eyed giant Cyclops, whom Odysseus meets in the *Odyssey*. There are 221 different versions of the story of the Cyclops, from places as far apart as Hungary, Sicily, Armenia, Finland and Russia. In the version from Thirsk in North Yorkshire, the one-eyed giant is a miller, preventing Jack from going to Topcliffe Fair (which is still celebrated today). But Homer's Cyclops is entirely Greek: he is the son of the Greek sea-god Poseidon, fully informed on such matters as the Trojan War, Greek customs of entertaining strangers, and Zeus' care for strangers.

VERY HUMAN GODS

Homer was said to have given the Greeks their gods, and he did so in the sense that he endowed them with personalities, something Hesiod never did. They were constructed as a quarrelling family, with Zeus at their head. They had their human favourites: Athena supported Achilles and Odysseus, Apollo urged on Trojan Hector. They passed their days like humans, talking, arguing, making love, eating, sleeping, drinking, getting angry with each other, complaining if ill-treated, sweating if they worked hard, and so on. In other words, they had an everyday life. Homer often described his human heroes as 'godlike'; that is because he has made his gods so like men. But Homeric gods were not the state gods of the *polis*, worshipped with grand state rituals – processions, games and other official ceremonies. Homeric worship, was a more personal business.

RELIGION WITHOUT DOGMA

Greeks possessed no definitive sacred books, such as the Bible or Koran (myths were not sacred in any sense; see p. 40). There was no centralized religious authority like a church. So beliefs, creeds and dogmas were not a feature of religion in the Greek world, nor did it make moral or spiritual demands. Consequently, you did not 'believe in' ancient gods as a Christian 'believes in' Christ. Rather, you acknowledged them, rather like a man on a cliff-top acknowledging gravity: they were powers that it was foolish to ignore. You did this by rituals, of which sacrifice was the grandest (see p. 43). But it was just a ritual, a special routine. The god had been worshipped and should therefore be pleased with you and benefit you. It was a *quid pro quo* relationship: 'you scratch my back and I'll scratch yours'.

PRIAM'S TREASURE

The British diplomat Frank Calvert began excavating around Hisarlik in 1865. He was joined in 1868 by the wealthy, indefatigable and rather dodgy German businessman Heinrich Schliemann. Between 1871 and 1879 Schliemann uncovered the ruins of a sequence of ancient cities, one developing on top of the other, starting in the Bronze Age and ending in the Roman period. This sequence he declared to be Troy. In the process he made 'Troy' even more ruined than it already was by driving through it a gigantic trench 86 yards by 15 (79 metres by 14), thereby removing 102,020 cubic yards (78,000 cubic metres) of mixed urban conglomerate. In Troy/Hisarlik II (2600–2250 BC) he discovered a vast collection of jewellery, gold and other items which he said was 'Priam's treasure'. He draped his wife Sophia in much of it, declaring her to be Helen.

THE FACE OF AGAMEMNON

In 1876 Schliemann turned his attention to Mycenae, where he found graves even more stuffed with gold and jewellery. The 'round' face of one body, complete with thirty-two teeth and wearing a heavy gold mask, was 'wonderfully preserved', prompting Schliemann to comment: 'This corpse very much resembles the image which my imagination formed long ago of wide-ruling Agamemnon'. *Really?* This comment was the source of the famous 'Today I gazed upon the face of Agamemnon' quotation. Gladstone argued that the face 'bore out the details of Agamemnon's murder'. Of *course* it did.

All this was total fantasy, of the same sort as ancient Greeks' fantasies about the historicity of their myths. But it caused tremendous excitement across the world and raised again the whole question of the relationship between Greek myth and history.

RACIAL BUNKUM: THE SWASTIKA

Swastika derives from the Sanskrit *svastika*. It means 'well-being'. When Heinrich Schliemann found swastikas in Troy, he associated them with swastikas found on early German pottery. This symbol became associated with Germanic theories of an Aryan super-race originating in Germany which invaded the Greek East, making Greeks part of the super-race too. When a swastika was found scratched on the pubic triangle of a statue of a Trojan 'goddess' made of lead, it became a fertility symbol, obviously emphasising the Aryan connection. That swastika was, of course, a fake: Schliemann had inscribed it himself. In 1933, the swastika flag was flown as the symbol of the German Reich.

PUSHKIN YOUR LUCK

'Priam's treasure' was taken by Schliemann to Berlin and put on display there. But it was stolen by the Russians during their assault on Berlin at the end of the Second World War in 1945. They denied it, saying it had just 'disappeared' in the general mêlée. The Russian curators, many rather concerned about this, were told to maintain their silence, or else. The treasure eventually emerged from the Pushkin Museum into the light of day, blinking and slightly embarrassed, in 1994. The Germans are demanding it back. The Russians point out that the Germans stole many of their treasures during their invasion in 1941. The argument rumbles on.

POLIS: THE GREEK CITY-STATE

Homer looked back to an aristocratic world of heroes from the deep past. In fact he was composing at a time when a quite different unit of organization was emerging that was to dominate the Greek world. It was the city-state, or *polis* (plural *poleis*; whence our 'politics', 'police', etc.).

The *polis* was first and foremost a small, strongly independent community controlling a geographically precise territory, typically an area of mountains, farmlands and sea. This was very different from the central command-and-control culture of Mycenaean Greece or the tribal culture typical of much of northern Greece. Wars with neighbours over borders were common. Athens and Sparta were far and away the largest *poleis*: Athens and its territory Attica covered 920 square miles (2,400 square km), Sparta three times that amount. As we have seen, Greeks took their *polis* culture across many areas of the Mediterranean, from the Black Sea and the coastal fringes of Turkey to North Africa, southern Italy, Sicily, southern France ('Gaul') and Spain. But they still saw themselves first and foremost as Greeks. At any one time, there were about 1,000 *poleis* around the Mediterranean.

THE AUTONOMOUS COMMUNITY

The ancient Greek *polis* was certainly small. Because of the nature of the terrain and the limited resources a *polis* could command, the average *polis* was only around 2,000 to 8,000 strong, of whom a quarter were male citizens. The explanation of Athens' power is that in terms of *citizen* population it became the largest of all *poleis*; in the fifth century BC it held about 430,000, of whom around 60,000 were citizens. Plato calculated the ideal size at 5,040; Aristotle thought in terms of 'the largest population within easy view of each other consistent with the needs of a self-sufficient life'.

And that is the point: there was no central Greek government telling *poleis* what to do, let alone any concept of a bureaucratic cross-*polis* state apparatus. The Greek world consisted of self-sufficient, autonomous *poleis*, each run by its own citizens in whatever way they chose, with its own laws, customs, rituals, coinage (etc.), each prepared to fight any other *polis* that threatened its territory, or to unite with it – or anyone else – if self-interest or necessity decreed. In the Persian wars (490–479 BC), for example, more Greeks fought on the Persian side than on the Greek; only thirty-one *poleis* actually opposed Persia. Greek *poleis* ferociously guarded their freedom and independence.

LIFE IN THE POLIS: THE WORKING DAY

Because *polis* is translated 'city-state', it is easy to assume that it was an urban community. Nothing could be further from the truth. The vast majority of Greeks were peasants; they survived by working the land, growing enough to feed themselves and hoping to create a small surplus to trade at market. How many Greeks ever went into the main city centre is a good question. In Attica, for example, peasants on their farms on the fringes could be some 30 miles (*c.* 50 km) from Athens – a long journey there and back.

In his poem *Works and Days*, the Greek farmer-poet Hesiod gives some sense of the unrelenting nature of peasant life in the ancient world. He saw farming as a matter of survival, when men 'will never cease from toil and misery by day and night'. He castigated his wretched brother Perses, who bribed his way into getting a larger share of a disputed inheritance than he did, but (presumably) wasted it and now lived in idleness and beggary. Serves him right, said Hesiod; that is not the way ahead.

TIPS FOR THE GOOD PEASANT LIFE

For Hesiod, it is only work that counts:

Do not put things off till tomorrow and the next day. That man never fills his granary. It is application that produces increase. The man who puts off work wrestles with ruin.

Look after the pennies, he recommends:

If you lay down even a little on a little, and do this often, that could well grow big; he who adds to what is there keeps hunger at bay.

Protect what you have:

What is stored away at home is never a worry; better to have things there in the house than outside.

The consequence could be dramatic:

It is through work that men become rich in flocks and wealthy, and a working man is much dearer to the immortals. Work is no disgrace, but idleness is; and if you work, you will soon find the idle man will envy you as you enrich yourself – for wealth is accompanied by honour and prestige.

The sentiment is very Greek: nothing beats being looked up to.

PIGGING IT

It is significant that in Hesiod men lived off cereal crops for the most part, not off meat, the food of Homeric heroes. The point is that sheep (wool), goats (milk and cheese) and cattle (traction power from oxen) were too precious to eat regularly. That left pigs: easy to feed, littering twice a year and a third of the price of sheep and goats (if prices for sacrificial offerings are anything to go by); further, they produced up to five times more usable meat and fat per animal than sheep or goats. That left a problem: how to preserve the meat once you had killed the animal. Salting and drying were the key. Meanwhile, small bits of pig – particularly the cheap, less tempting bits – were salted and made into sausages. The Greeks did not have a single word for 'sausage': they had eleven.

COMMUNITY AND COMPETITION

Community co-operation was important. Hesiod advises:

> Invite to dinner one who is friendly, and ignore your enemy. Most of all, invite the man who lives near you... a bad neighbour is as big a bane as a good one is a boon; he has got good value who has a good neighbour. Nor would a cow be lost, but for a bad neighbour. It is good to take a measure from your neighbour and good to pay him back the same, or better, so that if you are in need afterwards, you can rely on him for help.

But there was also a strong sense of competition, says Hesiod:

A man is keen to work when he sees his rich neighbour
ploughing and planting and putting his house in order, and
neighbour vies with neighbour as he hurries after wealth.
This competition is productive for men. So too potter gets
angry with potter, craftsman with craftsman, and beggar is
jealous of beggar, minstrel of minstrel.

GOOD AND BAD WOMEN

In a passage from his *Theogony*, Hesiod is uncompromising in his
attitude towards women:

Women are like drones which are fed by the bees in their
roofed hives and are their partners in crime. For the bees
are busy all day till the sun goes down and build white
honeycombs; but the drones stay at home in the shelter of
the hive and fill their bellies with the toil of others. High-
thundering Zeus made woman to be a similar curse to mortal
men and a partner in vexation. But Zeus produced a second
price for man to pay. If a man avoids marriage and all the
mischief women cause, and never takes a wife, he comes
to his declining years with no one to look after him in the
miseries of old age. He has enough to live on while he lives,
and when he dies his distant relatives divide up his property.
A man who does marry and has a good wife after his own
heart can balance evil with good while he lives; but he who
gets one of the hurtful sort of women lives with an open
wound in his heart and spirit, and an ill that has no cure.

Compare p. 45 above and contrast p. 62. This is the first example of misogyny in western literature.

FRIEND/ AND ENEMIE/

The '-phile' root in English means 'friend': Philippa is a friend to horses (*phil-hippos*), a philanthrope a friend to mankind (*phil-anthrôpos*). But in Greek, a *philos* was much more than a friend: he was someone who could be relied upon to provide support, advice, finance and backing, in any situation, especially emergencies. The more *philoi* you had and the closer your ties with them, the better; and it was a commonplace of Greek ethics that a man was valued by the extent to which he did active good to *philoi* and active harm to personal enemies. Such social values were endemic in Greek life; they encouraged a culture of potentially violent competition and of revenge. Getting one's own back was of great importance to Greeks: whatever else a Greek did, turning one or other of his cheeks was not one of them.

MILK

To many, milk is a staple of the western diet. Not so in the Greek world, because it went off so quickly: it was drunk fresh, or not at all. Since the enzyme that enables cow's milk to be digested beyond childhood is characteristic of northern Europeans, the milk of choice was that from goats or sheep. Even so, most of it was turned into cheese, or forms of curd and yoghurt.

IV

c. 700–593 BC

TIMELINE

c. 735–715 BC	Sparta conquers Messenia
733 BC	Foundation of Syracuse
c. 700 BC	Introduction of hoplite fighting
688 or 659 BC	Foundation of Byzantium
c. 650 BC	Messenian revolt: Lycurgus reshapes Sparta?
	Archilochus, poet from Paros
	Tyrtaeus, poet from Sparta
	Growth of the oracle at Delphi
632 BC	Cylon's failed coup in Athens; a curse laid on Megacles (I)
620 BC	Dracon's laws in Athens
600 BC	Foundation of Marseilles (Massalia)
	Thales, philosopher from Miletus
	Development of coinage

Development of the trireme

Sappho, poetess from Lesbos

Periander, tyrant of Corinth

594 BC   Solon and the laws of Athens

TYRANNY, POETRY AND SPECULATION

Spartans claimed to be descended from Heracles. Sparta had undergone its poverty-stricken Dark Age too, and emerged by ruthlessly reshaping their world: they conquered the neighbouring territory of Messenia and enslaved its whole population. After a revolt by the Messenians around 650 BC, Sparta tightened its grip on this 'enemy within' by turning itself into a military state. If the Spartan cultural and political 'founding father' Lycurgus ever existed, it may have been at this time.

The Greeks, who had gone east in 1000 BC, now started going west: to Cumae, near Naples (founded by Euboeans *c*. 740 BC) and to Syracuse (founded by Corinthians *c*. 733 BC). That region of southern Italy and Sicily was to become known by the Romans as Magna Graecia, 'Great[er] Greece'. Greeks also migrated into the Black Sea. They were risk-takers, in an uncertain world, driven by starvation, poverty or better opportunities – for example, more productive land or possibilities for exchange of goods (i.e. trade). At any rate, the migration is probably linked to the expanding population in Greece. Byzantium, a small town that was in a thousand years to become the mighty Constantinople (today's Istanbul), was also founded; and settlers from Phocaea founded a major town even further west than Magna Graecia – Marseilles (Latin: Massalia), far-sightedly introducing the vine.

In the course of these migrations Greeks brought goods such as wheat and olives as well as wine to the western Mediterranean. Trade between Greeks and non-Greeks increased, and the new Greek settlements abroad brought Greek skills and artefacts to their hinterlands, including southern Russia and the Celts of northern Europe.

Around this time hoplite fighting was invented – a major innovation in Greek warfare with implications for the dynamics of society, since the defence of a *polis* would now be in the hands of a broader range of citizens. Archilochus from the island of Paros and the Spartan Tyrtaeus broke into poetic song, while the Delphic oracle began to grow in importance.

In some parts of Greece tyrants, like Cylon (unsuccessfully) in Athens and Periander in Corinth, began to emerge – not necessarily oppressive figures but aristocrats seizing power for themselves and their followers in the newly formed *poleis*. The first so-called Greek philosopher/natural scientist, Thales from Miletus, speculated what the world was made from.

Meanwhile, the invention of coinage boosted the possibility of trade – and therefore of some people getting considerably richer than others – while the trireme, a new-style warship, revolutionized fighting at sea. On the island of Lesbos, the poetess Sappho sang poems that would result in her being called 'the tenth Muse'.

In 594 BC economic problems in Athens were sorted out by Solon, in a move that prefigured Athens' invention of democracy.

There is an energy, imagination and sense of adventure about the Greeks of this period, politically, culturally, intellectually and socially. But, as even this brief summary shows, a unified world it was not. No dominant *polis* had emerged, though the sheer size of Sparta and Athens was beginning to tell. Neither of them needed to send settlers abroad.

WHAT'S IN A NAME?

One possible explanation why Romans gave the name *Graeci* (our 'Greeks') to the people who called themselves *Hellênes* emerges from the eighth century BC, when Greeks first started moving settlements into southern Italy. One of the main movers was the island of Euboea, close to Greece's eastern coast; opposite it, on the Greek mainland, was a place called Graea. If they were among the first settlers, and local Italians asked them who they were, they would have said *Graikoi*, meaning 'men from Graea'. This term might then have been applied to everyone coming from that part of the world. Another possibility was offered by Aristotle: he said that in the deep past, only a small part of Greece was called Hellas, but its inhabitants were originally called *Graikoi* before they became *Hellênes*. Possibly. But the fact is that the answer still eludes us.

ONE HELOT OF A LIFE

In the eighth century BC Sparta annexed the territory of neighbouring Messenia and reduced the population effectively to slaves ('helots' lit.

'captives'). This turned Sparta into a powerful military state, consisting of three quite distinct categories by birth, all Spartans, all speaking the same language and worshipping the same gods but with very different functions:

Spartiates, the warrior elite;

the *perioikoi*, 'neighbours', free but inferior neighbours, serving in the army and having a say in their own but none in Sparta's affairs, self-employed peasant-farmers like most other Greeks (see p. 70), rich or poor, but using their skills as craftsmen and tradesmen in the Spartiate cause; and

helots, enslaved land-workers, maintaining the vital Spartan agricultural economy.

The Spartans now found themselves outnumbered about five to one by the helot population, so the problems of security were grave, even more so after a Messenian revolt around 650 BC. After that, they turned themselves into a military state, made themselves almost entirely self-sufficient, and constructed alliances across the Peloponnese, forming the so-called 'Peloponnesian League'. Their policy towards other Greek states became essentially a defensive one, driven by the big fear that their huge helot population might revolt or be helped to revolt. That is why secure allies across the Peloponnese were of such high importance.

Sparta was also known as Laconia (the Spartans' original homeland) or Lacedaemon (after an early king). Their army was easily recognizable, dressed in purple cloaks, with a lambda (Λ, equivalent to our 'L') on their shields, and marching in step to music.

EDUCATION FOR BATTLE

The Spartan emphasis was on rearing citizen male children, who were placed in army barracks at the age of seven. There they went barefoot, wearing a single homespun garment, all the year round. Kept hungry, they were encouraged to steal – severe punishment awaited not those who stole but those who got caught stealing. These correctly educated, fully trained Spartans, were known as Spartiates (the title had to be earned: it was not automatic). There was restricted access to marriage, and pederasty played its part: between the age of twelve and eighteen, every Spartiate male took an adult warrior as lover ('for such a love inspires modesty, ambition and a burning desire to excel,' the biographer Plutarch explains). It was the adult's job to ensure the young man became a true Spartiate. The story is told that, when one young man cried out in pain during training, it was his adult male lover who was punished for failing to instil the Spartiate code of gritted teeth. More females than usual may have been abandoned at birth, but citizen women were educated and socialized to be fitting wives and mothers.

These Spartiates were forbidden any profession but war: the result was effectively the Greek world's first professional army. In 600 BC, full Spartiates perhaps numbered perhaps 8,000–9,000 – far more fully trained hoplites than most other *poleis* had.

Question: what happened to the citizen Spartans who *failed* the Spartiate exam? We do not know. It may also be the case that promising sons of *perioikoi* or sons of Spartiate fathers by helot mothers could also try to qualify. But what we do know is that Spartiate numbers continued to drop.

SPARTAN BROTH

The Spartans' basic food was a black broth made of boiled pigs' legs, salt, blood and vinegar. Many stories were told about it. One lucky diner tasted it and said: 'Now I know why the Spartans don't fear death.' Dionysius, tyrant of Syracuse, ordered a Spartan slave of his to cook it. One mouthful was quite enough. The cook commented that, if you wished to develop a taste for it, you had to have trained like a Spartan and bathed in the (freezing) river Eurotas.

OIL TO THE GOOD

Climate and soil in Messenia and Laconia were ideal for the olive tree, and Spartans seem to have introduced the Greek habit of taking physical exercise naked, scrubbing down and finishing off by anointing themselves with olive oil. This is one of the ways in which Greeks differentiated themselves from barbarians: Greeks flaunted their stuff because they looked so good, while unfit barbarians kept their flabby bodies out of sight.

GOOD ORDER

Sparta's rigid, austere militaristic control over those it ruled made it famous for its *eunomia*, 'good order', very appealing to thinkers like Plato who had little time for messy democracy. Spartans believed that the man responsible for this state of affairs was Lycurgus, a misty, possibly mythical, figure to whom virtually all Spartan institutions and customs were ascribed. He introduced an education system that concentrated on turning men into a fighting force unmatchable for courage, skill and discipline. He invented a political system in which control was in the hands of the *gerousia*, a group of thirty distinguished senior citizens (over sixty), two of whom were hereditary 'kings'; this body discussed all business before presenting it to the assembly of Spartiates. He ensured that men's first duty was not to families or friends but to the state, and developed in them a culture of paranoia about the outside world. Young Spartans in training were for a time part of a secret organization, the *krypteia*, in which they were charged with murdering and spreading terror among the helots – as long as they were not found out.

LACONIC REPUTATION

Spartans were famous for being men of fearless courage and few words. The story was told of a young Spartan who had stolen a fox. He was hauled up before the courts, the fox tucked under his tunic. It started eating its way through his stomach. The boy said nothing and did not react, until he dropped dead.

As for pithy, laconic utterance: Lycurgus was once urged to turn Sparta into a democracy. He replied: 'Turn your own household into a democracy first.' When Philip of Macedon asked the Spartans if they wanted him as a friend or enemy, they replied: 'Neither.' An envoy spoke at great length to king Agis, and asked what he should report back. Agis replied: 'That throughout your speech I listened in silence.' The 301 Spartans defending Thermopylae (see p. 162) were told by the Persians that their arrows would blot out the sky. Dieneces replied: 'Excellent. Then we shall fight in the shade.' King Agis used to remark that it was not important to know how many the enemy were – just *where* they were. Asked where Sparta's walls were, king Agesilaus said: 'There', pointing to his men. When Panthoidas in Asia saw a great defensive wall, he said: 'Magnificent women's quarters.' Asked how far Sparta's boundaries reached, Agesilaus took up his spear and said: 'As far as this reaches.'

Spartan women told their sons to return either with their shield or on it (i.e. dead). When one young man complained to his mother that his sword was too short, she replied: 'Then lengthen it by a stride.' An enemy embassy announced that they were about to invade and, if they succeeded, Sparta would be razed. The Spartans replied: 'If.' The point about Spartan brevity is that it enabled Spartans to contribute forcefully and memorably to verbal debate without compromising their tight-lipped, all-action image.

ARCHILOCHUS FROM PAROS

The poet Archilochus was a tough-talking soldier, and his poetry is full of memories of his companions and their adventures on the field of battle and on the high seas – their successes and defeats, their various scrapes, and the politics behind it all. His work was very highly rated in the ancient world but survives only in fragments (for the survival of Greek literature, see p. 360). In the following passage he prefers the real fighter, however unglamorous, to the self-important, preening officer:

> I do not like the captain, tall-standing, legs apart,
> Whose cut of hair and whisker is his principal renown.
> Give me the little fellow, with the bigness in his heart,
> And let his legs be bandy, if they never let him down.
>
> (trans. D. L. Page)

And here he has presumably been caught unawares, perhaps in an ambush, and had to leave everything and run for it. No Homeric or Spartan heroics for him:

> Some Thracian sports my splendid shield:
> I had to leave it in a wood,
> But saved my skin. Well, I don't care –
> I'll get another just as good.
>
> (trans. M. L. West)

The island of Paros was also a centre for the worship of Demeter, the goddess of agriculture, and her cult was associated with recitations of scurrilous, erotic poems, designed (presumably) to encourage fertility. Archilochus let rip. Here is a sequence of suggestive fragments about a woman he enjoyed once but whose charms were long gone:

> Many a sightless eel have you taken in...
> And I used to explore your rugged glens
>   In my full-blooded youth...
> Such was the lust for sex that, worming in
>   Under my heart, quite blinded me
> And robbed me of my young wits...
>
> (trans. M. L. West)

Here are other fragments from his erotic poems:

> ... his tender horn...
> ... wet mound of Venus...
> Up and down she bounced like a kingfisher flapping on a
>   jutting rock.

Like a Thracian or Phrygian drinking beer through a tube
she sucked, stooped down, engaged too from behind.
And his dong... flooded over like a stall-fed donkey's...
... foam all round her mouth...
They stooped and spurted off
all their accumulated wantonness.
... through the tube into the vessel.
... a growth between the thighs...
I won't use surgery, I know another sovereign remedy
for a growth of this description.

(trans. M. L. West)

MEDITERRANEAN ADVENTURES

An Athenian inscription (*c.* 440 BC) reads: 'The colonists to Brea are to
go from the *thêtes* and *zeugitae*', i.e. the two poorest classes (see p. 104).
Since Greece was for the most part a poor country, Greeks were willing
to travel abroad to make their fortune. That said, it showed a great deal
of ambition and guts for people to transport themselves lock, stock and
barrel, and start up a new life, as many Greeks did from the 730s BC
onwards. It also suggests ready availability of transport and general
communication around the Mediterranean – more evidence of 'opening
up' – and a considerable degree of co-operation and organization too.
For those who went, their new life would offer the prospect of new
sources of wealth as well as new technologies. Greeks living abroad
would certainly not be the 'poorer neighbours'.

ARMS...

The term 'hoplite' derived from the Greek *hoplon*, 'a shield', though in the plural (*hopla*), it meant 'weapons' or 'armour'. Hoplites were citizens (mainly farmers) who could afford the armour: helmet, breastplate, greaves, round shield about a metre across, spear and short, single-edged 'hacking' sword. Up to half the male population could probably afford most of the gear, though whether they could all afford a bronze breastplate – a very expensive item – is extremely doubtful (one guess is that one in ten might have done so). Such involvement in the defence of their *polis* may well have encouraged these citizens to demand a greater role in its decision-making.

... AND THE MAN

The hoplite formation was basically a phalanx: row upon row of tightly packed men (the occasional reference to massed fighting in Homer suggests an origin). The shield was carried on the left arm by means of a hand-grip on the right rim, which the left hand grasped through an arm-band in the centre. It protected most of the hoplite and the right side of the man to his left. It was essential to keep this formation steady. The front line was backed up by rows of hoplites behind, ready to step into the breach if a man in front fell. The main weapon was the spear, used for jabbing, either above or below the enemy shield; the sword was used as a back-up. It looks as if the first engagement was essentially hand-to-hand combat, followed by general shoving when the enemy weakened. The aim was to get the enemy to turn and run.

It is important to stress that *most* battles in the Greek world were brief affairs – a single pitched battle, all over in a few hours. Victory depended most of all on morale – confidence – and the cohesion of the hoplite force (no breaking ranks). Only in exceptional circumstances did victorious soldiers run amok, slaughtering as they went, destroying infrastructure, raping and enslaving. They usually put up a victory monument and went home. They were farmers: they had work to do.

TYRTAEUS FROM SPARTA

The time came when every Spartan was made to listen to Tyrtaeus' poetry, which was composed when the Messenians were in revolt (see p. 80). It gives a powerful sense of what hoplite fighting was actually like – terrifying – and how essential for success it was that the line held, come what may:

> So let us fight with spirit for our land,
> die for our sons, and spare our lives no more.
> You young men, keep together, hold the line,
> do not start panic or disgraceful rout.
> Keep grand and valiant spirits in your hearts,
> be not in love with life – the fight's with men!
> ...
> Let every man, then, feet set firm apart,
> bite on his lip and stand against the foe...
> You know that those who bravely hold the line
> and press toward engagement at the front
> die in less numbers, with the ranks behind
> protected; those who run, lose all esteem.
> The list is endless of the ills that hurt

the man who learns to think the coward's
thoughts: for it's a bad place, as he flees the fray,
to have his wound, between the shoulder-blades,
and it's a shameful sight to see him lie
dead in the dust, the spear-point in his back.
Let every man, then, feet set firm apart,
bite on his lip and stand against the foe,
his thighs and shins, his shoulders and his chest
all hidden by the broad bulge of his shield.
Let his right hand brandish the savage lance,
the plume nod fearsomely above his head.
By fierce deeds let him teach himself to fight,
and not stand out of fire – he has a shield –
but get in close, engage, and stab with lance
or sword, and strike his adversary down.
Plant foot by foeman's foot, press shield on shield,
thrust helm at helm, and tangle plume with
plume, opposing breast to breast: that's how to fight,
with the long lance or sword-grip in your hand.

(trans. M. L. West)

THE DELPHIC ORACLE

Of some 300 oracles in the ancient world, about 120 were in Greece.
From its origins around 800 BC, when the first dedications there are
found, the oracle at Delphi became the most famous of them all. What
form the consultations took in its early days we do not know; but we
have some information about how the oracle worked in the classical

period. The priestess and voice of the oracle – the Pythia, a female who remained chaste and served for life – was not on constant duty: she was available only one day a month for nine months of the year, but could be consulted in an emergency. The consultation took place inside the temple of Apollo. The consultant paid a temple tax for the privilege and offered up a sacrifice outside the temple (unless it was a regular day for consultations, when the priests of Apollo obliged). If the offering was accepted, the consultant entered the temple and offered up another sacrifice (more expense). The local *prophêtai* ('interpreters') then accompanied him into the inner shrine, where the Pythia, purified and with a laurel wreath on her head, heard and responded to the question. The answer she gave was then 'interpreted' in some way by the *prophêtai*.

BACKING A WINNER

Virtually all of the 500 or so genuine oracular responses – genuine because the questions and answers were inscribed on stone for all to see – simply asked for religious advice. For instance, a portent has appeared in the sky: what shall the Athenians do, or to what god shall they offer sacrifice and pray for better consequences from the portent? Answer: it is to the Athenians' advantage to sacrifice to... and a string of gods follows. The oracle served as a sort of citizens' advice bureau, designed to act supportively towards the consultant.

But the oracle also had a reputation at a different, far more dramatic level – such as telling Oedipus that he would kill his father and marry his mother. This is clearly mythical fantasy. On the other hand, the oracle also had to give advice on tricky political matters (for example, the

Persian wars). How did that work? What difference did an oracle make? One gets the sense that there must have been a team of international diplomats on permanent call – except that there were no such bodies. On Delphic 'inspiration', see p. 161.

TYRANTS

However any *polis* ruled itself, there came a period for many when, with the support of influential friends, some of the wealthy in some *poleis* staged a sort of military coup and ruled as *turannoi*, 'tyrants'. *Turannos* is a non-Greek word (it is Lydian) – as if it were a wholly alien concept in the eyes of a *polis*-based society. In fact, to start with, the term meant nothing worse (or better) than ruler. But it was a form of unconstitutional one-man rule, and independent-minded Greeks were not on the whole favourable to such a set-up.

CURSE AND CRIME

By about 650 BC, Athens seems to have been in the charge of *arkhōn*s – annually appointed officials, probably drawn for the most part from the nobility. When they had served their term of office, they joined the Areopagus, which may have been a general advisory body with some jurisdiction over the laws. But in 632 BC Cylon, an aristocrat and Olympic victor, who enjoyed all the kudos that such success brought, tried to make himself tyrant. He failed. His followers, who were taking refuge as suppliants (see below) at an altar of Athena, were killed. This was against all precedent, and the *arkhōn* at the time, Megacles (I), was cursed for allowing it and exiled. In 620 BC the lawgiver Dracon drafted Athens' first criminal code, and extremely draconian (i.e. severe) it was too, since Dracon argued that, as small crimes deserved the death penalty, so must big ones (his laws were 'written in blood, not ink', a later politician said). But there was clearly trouble and violence in Athens at the time; later writers ascribed this to the 'poor becoming enslaved to the rich', and Dracon's code may have been a response to the turmoil. In 594 BC Solon was called upon to sort it out (see p. 103).

SUPPLIANT RIGHTS

Not many Greeks, even in the direst circumstances, would become 'suppliants'. This meant willingly humiliating oneself by indicating one's abject helplessness and distress before begging help from a man or a woman. But sometimes needs must (even the great Odysseus supplicated the young girl Nausicaa in the *Odyssey*), and, since Zeus was god of supplication, suppliants came under divine protection. Full physical supplication entailed kneeling before someone and holding their knees and chin – partly to restrain them symbolically from movement or speech during the plea – and begging them for help; or attaching oneself to an altar or some other object of religious significance. (In the case of Cylon's followers, they tied a rope to the altar and held on to it when they were persuaded to leave, on the assumption that its 'force' would still be felt.) As long as that position and contact were maintained, the supplicatee was almost duty-bound to honour the request, though there were circumstances in which the supplicatee could reject it without fear of divine retribution.

THE CURSE OF THE ALCMAEONIDS

Megacles (I) was an Alcmaeonid, i.e. of the family of Alcmaeon, and archon in Athens. The murder of Cylon's followers resulted in his and his family's exile from Athens. Even the bones of buried Alcmaeonids were dug up and flung outside Athens' city limits: one could not have such cursed remains polluting the city. This family would have tremendous future influence in Athens, and its enemies would constantly try to use this curse to diminish it.

TYRANT THEORY

Aristotle (p. 307) distinguished two sorts of *turannos*. One sort, knowing that the people hated him, rendered them incapable of moving against him by adopting three main strategies: he stamped out anyone with any independence of mind or spirit; ensured no one had any trust in anyone else; and deprived his subjects of the chance of building up a power base. So he kept the people leaderless, obsequious, uneducated, disassociated, poor, working and under a constant watchful eye.

The alternative tyrant ensured that people did not want to move against him. So he appeared more like a responsible manager of a household than a tyrant; led a life of moderation, as a trustee of public resources; embraced men of drive and ability so that they did not think they could do better under a different regime; made sure that his subjects did not feel ill-used by him; and did all in his power to keep both rich and poor onside and reconciled to him and to each other. So, by ensuring people were not reduced to 'impotent submission', he had a chance of staying in power for longer. Such tyrants, Aristotle concluded, were only 'half-wicked'.

THE BEGINNINGS OF PHILOSOPHY?

All over the Mediterranean, people were thinking about where the world came from and what men were doing on it. Jews, Egyptians, Phoenicians, Persians, Babylonians – all had their own 'takes' on the issues. If we wish to argue that Greeks invented philosophy, we do so in the sense that they did not see sacred books, priests or rulers as ultimate authorities on what to think. Rather, they tried to keep the gods out of their speculations, relying more on their own capacities to reach humanly intelligible conclusions; and then they argued ferociously about them in public, without fear or favour.

Diodorus, a first-century BC Greek historian from Sicily, put it like this (note that by 'barbarians' Greeks meant those who did not speak Greek: instead they went *bar-bar-bar*):

> The barbarians, by always sticking to the same things, keep a firm hold on every detail. But the Greeks, aiming at the profit to be made out of the business, keep founding new schools and argue with each other over the most important matters of speculation. As a result, their pupils hold conflicting views, and their minds, vacillating throughout their lives and unable to believe anything with firm conviction, simply wander in confusion.

Precisely: dogma was out. Everything was up for grabs. See p. 355 for the battles students fought in support of their professors!

LAW OF RULES

It is easy to assume that Athens was the 'home of philosophy'. But in fact it was among Greeks on the west ('Ionian') coast of Asia Minor, stimulated by contact with Near Eastern thought, that debate was stirring in the sixth century BC. These sages certainly knew their onions, but it needs to be said that while they thought they could account for everything, their commitment to methodical, detailed, accurate and relevant observations was very limited.

But at the same time, they believed that Nature was not random. It was rule-governed. Further, its rules encompassed the whole ordered universe (the *kosmos*) so that everyday phenomena external to the earth – eclipses, thunderstorms, movements of the stars and so on – as well as natural disasters such as earthquakes could be explained by these 'rules'. As the fifth-century BC atomist Leucippus said, 'Nothing happens at random, but everything from a scientific principle and necessity.' But the important point is this: though their theories were mostly false and their conclusions mostly nonsense, they gave *reasons* for their conclusions and *argued* for them in *public*. Nor did they allow supernatural explanations: that was cheating, since the world had to be *humanly* intelligible. Otherwise, why bother? No one could understand the mind of a god. All this was of the highest importance for western intellectual development. If they got it wrong, so have many subsequent philosophers and scientists...

But none of their work encouraged Greeks to think that they should not acknowledge the gods. That would have been a very stupid thing to do indeed.

NATURAL PROPERTIES

Phusis, 'nature' (our physics), was at the heart of early Greek thinking. It comes from the Greek word *phuô* ('I grow'), and how things grow is related to their particular properties. This is what modern science investigates, and ancient science tried to do so too. From the notion that matter has properties, it was a short step to ask: 'Well, if things grow, what do they grow from? What is it that makes them grow? How did the universe grow? What did it start from?'

WATER, WATER EVERYWHERE

Thales (*c*. 624–546 BC), a Greek from Miletus, was a *phusikos*: 'a student of the nature of things'. Aristotle thought Thales was the first person to try to think rationally about nature because he offered *argument* as against those (like Hesiod) who simply told stories. Thales started the trend for asking 'What makes the world as it is?' and came up with the answer: water. Life and all nature needed water to grow; and water could not be generated – it was just 'there'. Further, water was able to take on solid, liquid and gaseous forms: it could explain how water changed into everything else. But Thales never tried to *test* his theory. That idea, so crucial to us, was another two millennia in the making. As one of the Greeks' Seven Sages, Thales was also responsible for the saying 'Know yourself'. Very Greek was his reply to the question 'How best can one bear adversity?' – 'If one sees one's enemies doing even worse.' If you cannot be a winner, it is some compensation if your enemies aren't either.

COINAGE

Coinage was invented in Lydia (a state in Asia Minor) around 620 BC. Fairly quickly it caught on, and from about the 550s BC coinage came to play an increasingly important part in the Greek economic systems. It could be used as a means of exchange, payment, store of value, unit of account, and so on – extremely useful when dealing with different states. It would also pay for mercenaries, of whom there were a great number in Greece from the seventh century BC: soldiering could make a very decent living (see p. 248). Over time, as markets expanded, quite complex transactions became possible. It was far more efficient than bartering, even more so when a culture of credit developed, though Greeks (and Romans) had some moral reservations about interest-bearing loans.

SAFE AS TEMPLES

Greeks tended to store public money in temples for safe-keeping under the eyes of the god. Temple finances were further increased by those paying tithes and offering benefactions, as well as by rents from sacred property, taxes and fees for services, etc. So temples became guardians of vast stores of public wealth which they could advance as loans to governments and cities.

THE TRIREME REVOLUTION

The trireme was the fastest and finest man-of-war in the classical period. It revolutionized naval warfare. It was a long, slender ship with a low draught; the dimensions attested by the fourth-century BC remains of the ship-sheds at the Piraeus were 115–21 feet (35–7 metres) by 11 feet (3.5 metres). A trireme had 170 rowers, in three superimposed banks, plus commanders, marines and archers: about 200 in all. Its chief armament was the bronze ram (an extension of the keel) used to ram into and cripple enemy ships. It could reach a steady speed of 7–8 knots, or even up to 13 knots for a short burst. But with its big crew and its need to be as light as possible, it carried few provisions and was usually beached at night for crews to eat and sleep. Except in unusual circumstances, the crew rowed only when fighting; the trireme had masts to catch the wind for long journeys. Being light and rather unstable, it could not be used in rough weather.

TRAINING UP THE CREW

Rowing a trireme effectively was a highly skilled job which required considerable training: it was here that Athens excelled. The military man and historian Xenophon (fourth century BC) gives an account of a voyage which a commander used to get the men in shape. Unusually, he made very little use of his sails:

> By proceeding under oars in this way, Iphicrates made his crews fitter and his ships faster. And when the expedition was due for its morning or evening meal at any particular place [the crew slept and ate ashore], he would order the leading ships back, turn the line round again to face the land and make them race at a signal for the shore... On daylight voyages he trained them to form line ahead or line abreast at a signal, so that in the course of their voyage they had practised and become skilled at the manoeuvres needed in a naval battle before they reached the area of sea which they supposed to be in enemy control.

SAPPHO

Sappho's fame was such that she was known as 'the tenth Muse' (there were nine of these famous goddesses of culture). She lived on the island of Lesbos (whence our 'lesbian'), off the west coast of Asia Minor, in the sixth century BC. Like Archilochus' work, hers survives only in fragments and quotations. If we can trust that her poetry is autobiographical – not something that can be automatically assumed – she herself was lesbian but also had a daughter Cleis. She wrote intense, personal poems about family, friends and lovers. Much of her poetry is addressed to groups of women, of whom she appears to be the leader in some capacity or other. Perhaps she taught them music or poetry. Some of her poems celebrate marriage or public festivals, from the female point of view. Incidentally, we use the Latin version of her name: in Greek she was *Psapphô*.

It should not be assumed, however, that Sappho was the only female poet of the Greek world; it is possible to count sixty-four in all, real and imagined, though the fragments of only very few of their works survive.

TYPICAL BLOKE

In perhaps her most famous poem, Sappho reflects on her feelings at seeing a man apparently quite unmoved by the presence of a woman who means a great deal to her (square brackets indicate a gap in the text):

> He looks to me to be in heaven,
> that man who sits across from you
> and listens near you to your soft speaking,
> your lovely laughter: that, I vow,
> makes the heart leap in my breast;
> for watching you a moment, speech fails me,
> my tongue is paralysed, at once
> a light fire runs beneath my skin,

my eyes are blinded, and my ears drumming,
   the sweat pours down me, and I shake
all over, sallower than grass:
I feel as if I'm not far off dying.
   But no thing is too hard to bear;
   for [God can make] the poor man [rich,
or bring to nothing heaven-high fortune.]
                      (trans. M. L. West)

This is not a poem about [Sappho's jealousy. The sole point of the man is that he is wholly insensitive to the woman's charms; he is merely the starting point for Sappho's reflections on the intense physical feelings that the woman in question arouses in her.

PERIANDER: THE BAD TYRANT

A tyrant is as tyrannical as his press, which makes judging Periander of Corinth rather difficult. Aristotle, in the fourth century BC, recorded some repressive measures and noted that he needed a bodyguard (always a sign of the tyrant) but otherwise judged him 'moderate, raising no new taxes but satisfied with those on markets and harbours, and not unjust nor insolent but hating wickedness'. Doubtless his enemies put it about that he came to power by killing all outstanding Corinthians and his own wife, afterwards making love to her corpse; burned every Corinthian woman's fine dresses to honour her spirit; sent 300 boys from Corcyra (Corfu), where his son had been killed, to Lydia (Asia Minor) to be castrated; and so on.

PERIANDER: THE GOOD TYRANT

Periander may have had some bad press, but at the same time he was judged to be among Greece's Seven Sages. He was supposed to have said that it was better to be guarded by the citizens' goodwill than the spears of a bodyguard. He certainly helped to turn Corinth into a wealthy, flourishing place. He was also responsible for starting a project of the utmost importance: a passageway across the narrow isthmus of Corinth. This connected the distant Aegean Sea (to the east and Asia Minor) with the Adriatic (to the west and the route into Italy), and avoided the need for ships to slog south all the way round the Peloponnese.

THE CORINTHIAN WAY

Periander's wagon-way across the isthmus was 12 to 16 feet (3.6 to 5 metres) wide, with a channel in the middle 5 feet (1.5 metres) wide. It followed almost the identical route of what would in 2,500 years' time become the Corinth Canal. The light, narrow trireme, braced with ropes and padding, would be easily hauled across by its 170 crew. But the channel was too small for a big, round-bottomed, sail-driven merchantman. So those ships would unload cargo – especially heavy, expensive cargo such as marble, metal ore, roof tiles and timber – on one side, haul it over the wagon-way, and load it up on a different ship on the other side (there were harbours on both sides). All this with, of course, a very nice toll fee exacted by Corinth as well, thank you very much. It helped make Corinth a wealthy, powerful place. An ally of Sparta, Corinth was often a little too hot to handle for that conservative state.

FROM NERO TO THOMAS COOK

The first person actually to start digging the Corinth Canal was the Roman emperor Nero in AD 67. He declared the canal project open by striking the first blow with a golden shovel – a melancholy precedent that kings, queens, presidents and chairmen have been wearily following ever since. He dug about a mile at the west side, half a mile at the other. But revolution against him in the Roman empire put an end to this effort.

The canal proper was finally started in 1882 and opened in 1893. It cost the French company responsible for its construction 60 million French francs and bankrupted it. Thomas Cook's, the travel agent, went mad with excitement. In hushed, reverential tones of the sort that now greet a new telephone, the *Cook's Handbook* pointed out that the canal was 'fitted with Electric Light so that the canal is navigable both by day and night'.

CORINTH – CITY OF FUN

In 464 BC, Xenophon from Corinth won two victories at Olympia. He had promised to endow Corinth with a hundred sacred prostitutes if he was successful, and Pindar, the go-to poet for Olympic victory poems, duly celebrated the donation. It begins:

> Young women, hostesses to many, handmaidens of
> Attraction in wealthy Corinth...

and ends:

> Queen of Cyprus [i.e. Aphrodite], Xenophon has brought
> you a herd of a hundred grazing girls, and takes delight in
> fulfilment of his vows.

The geographer Strabo thought Corinth's wealth was partly down to these women:

> The temple of Aphrodite was so rich that it owned more than a thousand temple slaves, courtesans, whom both men and women had dedicated to the goddess. It was because of these women that the city became crowded and wealthy; for ship captains easily spent all their money on them.

Corinth's reputation for licentiousness was well deserved. While *Private Eye* refers to 'Ugandan discussions', the comic playwright Aristophanes talked of 'Corinthing'. St Paul visited Corinth between AD 50 and 52, and his two letters to the Corinthians express great concern about the effect of pagan Corinth on the church.

SOLON: THE ROAD TO DEMOCRACY

Another of the Seven Sages, Solon was a remarkable man: his reforms complete, he legislated that they should last for ten years, and promptly departed from Athens, leaving the Athenians to get on with it. If only...

Solon was *arkhôn* in Athens in 594 BC at a time when there were serious social problems, especially the poor becoming enslaved to the rich. Revolution was in the air. He legislated on a number of fronts, and the laws were inscribed, in wood or stone, in public places for all to see:

- Helping the poor by ensuring no man could be enslaved because he could not pay his debts (as a result, debt never became a political problem in classical Athens).

- Widening political power so that some posts were reserved for the wealthy rather than hereditary aristocrats (this would doubtless have pleased his wealthy backers; at the same time, he divided Athenians into four classes by wealth).

- Giving the poor some say in the Assembly and law-courts, e.g. ensuring that appeals could be made against legal decisions.

- Establishing a Council of Four Hundred – a steering committee to prepare business for the Assembly.

These measures shifted power – marginally – away from noble families to the people. He also welcomed back the Alcmaeonid family, who had previously been banished (see p. 92).

His reforms did not solve all the problems – a period of tyranny in Athens would ensue – but they did lay a firm foundation on which radical democracy was invented in 508 BC, and his reforms remained largely unchanged till Athens' defeat by Sparta in 404 BC.

Incidentally, most of what we know about Solon derives from his own writings – *poetry*, of course (see p. 36).

GENES, MONEY AND POWER

One of Solon's most influential moves was to categorize Athenians by wealth, i.e. by the value of the property they possessed (*not* by taxable income, for instance, since there were no such things as jobs with an income that could be taxed; see Hesiod, p. 70). Solon divided the citizens up into four classes:

pentakosimedimnoi	the wealthiest
hippeis	wealthy enough to serve in the cavalry

| *zeugitai* | could equip themselves as hoplites (see p. 87) |
| *thêtes* | the rest |

Originally, an *arkhôn*ship (i.e. real political power) was in the hands only of aristocratic families. However, defining citizens by wealth, not birth, meant that it was possible to extend the range of citizens who could hold a post, either because citizens became wealthier or because posts were opened up to poorer citizens.

To anticipate future developments in the *arkhôn*ship: in Solon's time the top two classes could become *arkhôn*s; in 501 BC, elected *stratêgoi* (military commanders) took over some of the *arkhôn*'s duties (p. 140); in 487 BC, *arkhôn*s were appointed by lot; in 458 BC, anyone in the third grouping could put their name into the hat for an *arkhôn*ship (p. 171); and in the fourth century BC, the last group could do so as well.

ϟΥϹΟΡΗΑΝΤΙϹ LAW

The legal system which Solon developed had no room for police or a state prosecutor. But that raised a problem. If there was no state prosecutor, how could offenders who had not actually harmed any *individual* (e.g. by flouting citizenship laws) be brought to book? Solon's answer was based on the argument that 'the best governed state is one in which those who are not wronged are as diligent in prosecuting criminals as those who have personally suffered'. So for certain types of offence, the principle was established that 'anyone who wanted to' could bring a case, often with a fixed reward for winning.

It was a nosy parker's dream. Athenians called such people *sukophantai* (derivation unknown), and they were deeply loathed. The sycophant naturally posed as a public benefactor, arguing high-mindedly that he was only 'serving the national interest', but Athenians saw them as interfering busybodies with a single end in view: making fast and easy profits out of the innocent.

HAPPINESS IN YOUR END

When Solon was visiting Lydia (so the historian Herodotus tell us), the Lydian king Croesus sent him on a guided tour of his fabulous treasuries. He then asked him who was the happiest man in the world, 'supposing the answer would be himself'. It turned out not to be: he did not even come second, let alone first. 'So what about me?' whined Croesus. Solon's magnificent reply pointed out that 'the god is envious of human prosperity and disruptive... and man is entirely a creature of chance'. Croesus might indeed seem to be rich and rule many people, but

> I will not answer your question until I know that you have died happily. Great wealth can make a man no happier than moderate means, unless he has the luck to remain prosperous right to the end... So until a man is dead, keep the word 'happy' in reserve. Till then, he is not happy, only lucky... Look to the end, no matter what you are considering. Often enough the god gives a man a glimpse of happiness and then utterly uproots him.

The story can hardly be true – Croesus became king of Lydia only in 560 BC – but time came to reveal the wisdom of Solon's words (for Croesus' fate, see p. 123).

LE<ALIZIN< BROTHEL$

St Augustine, writing in the fourth century AD, regretfully admitted that if prostitutes were banned, society 'would be reduced to chaos through unsatisfied lust'. Solon got there well before him: he instituted a legalized brothel in Athens. He did this, we are told, because of the crisis developing in the lives of Athenian youth. They were, he felt, under the compulsion of nature, but were going astray in directions that were not appropriate. So, as Athenaeus (see p. 363) tells us, Solon

> purchased and stationed women in various quarters, equipped and ready for all alike. They stand there naked, so that you will not be deceived. If you are not quite yourself, or there's something annoying you, their door is open – one obol a time. No prudishness, no bullshit, no pulling away – you just get on with it. You leave, that's it. Tell her to jump in a lake if you want – she is nothing to you.

But there was more to it than that. Solon saw that, to justify a rather shady public institution, popularity was not enough. The venture needed a higher purpose, and he decided that temple construction fitted the bill perfectly. So he diverted the profits into building a temple to Aphrodite *Pandemos* ('of all the people') – quite a useful temple too, costing about 500 talents, i.e. 18 million obols. It says a lot for the youth of Athens.

WATER WORK$

Attica did not have sufficient water from streams, lakes or springs. So Solon passed a law that if you lived more than 800 yards (740 metres) from a public well, you should dig your own; but if you dug to a depth of 20 yards (18 metres) and *still* could not find any water, you could use some of your neighbour's (see p. 136).

THE PENALTY FOR TREASON

Solon passed a law against tyranny, or subversion of the people. In the democratic period (see p.188), this had become a treason law, which the people's Assembly imposed ruthlessly. Here is the sentence passed on two traitors as a result of the oligarchic coup in 411 BC (see pp. 185, 232 on Antigone). Phrynichus, the instigator of the coup, was assassinated.

Archeptolemus son of Hippodamus of Agryle, being present, and Antiphon son of Sophilus of Rhamnous, being present, were found guilty of treason. They were sentenced to be handed over to the authorities, their property to be confiscated, with the tithe consecrated to the goddess, their homes to be levelled to the ground and markers placed on the sites, inscribed 'the property of Archeptolemus and Antiphon, the traitors'; and their heads of their deme to make an account of their property. It shall not be allowed to bury Archeptolemus and Antiphon at Athens or in any Athenian dominion. Archeptolemus and Antiphon and their posterity, both bastards and legitimate, shall be without citizen-rights. If anyone adopts a descendant of Archeptolemus and Antiphon, he shall lose his citizen-rights. The Athenians shall inscribe this on a bronze stele and set it up in the same place as the decrees about Phrynichus.

V

593–493 BC

TIMELINE

586–553 BC	Pythian, Nemean and Isthmian Games established
566 BC	Festival of Panathenaea
c. 560 BC	Athenian black-figure pottery on the rise
	Croesus king of Lydia
c. 546–528 BC	Pisistratus *turannos*
546 BC	Cyrus of Persia defeats Croesus
534 BC	Pisistratus introduces the Dionysia
528 BC	Hippias and Hipparchus tyrants of Athens
c. 520 BC	Athenian red-figure vases
514 BC	Hipparchus assassinated
510 BC	Hippias expelled
508 BC	Cleisthenes invents democracy
499 BC	The Ionian revolt: Greek cities in Asia Minor against Persia
494 BC	Persians regain Asia Minor; destruction of Miletus

ATHENS: FROM TYRANNY TO DEMOCRACY

We now turn to Athens' fortunes after the Solonian revolution: the tyranny of Pisistratus, the fortunes of the Alcmaeonids, the overthrow of the tyranny and the invention of democracy in Athens. We also follow the story of Croesus, king of Lydia, in Asia Minor, and the growing threat of Persian power under King Cyrus.

Athens was now a flourishing city. Envious of the Olympic Games and other games that had sprung up – at Delphi (Pythian Games), Corinth (Isthmian) and Nemea (Nemean) – it initiated the Panathenaea in 566 BC. At this 'All-Athenian' ceremony, games and music competitions were staged, and a great civic procession marched up to the Acropolis; every four years, a robe was woven and dedicated to Athena. Building in Athens went on apace: a temple to Athena was begun on the Acropolis, and many statues dedicated there. These did not come cheap. On the artistic front, from about 560 BC, Athenian black-figure pottery became the most popular tableware (ousting Corinthian, on which it was based), and Athenian craftsmen were much in demand.

The advent of Pisistratus as *turannos* about 546 BC enhanced these cultural and economic developments and hence Athens' unity and self-confidence: the Dionysia, a festival of tragedies in honour of the god Dionysus, was started. A feud with the Alcmaeonid Megacles (II), son of Alcmaeon, who had supported Pisistratus but then fallen out with him, saw the Alcmaeonids retire to Delphi. There they won the contract to rebuild the temple of Apollo at Delphi which had been destroyed by earthquake in 548 BC. This would put them in very good stead with the oracle in the years to come.

When Pisistratus died in 528 BC, his sons Hippias and Hipparchus took over from him. They maintained their father's cultural interests, introduced Attic coinage (the famous Attic 'owls') and started the temple of Olympian Zeus, but were prone to assassinating rivals. At the Panathenaea of 514 BC, Hipparchus himself was assassinated, and those who wished to remove Hippias looked for support outside Athens. They found a willing helper in Sparta. Sparta's first effort failed, but assisted by the Delphic oracle which – surprise, surprise – told everyone to throw out Hippias, Sparta finally succeeded in 510 BC. Hippias was expelled and the Alcmaeonids returned.

As the Athenians set about restoring 'constitutional' life, the Alcmaeonid Cleisthenes in 508 BC invented a brand-new system of government: the world's first and last democracy. The Spartans were not impressed, since this meant that their man in Athens, Isagoras, was not at the helm. The Spartan king Cleomenes organized an attack in 506 BC, but his forces withdrew and his allies from Boeotia and Chalcis were defeated. As Herodotus said: 'It is plain enough, not in this instance only but everywhere else too, that freedom is an excellent thing.'

Meanwhile, in Asia Minor, the Greeks who had established settlements along the west coast were feeling the heat, first from Lydia, which had subjugated many Greek *poleis* by about 560 BC. But the Lydian king Croesus was a benign ruler and keen admirer of Greek culture. The Persians further east were rather less impressed. Under their king Cyrus they conquered Croesus in 546 BC, imposed their own *turannoi* on the Greek settlements, exacted large taxes from them, and continued pushing west into northern Greece (Thrace and Macedonia). The Ionian revolt of 499 BC saw the Greek cities of Asia Minor throwing out their *turannoi* and – with the help of Athens and Eretria – burning Sardis. This had been the previous capital of Lydia and was now the Persians' local administrative headquarters. In 494 BC the Persians under their king Darius (in Persian: Dārayava(h)uš) retook the lost territory, destroyed the Greek fleet off Miletus, burned Miletus itself and sent its people into slavery. The Greek settlements in Asia Minor were a lost cause. Darius now set his sights further west, deciding to punish the Greeks and establish a foothold in Europe.

We start with the expansion of the Games, and then turn to Croesus. The wonderful stories associated with him are down to Herodotus, the father of history and one of the world's great storytellers.

WREATHED IN GLORY

The prize for the winners at Olympia was a simple wreath of olive. In fact there were four 'crown' games, as they were known, where the prize for victory was a wreath: olive at Olympia, celery at Nemea, laurel at Delphi and pine at Isthmia. These 'crown' games were the most prestigious. Cash and other benefits flowed to the winners both from the ecstatic towns where the athletes were raised and from invitations to compete elsewhere. 'Money' games soon sprang up, where prizes in cash or in kind were on offer. As a result of Alexander's conquests in the east and, later, the expansion of the Roman empire across the Mediterranean, these Greek games gradually turned into a form of universal entertainment, with professional, full-time athletic guilds touring the world, rather like the Harlem Globetrotters, often demanding appearance money too. The distinction between 'professional' and 'amateur', so often invoked to contrast modern and ancient athletics, is not an ancient one.

PEACE DIVIDEND

When the three Greek 'sacred heralds' spread out from Elis to announce the forthcoming Olympic Games (*not* carrying an Olympic flame: see p. 275), they proclaimed a truce (of sorts) for up to three months before and after the five-day event. Its purpose was not political (war was endemic in the Greek world) but social: to ensure safe passage for the myriad Greeks from all over the Mediterranean who travelled to watch. In fact, only open warfare by or against the people of Elis was actually forbidden during the truce (though in 364 BC an invasion by Arcadia did interrupt the pentathlon). The result was that the games were celebrated every four years for over a thousand years – an astonishing record (compare the modern Olympics, instituted in 1896 and already cancelled three times by war – 1916, 1940 and 1944).

WHERE SECOND IS THE FIRST LOSER

The Greek word *athlêtês* means 'one who competes for a prize', and ancient Greeks were fiercely competitive people, never more so than at the games, where only winning counted, and winning as individuals too: there were no team events, let alone prizes for second or third. Nor were there any records. What counted was beating the opposition on the day – and that was all. That said, riders of horses and chariots did not get the honours. The mare Breeze threw her rider at the start, but still ran a perfect race, came first and got the prize for the sponsor: it was the sponsor (see Alcibiades, p. 236), not the driver, whom Pindar, the fifth-century BC court poet, celebrated with a victory ode. Pindar characterized winning at Olympia as the closest one could get to divine bliss, but warned that life could not continue like that.

Not everyone could be a winner. Sarcastic stories abounded about hopeless losers like Charmus, who came seventh in a field of six (a friend who ran on to encourage him beat him; the joke continued: 'if he had five more friends he would have finished twelfth'); and Marcus, so slow that the groundsman locked him in the stadium for the night, thinking he was a statue.

CONTACT SPORTS

Wrestling, boxing and the *pankration* ('all-strength') were subject to no time limits or weight classes, let alone a 'ring'. Men fought till one or the other was technically defeated or simply submitted. In wrestling, the aim was to throw your opponent three times, a fall defined as touching the ground with the knee. Breaking bones was allowed ('finger-breaker' was the epithet of Leontiscus from Sicily). Boxing was seriously brutal. No punches were prohibited. Men were killed in this sport, but it did not count as homicide. The *pankration* combined wrestling, judo and boxing. Everything was allowed except gouging and biting. You won by making the opponent give up. Most of the time seems to have been spent rolling around on the ground. All three disciplines were overseen by judges holding a stick, who beat any contestant seen to be fouling.

NO-WIN WINS

Athletes had to do the gods honour by showing their commitment to the Olympics. As a result, there was a firm rule that all competitors had to arrive a month before the games for practice. We are told of a Greek from Alexandria, Apollonius, who arrived late, saying that adverse winds had kept him back. However, a fellow Greek from Alexandria revealed this as a lie: Apollonius had been busy picking up cash prizes in games in Asia Minor, and that was why he was late. He was disqualified. The consequence of individual entry, with a month's practice beforehand, was that it was possible to win without competing at all. The reason was that opponents checked each other out in the one-month practice period and, if they knew they had no chance, pulled a hamstring or similar and quietly disappeared. Many athletes, especially in contact sports, announced on their victory monuments that they had won *akoniti*, 'without dust', i.e. without a single fight.

TRANSFER MARKETS

In the Greek world there was a transfer market in athletes. For example, in 488 BC Astylus from southern Italy won the 200 metres and long distance. He then repeated this triumph in 484 and 480 – but as a Syracusan! He'd been tapped up by the ambitious Greek tyrant of Syracuse, Hieron, himself a keen competitor in the games, and hired for a vast fee.

SEX AND THE GAMES

The one-time world heavyweight boxing champion Lennox Lewis, arguing that women weakened a boxer, avoided sex for three weeks before a big fight. The theory has certainly been around for some time. In the ancient world it was based on the idea that semen was a vital factor in keeping a man strong. The doctor Aretaeus, in the first century AD, said:

> If any man is in possession of semen, he is fierce, courageous and physically mighty, like beasts. Evidence for this is to be found in athletes who practise abstinence.

Even involuntary nocturnal emissions were thought to be enfeebling, threatening one's endurance and breathing. The doctor Galen, in the second century AD, recommended that athletes take precautions against them:

> A flattened lead plate is an object to be placed under the muscles of the loins of an athlete in training, chilling them whenever they might have nocturnal emissions of semen.

Incidentally, if sex before exercise was regarded as potentially deleterious to health, exercise before sex was strongly recommended, especially foot-races and horse-riding.

DIVINE NUDES

At the Panathenaic Games (see p. 125) there were competitions for 'fine manliness' – athletic prowess and physical beauty combined. Such competitions, the fact that athletes competed naked, and the culture of pederasty (see p. 253) must have had some bearing on the development of the male nude statue, whether of gods, heroes, athletes, or warriors. They stood for a range of qualities: athletic or military prowess, civic virtue and sexual desirability in male eyes (note how dainty the penises were, as also on pederastic scenes on vases; big ones were characteristic of barbarians and the ugly). Greeks generally believed that male beauty and goodness somehow went hand in hand, and such statues seem to be striving to illustrate such perfection – a combination of naturalism and idealism so perfect indeed that no male body ever really looked like that. It seems, in fact, as if Greek sculptors reckoned they could imagine and represent the divine. Maximus of Tyre (second century AD) made the point:

> The Greek manner of honouring the gods recruits whatever is most beautiful on earth, whether in terms of raw material, human shape or artistic precision... the best human bodies are vehicles of the divine.

As a result, if you were to be counted as a hero in any sense – someone elevated onto a different plane of existence, in life or death – nudity was your appropriate garb. The convention, eagerly embraced by rough Roman generals (see p. 358), has thankfully gone out fashion.

FIGHTS TO THE DEATH

In the Olympic Games of 564 BC, Arrichion was fighting in the *pankration* against an unknown opponent. He was undefeated, but his opponent had him in a leg-lock and was slowly throttling him with his arm. With an enormous effort, Arrichion threw him off, and with a vicious kick dislocated his opponent's trapped ankle. His adversary signalled that he had given in – but Arrichion was already dead. Still, he was awarded the crown.

In 400 BC, we are told of two boxers, Damoxenus and Creugas, still slugging it out as night drew on. They agreed that, to finish it, each should deal the other an unopposed blow. Creugas hit Damoxenus on the head, without knocking him out. Damoxenus then struck Creugas under the ribs, with fingers extended. His nails were so sharp that his fingers pierced Creugas' stomach and he then tore out his entrails. Creugas died on the spot, but he was awarded the crown on a technicality – his opponent had delivered not one blow but two: into the stomach and out again.

THE FATHER OF HISTORY

The purpose of Herodotus' 'researches/enquiries' (*historiai*), as he says at the start of his *Histories*, was:

> to ensure that the passage of time will not obscure human achievements, and that great and astonishing deeds, some Greek, some non-Greek, do not go uncelebrated. Particular attention has been paid to the reasons which brought the Greeks and Persians into conflict with each other.

Herodotus came from Halicarnassus (modern Bodrum) on the coast of Asia Minor, visited Athens, and finally settled in Thurii (southern Italy). He was born around 484 BC and died after 431. His is the first work in Greek prose to survive. His *historiai* took him all over the Mediterranean as he compiled this one work (in nine books) – a history of the Greek and Persian peoples, culminating in the Persian wars (490–479 BC).

ALL HUMAN LIFE IS THERE

Wherever the Persians went as they spread west, north and south, Herodotus seems to have gone. Personal visits apparently took him as far as Aswan, Babylon and southern Russia, and he talked to just about everyone. Anthropologist, sociologist, ethnographer and historian, Herodotus embraced all human life. He came across a myriad different peoples – Egyptians, Lydians, Scythians, Persians, North Africans and literally hundreds more – and their characteristics, institutions, beliefs, and 'great and astonishing deeds' lie at the heart of the *Histories*. Here we learn how to build a pyramid; about Indian ants the size of small dogs which quarry for gold; and about the Babylonian national health service (they do not have one: the ill are placed in the streets and must listen to the advice of others who have had the complaint). Women tend not to feature greatly in ancient historical accounts of events, but Herodotus names 375 of them, most from monarchic or tyrannical familes, many quite as nasty as any male.

RECIPROCAL (DIS)FAVOURS

Herodotus' undertaking is on a massive scale, staggering in scope and conception. It takes him right back into 'mythistory' to locate the start of the east–west conflict (e.g. the Trojan War) but he finds the mainspring some 200 years before his time: the palace revolution in 680 BC that led to the Lydian king Croesus' family coming to power. His key perception is that events were driven by that central obligation in the ancient world:

to reciprocate – with those who had done you a favour, by means of favours, and with those who had done you harm, by harm (see p. 74). He saw reciprocal obligation spreading its tentacles from person to person, from nation to nation; it was this that bound together peoples from Spain to the Caspian, from southern Russia to Africa – 940 of them named in all – into Herodotus' stupendous complex. And all without books, or libraries, or (wonder of wonders) the internet.

THE FIRST HISTORIAN

Many people wrote accounts of the past before Herodotus did (consider, for example, the early books of the Old Testament). But Herodotus can claim to be the world's first *historian* (as opposed to compiler or recorder) for the following reasons:

(i)   No less than 1,086 times he intervenes in his own narrative to qualify it by adding (for example) 'I am only repeating what X says', 'Whether their explanation is valid, I am not qualified to say', 'I would be amazed if this story were actually true', and so on. In other words, he was open to doubt, happy to report what he was told but 'under no obligation to believe it entirely – something that is true for the whole of my narrative'. It is this ceaseless questioning and doubting that mark him out as radically different from everyone else.

(ii) Like early Greek natural scientists, Herodotus demanded that accounts of the world be humanly intelligible (see p. 94). This meant not allowing divine intervention any significant place in his explanation of why people behaved as they did. Now and again, where express occurrences did indeed seem humanly inexplicable, Herodotus would point to some divine power, but he did not expand such inexplicability into a grand law of history. For Herodotus it was human failings that brought disaster.

TESTING THE ORACLES

The Lydian king Croesus was aware that Cyrus, king of the Persians, had defeated his northerly neighbours the Medes and had his eyes on the rich pickings of Croesus' kingdom further west. So, he decided he had better consult a reliable oracle first, and check whether attacking Cyrus would be an intelligent move or not. This landed him with a problem: which of the many oracles could be guaranteed to tell the truth? Clearly a little market research was called for. So Croesus sent delegations to all the major oracles in Greece with the following question: what was Croesus doing on the hundredth day after the delegation in question had left Lydia? Only the Delphic oracle's answer survives. It ended as follows:

> I smell the smell of a hard-shelled tortoise,
> Boiling in a bronze cauldron with the flesh of a lamb.
> Bronze is the cauldron and bronze its lid.

And it was right. After he had sent off the delegations, Croesus thought long and hard about what he could possibly do on the hundredth day that no one could ever guess in a million years. His solution was to chop up a tortoise and a lamb and boil them together in a bronze cauldron with a bronze lid. And Delphi got it. Apparently.

DELPHIC RESPONSE

After Croesus had convinced himself that the Delphic oracle would never let him down, Herodotus tells us that he enquired what would happen if he fought the Persian king Cyrus. 'You will destroy a great empire,' the oracle replied. Croesus was overjoyed, but still followed it up by asking if his reign would be a long one. 'When a mule is king of Persia, run for your life,' came the answer. This seemed to settle the matter. Croesus took on Cyrus and was duly defeated. Made captive, he sent to the oracle to ask what on earth it was up to. The oracle replied that to the first prophecy he should have enquired 'Which empire?', and on the second he should have reflected that Cyrus was the mule in question, being the son of parents of different races – a noble Mede mother, but a base-born Persian father. Herodotus goes on: 'When the reply was reported to Croesus, he admitted that the god was innocent and he had only himself to blame.' He should have listened to Solon (see p. 106).

RICH AS CROESUS

The Lydians had a reputation for being very civilized and agreeable people – great party-givers, terrific dress sense, superb musicians and inventors of the seven-stringed lyre. Their capital, Sardis, was a city of opportunity and luxury for everyone, including Greeks. They invented gold and silver coinage, and therefore, as far as we know, the retail trade. So if anyone was to become a by-word for wealth, it is not surprising that it was a king of Lydia.

Incidentally, the invention of retail trade, which created a middle man in the process of exchange between the producer and the customer, was not a move Greeks were much in favour of, smelling as it did of potentially crooked dealings (on which see p. 96).

GOLDEN BOOTS

The Athenian Alcmaeon, son of Megacles (I), who gave his name to the Alcmaeonid family (see p. 92), had done Croesus a favour in helping him consult the Delphic oracle, so the king invited him back to Sardis to thank him. He told Alcmaeon he could take back to Athens as much gold as he could carry at one time. Faced with this stimulating challenge, Alcmaeon put on a very large, loose and baggy cloak and a pair of the biggest boots with the widest tops he could find. When he had been led into the treasury, Alcmaeon proceeded to fill them. Literally. He then crammed his cloak with as much as it could hold, sprinkled gold dust on his head and stuffed more into his mouth. He then staggered out, cheeks bulging, hardly able to drag himself along in his boots, looking like some outlandish alien. Croesus took one look, fell off his chair laughing, granted him everything he had taken, and proceeded to double it. That was the source of the Alcmaeonids' massive family wealth (says Herodotus) and from then on life for Alcmaeon became one long downhill struggle. He opened a stable and won the chariot-race at the Olympic Games on the strength of it.

FESTIVAL MANIA

One feature of Greek culture at this time is passion for competition and display between citizens and cities, and the prospect of kudos that it brought. (It was in this spirit that Cylon, boosted by his victory at Olympia, tried to become tyrant of Athens; see p. 91.) The 'All-Athenian'

Panathenaea featured sacrifices to Athena and Poseidon; special games
– mock battles, jumping on and off a chariot, and a four-horse chariot-
race, for which the winner won 140 amphoras full of Athenian olive
oil (each amphora containing about 5 gallons/22 litres); competitions
in music and poetry (for which there were financial prizes); and, in
particular, recitations of the Homeric poems, implying that by now a
fixed version of the poems was available (see p. 59). The climax of the
festival was a huge sacrifice to Athena. Every four years, a special robe
was woven in which to dress the very ancient statue of Athena housed
in the temple of Erechtheus (not the Parthenon) on the Acropolis. More
and more such festivals came to be laid on, with the promise of glory
for winners. Ancient Greeks set a very high store on winning in front of
adoring masses in both sporting and cultural events.

STONY BOTTOM

Another festival which might have been established under Pisistratus
was the City Dionysia, at which many great Greek tragedies were
staged. This theatrical showcase was in honour of the god Dionysus
and lasted three days. It featured nine tragedies (three trilogies by
three playwrights), three rollicking satyr-plays (one after each trilogy),
three comedies (at least), and twenty performances by choruses (see
pp. 187, 220). It all makes Wagner's *Ring Cycle* resemble a newsflash.
The Athenians adored every minute of it, despite the stone seating.

DANGEROUS DEITY

The popularity of Dionysus (his other name was *Bakkhos*, or Bacchus
in Latin) can be judged by the fact that no god was more frequently

represented in ancient art. His mother was the human Semele, blasted to smithereens by a jealous Hera when she found Semele was carrying Zeus' child; but Zeus rescued the baby and stored it in his thigh till it was ready to be born. Dionysus was essentially a god of transformation, perceived as both man and animal, male and effeminate, and especially associated with the theatre (transforming actors and audience), alcohol, the annual cycles of nature and life in death. As such, he was not the most comfortable of gods, threatening chaos in place of order. 'Raw flesh-eater' was one of his titles; Euripides calls him 'most terrible and most sweet to mortals' in his tragedy *Bacchae*, which features a chorus of Dionysus' ecstatic female followers in the grip of divine mania. No wonder Dionysus was such a hit with the public, though it must be said that there were no actual rites of Dionysus that indulged this sort of extreme behaviour. Festivals of Dionysus normally featured alcohol, obscenity, revelry, cross-dressing, plays and processions carrying vast *phalloi* through the streets – nothing, in other words, to upset even the most conservative horse, and a very welcome change from the daily grind of peasant life.

EUPALINOS' TUNNEL

The Tunnel of Eupalinos on Samos, named after the Megarian engineer who designed it, was constructed to secure the island's water supply in time of siege. The excavation was sponsored in the sixth century BC by Polycrates, the tyrant of Samos and described by Herodotus. Dug through the solid limestone of a mountain from each end simultaneously (at the rate of about 3 tons a day), the tunnel was 8 feet (2.5 metres) in diameter and ran under the mountain for 3,280 feet (1,000 metres) in a straight line into the city. The two ends of the tunnel were only 16 feet (5 metres) apart horizontally when they 'met', while the vertical deviation over the whole tunnel was only about 3 feet (1 metre). Pipes and channels dug inside the tunnel carried the water. This was necessary because it was impossible to be certain that the gradient of the tunnel itself could provide the required flow. It is now a UNESCO world heritage site.

AESOP

Herodotus places Aesop in the sixth century BC, describing him as a slave of one Iadmon from Samos. Whatever the truth of that – there is such disagreement about his life that many doubt he ever existed – the first collection of his fables was made about 300 BC (see p. 317), and they have enjoyed a flourishing existence, in prose and verse, ever since. The fables generally feature a conflict between talking animals that stand for human types, usually the rich and powerful against the poor and weak. They stress either the folly of taking on a stronger power, or the cunning which the weaker must deploy if he is to stand any chance of success; and they often warn that nature never changes. In other words, the fables present a world where truth is black and white. Since real human motives and character are usually devious, the lessons of the fables are better presented by non-human types, primed to behave in standard ways – the brave lion, tricky fox, feeble mouse, and so on. The lessons thus conveyed are clean, decisive and instantly applicable.

JACKDAWS, PIGEONS, DONKEYS AND FOXES

In one of Aesop's fables, the jackdaw had noticed that pigeons in the nearby coop were well fed. So he coloured his feathers to look like theirs and joined them, taking care not to make any sound. At first the pigeons were fooled, but one day the jackdaw forgot where he was and let out his familiar cry. The pigeons promptly chased him off. Dejected, he returned to his fellow jackdaws, who mistook him for a pigeon and also chased him off. Moral: be content with what you are.

The donkey and the fox became friends and, setting out to hunt, met a lion. Sensing danger, the fox said to the lion that he could have the donkey to eat if he left him (the fox) alone. The lion said that seemed very fair, so the fox led the donkey straight into a ditch. The lion, seeing that the donkey was his in any case, picked up the fox and threw him in too. Moral: if you set traps for your friends, you may find yourself caught in one as well.

ANIMAL MAGIC

It cannot be said that any ancient cultures set out to be kind to animals. Greeks were (on the whole) not intentionally cruel, but rather indifferent, especially when animal interests clashed with those of men. Plutarch (c. AD 46–120) is more sympathetic than most. In his dialogue *On the Cleverness of Animals*, he has much to say about animal intelligence. His six speakers first establish that animals are rational because they, for instance, plan for the future, have memory, care for their young, show gratitude and can be courageous and big-hearted. Then, using hundreds of examples, they debate whether land or sea animals are superior.

Aristotimus argues for land animals. Dogs put pebbles into a half-empty jar to bring the liquid to the top for drinking. Geese flying through eagles' territory carry stones in their beaks so they do not give themselves away by honking. Then what of the dim circus elephant, who, tired of being punished for forgetting his tricks, practised by moonlight to get them right? Cows in Persia can count: they lift a hundred buckets of water a day to irrigate the king's park – but not one more.

Phaedimus replies for marine animals. Fish must be brainy, being almost uncatchable. Sacred crocodiles in Egypt recognize the priests' voices when they call, and open their mouths to have their teeth cleaned. Tunny fish are experts in optics and maths: having weak right eyes, they always keep their left eye to seaward to watch out for danger, and they feed in schools formed into perfect six-sided cubes. Dolphins have rescued countless humans from the sea. And so on and on and on...

BLACK FIGURES TO RED

Around 600 BC, Athens adopted from Corinth the technique of 'black-figure' decoration on pottery. Very simply, the figures painted on the pot were black silhouettes, into which were incised details with a sharp instrument which revealed the colour of the clay beneath. This made for easy, if restricted, precision of detail. Working with an average-size kiln, a potter could produce about six medium-sized pots a week, i.e. 300 a year, though failed firings or rain would cut the number down. About 20,000 black-figure pieces survive, illustrating the vast range of scenes covered, from myth to everyday life, many of very high artistic quality. They swept the domestic and international market.

Around 520 BC, Athenian potters dropped incisions and fully painted the figures instead, reworking the firing technique to produce red figures on black backgrounds. These figures were more lively and realistic than the black-figure silhouettes, and figures could be painted in different perspectives too. Again, artistic standards were extraordinarily high. Of these about 40,000 survive.

That said, most potters were in business, working to make a living from a market for cheap, everyday pottery.

UNMYTHABLE STORIES

Greek pots regularly depict stories from myth, but there were many other ways in which Greeks learned about them. Mothers told them to their children; they were turned into song to be performed at public festivals; they were recited in epics and performed in tragedies; they were used as examples of behaviour in speeches and funeral orations. They were in fact common currency, appearing in vase-paintings and as the subjects of monumental sculptures in temples all across the Greek world.

WHAT IS A MYTH?

At its most basic, a myth is a story, a sequence of events. It is a traditional story, one that has been handed down from the distant past and has a special relevance to the society which tells it. Ancient Greeks themselves broadly defined the functions of myth as preserving the past, teaching the young, explaining the reason for rituals, customs, names (etc.), and offering pleasurable consolation for present sorrows. Philosophers regularly used them as a source for examples of behaviour. There are many modern theories of their deeper significance.

MYTHTERY HITHTORY

It is often argued that myth is 'history in disguise', i.e. it somehow reflects historical events and people from the deep past, distorted over the passage of time. Euhemerus (fourth century BC) was the first person to try to rationalize all myths in this way, including gods who, he reckoned, were historically nothing but larger-than-life humans. Though earlier Greeks were keen on rationalizing myths, it was Euhemerus who elevated the idea into a complete system. Euhemerism still exerts its lamentable grip.

ALL CHANGE

Thales (see p. 96) from Miletus started the ball rolling on the question of the nature of the world, and Heraclitus (*c*. 500 BC) from Ephesus, a most controversial and enigmatic thinker, took up the challenge. One possible interpretation of his thinking goes as follows: the cosmos may look stable, but it is constantly changing. This change comes about because the cosmos is basically fire, though not all of it is alight at once. Fire is the great catalyst, and it is this that generates the change of the cosmos into other substances. It turns the cosmos into a sort of war between substances, coming and going, ever-changing, but there is an underlying stability to this cosmos because change can happen only between opposites, and opposites (when you come to think about it) are merely different aspects of a single phenomenon. Thus hot and cold, wet and dry, living and dead are defined by their relationship to each other: they are not irreconcilable because you cannot have one without the other. Heraclitus glories in these apparent paradoxes: the road going up is the same as the road going down. You cannot step into the same river twice. In one fragment, Heraclitus identifies day/night, summer/ winter, war/peace, famine/plenty as different manifestations of god. So in a sense all things are One, a balance of contrary exchanges. It is only *by* changing that some things stay the same.

Incidentally, when he realized he was dying, he stretched out in the sun and told his slaves to cover him in cow dung. On the second day he died.

A HORSE'S GOD?

Active around 550 BC, Xenophanes came from Colophon in Asia Minor. He was among a number of Greek thinkers who were not entirely comfortable with the Homeric vision of gods looking and behaving rather like men (see p. 66). He pointed out that Homer 'ascribed to the gods everything that men regard as shameful and blameworthy – stealing, adultery, deceit', and wondered about man's tendency to make gods like men. 'If oxen, horses and lions could draw,' he remarked, 'horses would draw gods like horses (etc.)...', while 'Ethiopians [= 'blacks'] say their gods are snub-nosed and black'. This raised an important broader question, on which Herodotus and later Greeks pondered again and again: to what extent are our beliefs based on convention or custom? Are there *any* firm realities?

Incidentally, on the question of gods, Xenophanes envisaged 'God as one, supreme among gods and men, and not like mortals in body or in mind'. Xenophanes was, in other words, a henotheist ('single god') – one who believed in a supreme god while acknowledging there could be others. And the god he imagined was not one that could be accused of being anything like a mortal.

BAD SPORTS

Xenophanes was among those who did not approve of the Olympic Games:

> Honoured is the winner at Olympia by his fellow townsmen,
> with the best seats at games and festivals, a public pension
> and gifts of treasure from the city. But he does not deserve it.
> My wisdom is better than the strength of men and horses.
> A city may have a noble boxer, but that will not make it
> better ordered, nor keep its granaries filled.

Others agreed. Diogenes the Cynic, meeting an athlete who boasted how fast he was, replied: 'But not faster than a rabbit or deer, the swiftest of animals, and also the most cowardly' (see p. 286). Plato puts his finger on the commitment required of the athlete when he says (sneeringly) in his *Laws*: 'to dedicate your life to winning a victory in Delphi or Olympia keeps you far too busy to attend to other tasks'. Aristotle comments:

> The athlete's habit of body neither produces a good condition
> for the general purposes of life, not does it encourage ordinary
> health and the procreation of children... some exertion is
> essential for the best way of life, but it must be neither
> violent nor specialized, as is the case with athletes. It should
> rather be a general exertion, directed to all the activities of a
> free man.

But Aristotle was not hostile to the games *per se* – just to the extremes to which they drove people for such a meagre reward.

UNREAL WORLD

Parmenides from Elea in southern Italy, who was active around 500 BC, very nearly brought all Greek philosophy to a juddering halt. From the fragments of his work that survive, it seems that he challenged the whole idea that there was a single originating 'material principle' (e.g. water) from which everything else derived. Indeed, he argued that any change of any sort was impossible! To the assertion 'But we see change every day of our lives', Parmenides' stunning riposte was: no, you don't. You only *think* you do. In other words, the world we live in is an unreal, fantasy world.

This was to throw philosophers into confusion – with, as we shall see, remarkable results.

PATENT INVENTION

It is claimed that in 500 BC the Greek city of Sybaris in southern Italy invented the patent. The city granted the cook who invented a very special dish the sole right to cook it for one year, 'in order to encourage competition and get others to excel with similar inventions'. Sybaris gives us 'sybaritic' – the city was famous for its love of luxury.

THIRD TIME LUCKY

The Athenian tyrant Pisistratus had three shots at gaining power. Herodotus describes his second attempt as follows:

> This was quite the stupidest scheme I have ever heard, all
> the more so because the intelligence of the Greeks, and their
> general lack of gullibility, have long differentiated them from

other peoples, while the Athenians, who fell for the trick, are supposed to be the most intelligent of the Greeks.

It involved Pisistratus dressing an unnaturally tall, beautiful woman to look like Athena and driving into Athens with her, while outriders went ahead announcing that the goddess had come to honour him above every other mortal. It worked, but not for long. The reason was that Megacles (III), the Alcmaeonid, had agreed to help Pisistratus if Pisistratus married his daughter. Pisistratus did, but insisted on having only anal sex with her. His reason was fear of having children with the curse of the Alcmaeonids hanging over them (see p. 92). When Megacles heard of this, he gathered his allies to drive Pisistratus out. But Pisistratus used military might to seize power at the third attempt, sending the Alcmaeonids (among others) into exile.

THE MULTI-PURPOSE OLIVE

One essential step Pisistratus took was to find land for the landless. The result was an expansion in the growth of one of the ancient world's most important crops: olives. Olives are the original multi-purpose fruit. They are food; their oil was used for cooking, flavouring, lighting, moisturizing and cleansing; and they served as a medicine, animal feed, fertilizer, wood-preserver, water-proofer, insecticide and general lubricant (and even, as Marie Stopes much later confirmed, an excellent contraceptive). The early pickings (August to October) were used to produce delicate grades of olive oil as bases for such things as medicines; the final picking (December), when the olives were black, provided olives for food and oil for cooking. Olive oil was always Athens' main export, in exchange for grain from Egypt and especially Crimea.

OLIVE FOR EVER

The olive tree can be extraordinarily long-lasting (one found in Crete has been estimated at over 2,000 years!) and can thrive in poor soil, though it cannot bear extreme cold (this limits its spread into northern Europe). It is amazingly tough: it may be killed by disease, fire or other damage, it may be buried under motorways, but given the chance, new suckers will emerge to rejuvenate it. It is also evergreen, which lends it a sacred importance: olive oil was used to anoint kings and priests, and was seeped into the bones of dead martyrs and saints. It bears fruit after five or six years and needs little maintenance once it is established.

THE WET WAY TO A LONG LIFE

With very few exceptions, no village, town or city in the ancient world was ever founded without an on-site water supply – whether lake, river, spring, fountain or well (ancient Byzantium was a major exception). Private homes could also install tanks (cisterns) or dig a well; towns could build large cisterns or reservoirs – all the more important in the Mediterranean, with its hot, dry summers.

All these things made urban life possible and pleasurable. So Pisistratus knew what he was doing when he built public amenities such as drainage systems and elegant fountain houses where water could be drawn (these were highly convenient anyway, making popular meeting places and centres for community activity). Athens was a city on the rise, where growing trade brought prosperity and self-confidence to the citizens. Unlike many tyrants, Pisistratus died in his bed.

ᐸAY REVENᐸE

Of Pisistratus' two sons who took over on his death, Hippias wielded the political power, while Hipparchus was the cultural mover and shaker. He welcomed to the city poets like Anacreon and Simonides, and famous musicians who greatly enhanced Athens' dramatic performances and therefore cultural and artistic reputation (the arts counted for a great deal in the Greek world). He was assassinated, however, in 514 BC, by Harmodius and his lover Aristogeiton. Hipparchus had already tried to seduce Harmodius; having failed, he attempted to humiliate him. After the two had stabbed Hipparchus to death during the Panathenaea, they were caught and killed. Nevertheless, their fame as 'tyrant-slayers' was assured and they were celebrated in patriotic poems sung at symposia.

THE ᐸREEK BULLINᐸDON

Wine, women, boys and song are the themes of Anacreon's poetry. He is said to have died, appropriately, by choking on a grape pip. His poems were composed to be sung to a lyre accompaniment, at symposia – upper-class male drinking parties (*sun-*, 'all together' + *posis*, 'drink') of perhaps fourteen to thirty men.

A symposium was a private occasion on which aristocrats, linked by status, age, wealth and common interests, drank, talked, plotted, celebrated, recited poetry, sang and shagged the night away within their own four walls. The wine, which was up to about 18 per cent alcohol, was diluted one part wine to two or three of water – only barbarians drank wine neat – in a large mixing bowl, which was constantly refilled. The going could get tough. The wise man was advised to leave after three mixing bowls:

the fourth leads to violence, the fifth to uproar, the sixth to
revel, the seventh to black eyes, the eighth to summonses,
the ninth to vomiting and the tenth to madness and throwing
things about.

The revelry regularly reached a public climax in the *kômos*, when
the plastered symposiasts spilled out onto the streets in a display of
exhibitionist behaviour designed to show how unconventional they
were, demonstrate their power and lawlessness, and generally thumb
the nose at ordinary citizens.

LUBRICATING THE MUSE

Drinking and writing have long been associated. The poet Simonides
said that wine and literature were discovered at the same time. The
tragedian Aeschylus used such extraordinary language that people
assumed he composed in a vinous frenzy. 'Drink water and you'll never
produce a work of art,' said the Greek comic playwright Cratinus.

THE BIRTH OF DEMOCRACY

The assassination of Hipparchus changed the tenor of political life in
Athens. Out for revenge, Hippias initiated a bloodbath, but he also
married his daughter to a man whose father, tyrant of Lampsacus in
Asia Minor, had close connections with the Persians. He was looking for
a bolt-hole in case of trouble, which duly arrived in 510 BC. Encouraged
by the Alcmaeonids and the Delphic oracle (see p. 112), and probably
keen to draw Athens into alliance, the Spartans attacked Hippias' army
and forced a capitulation. The reign of the *turannoi* was at an end.
Hippias at once made for Persia to look for support there.

Now began a struggle for power in Athens. It came down to Isagoras, a personal friend of the Spartan king Cleomenes, and Cleisthenes, an Alcmaeonid who had encouraged Sparta to intervene. Isagoras used the curse on the Alcmaeonids (see p. 92) to have Cleisthenes banished, and Cleomenes arrived with a small force to install Isagoras as 'president'. The Athenian people rose up and threw them out. Cleisthenes was recalled and instituted the reforms that were to usher in the world's first (and last) democracy.

THE FIRST STEPS TOWARDS DEMOCRACY

The purpose of Cleisthenes' reforms was to continue Solon's reforms, breaking down barriers and exclusions so that *all* citizens could be involved in making decisions about Athens' political future.

(i) First, he created ten 'tribes'. These would be responsible for appointing some officials. Each tribe was made up of a number of 'demes', i.e. villages (*dêmoi*, sing. *dêmos*). The demes for each tribe would be drawn from three different parts of Attica: some from the coastal area, some from inland, and some from in or around Athens. Result: each tribe would fully represent the people of Attica as a whole.

(ii) The demes – of which there were 139 – would each provide (by proportional representation) members of the new 'Steering Committee' (*boulê*) of 500, which would prepare business for the new Assembly. Every community, then, would be represented on the Steering Committee, shaping Athens' political future.

(iii) Finally, the Assembly (*ekklêsia*) would be one of *all* male citizens over 18. Solon had given this body a formal status (see p. 104), but under Cleisthenes' revolution it would become *the* decision-making body. In time, every question confronting Athens would be submitted to it for debate and final decision.

After the rule of the *turannoi*, this must have seemed like a considerable release, but it was only opening up the political system to everyone equally, not giving them total control. That would come in time (see p. 170 for democracy's further development).

JAW-JAW, NOT WAR-WAR

Greeks defined three means of getting your own way: force, treachery and persuasion. Given Greek hostile, competitive social values, with the emphasis on winning at all costs, it is not surprising that the first two were regularly deployed, with often violent repercussions. One of the purposes – or at least consequences – of radical democracy was that political problems were to be settled not by men wielding baseball bats, but by peaceful, verbal persuasion in the Assembly. Words, not weaponry, were now (in theory) the way to power in Athens.

501 BC: A STRATEGIC MOVE

The word 'strategy' derives from the Greek *stratêgos*, 'leader of a military force' (army or navy). A move that was to have great significance occurred in 501 BC – the details are obscure – when it was decided to elect ten *stratêgoi* annually, all of equal status, one from each tribe. While political power still remained in the hands of the nine *arkhôn*s – one of whom may have been made commander-in-chief – it did not do so for long. The *stratêgoi* were soon to become not merely the chief military leaders but also the main political players – even more so in 487 BC, when the nine *arkhôn*s began to be appointed by lot.

A MAP OF THE WORLD

In their steady drive west the Persians had made the Greek adventurer Aristagoras deputy governor of the important town of Miletus in the region of Ionia on the west coast of Asia Minor. He stitched up a deal with Artaphrenes, Persian satrap (governor) of Lydia, to bring the rich, fertile island of Naxos under Persian control. To Persian fury, the whole thing fell apart, and Aristagoras was in big trouble.

So he decided to foment revolt against the Persians among the Ionian Greek cities, and he went to the Greek mainland to ask for help from Sparta. He brought a bronze map of the world with him, showing the Spartan king Cleomenes just how wealthy Asia Minor was: it was there for the taking! Cleomenes said he would give him an answer in two days. The answer came in the form of a question: how long would it take to reach the Persian king's palace in Susa? Three months, said Aristagoras. Cleomenes told him to leave at once: no Spartan wanted to be three months' journey from the sea. So Aristagoras resorted to bribery, eventually putting fifty talents on the table. At this point Cleomenes' daughter Gorgo, aged eight or nine at the time, said: 'Father, this man will corrupt you if you don't get up and leave.' Which Cleomenes did.

ATHENS SAILS INTO TROUBLE

Having failed to get support for his rebellion in Sparta, Aristagoras made for Athens. There he persuaded the new democratic Athenian Assembly, worried about Hippias' defection to the Persians, to provide him with twenty ships. Herodotus commented: 'These twenty ships proved to be the beginning of misfortune for Greeks and non-Greeks alike' – because the consequence would be the Persian wars.

The Ionians did have one major success: they took and burned Sardis. But it did not last. When the Persians were back in control in 494 BC, their king Darius asked who these Athenians were and, being informed, ordered an attendant to repeat three times, whenever a meal was served: 'Master, remember the Athenians.' And he did.

HISTORICAL TRAGEDY (I)

The tragedian Phrynichus was said to have been a pupil of Thespis (whence 'thespian'), the supposed inventor of tragedy. In the 490s BC Phrynichus produced one of the few plays about a known historical event: the *Sack of Miletus* (another is Aeschylus' *Persians*; see p. 168). This had been carried out by Persians in the course of the Ionian revolt, against a town that had originally been settled from Athens and was one of the most famous of its day. The play does not survive, but we know that it did not go down well with the audience because (as Herodotus tells us) 'it reminded them of their personal misfortunes'. It was decreed that no play should ever again be produced on that subject.

VI

493–450 BC

TIMELINE

493 BC	Themistocles and Piraeus harbour
490 BC	Battle of Marathon
487 BC	*Arkhôn*s and ostracism
486 BC	Death of Persian king Darius
483 BC	Silver mines at Laurium
481 BC	Greek preparations for Persian attack
480 BC	Battles at Thermopylae and Artemisium
	Battle of Salamis
479 BC	Battle of Plataea: the Persian defeat
	Pausanias against the Persians
478 BC	The Delian League
	Walls for Athens
476–469 BC	Cimon against the Persians
472 BC	Aeschylus' *Persians*

470s BC	Carystus forced into the Delian League; Naxos forced back into it
	Themistocles ostracized
465 BC	Thasos forced back into the Delian League
461 BC	Ephialtes and Pericles: democratic reforms in Athens
460–c. 445 BC	'First' Peloponnesian War
458 BC	Aeschylus' *Oresteia*
454 BC	Persians destroy Athenian fleet in Nile delta
	Delian League treasury moved to Athens
451 BC	Athenian citizenship law

FROM PERSIAN EMPIRE TO ATHENIAN – TYRANNY?

Themistocles, who was to be a big player in Athens' history, foresaw (it appears) that if Athens was to be a power in the land, it had to be master of the sea. So as *arkhôn* in 493 BC he started to fortify Piraeus' three rocky harbours, to take the place of the shoreline at Phalerum where Athenians had previously beached their ships. In 490 BC the Persian king Darius launched his revenge attack against Athens for her part in the Ionian revolt. The Persians landed their army at the beach at Marathon, where the Athenians decided to march out to meet them. The speed of the Athenian assault under Miltiades took the Persians by surprise, and they were defeated.

Knowing they would be back, the Athenians took steps to strengthen internal unity: they decided to appoint their nine *arkhôn*s by lot and to remove political trouble-makers by ostracism. In 486 BC Darius died, to be succeeded by his son Xerxes. In 483 BC Themistocles persuaded the Athenians to spend rich new veins of silver at the Laurium mines on building a fleet of 200 triremes. Xerxes now planned his twin invasion: the army to march by land and attack through the north of Greece, accompanied all the way by the fleet. In autumn 481 BC and spring 480 BC the Greeks met to form a (rare) alliance to face the threat; it was agreed that Sparta and its general Eurybiades should lead it. They decided to try to stop the Persian army at the narrow pass of Thermopylae. The heroic defence by land under the Spartan Leonidas failed; the Athenian fleet at nearby Artemisium had better fortune, but sailed back south after the land defeat. The Persians took and burned Athens, but were defeated by sea at Salamis. Xerxes returned to Persia, taking the fleet with him, but leaving his general Mardonius to deal with the Greeks by land. In 479 BC the Greek army led by the Spartans defeated them at Plataea.

The Athenians, determined to keep Persia out of the Aegean and liberate the Greek cities in Asia Minor, decided in 478 BC to form a naval alliance of *poleis* (which *we* call the Delian League because its treasury was on the island of Delos): each member was to contribute annually either cash or ships. Further, Themistocles oversaw the rebuilding of Athens' defensive walls which, twenty years later, were extended all the way down to the Piraeus. Athens could now supply itself by sea if an enemy army occupied the land. From 476 BC the Athenian Cimon, son of Miltiades, continued to drive the Persians out of the Aegean. Meanwhile, Athens forced the island of Carystus to join the Delian League and prevented the island of Naxos from leaving it. But when after 469 BC Cimon destroyed the remainder of the Persian fleet, the League was not wound up. Indeed, in 465 BC Athens attacked the island of Thasos to prevent it leaving. Was it a League of the free any more?

In Athens, Themistocles and Cimon, both warmongers, were ostracized; the powers of the Areopagus were cut back by Ephialtes in 461 BC, after which he was assassinated; and Pericles introduced pay for jurors, opened up the *arkhón*ship to poorer Athenians, and in 451 BC defined citizens as those with an Athenian mother and father. The democracy was becoming radicalized.

In 460 BC the Athenians started building a land empire, taking on Sparta's allies by land and sea (the 'first Peloponnesian War'), and continued attacking Persia. But in 454 BC their fleet of 200 ships, supporting Egypt's revolt from Persia, was wiped out in the Nile delta – a devastating blow. At the same time, the Athenians moved the treasury of the Delian League from Delos to Athens, dedicating one sixtieth of the League's revenues to Athena: the treasury was now for Athens to use as it pleased, hardly the action of the leader of a free alliance.

As a direct consequence of this empire-building, Athens turned itself into a city unlike any other. Its population was larger than any other city; its allies were numbered in hundreds; its navy outnumbered and outclassed all others; its army was numerically huge, if not a match for the Spartans; and economically it was unequalled in the Greek world. From now till 338 BC, it was at war (on average) for four years in every five.

THE POLITICS OF GOOD CITIZENS

Ancient Greeks were peasant farmers, and the main activity of the ancient subsistence economy was agriculture. The aim was self-sufficiency. Living in small city-states of 2,000–3,000 people (populous Athens was the exception, not the rule), these peasants had one priority – survival

– and in political terms that meant security: claiming and defending territory so that inhabitants could live in peace. In these circumstances bravery, not money, was at a premium: the job of the *polis*, in as far as it had one, was not primarily to raise money but to fight successfully. So the state needed brave citizens.

Here language came into the equation. The Greek for 'brave' was *agathos*. It had its root in the ideal of manliness – it was a male virtue. It also meant efficient, excellent, good *at* something, and good in the sense of 'virtuous'. Ancient political thought, in other words, was all about the production, not of money, but of 'good citizens': only they could make the good decisions that a true democracy needed.

THE FIRST OF THE SOPHISTS

Themistocles was said to have been an admirer of Mnesiphilus, whom the second-century AD biographer Plutarch described as neither an orator nor a natural philosopher, but rather a man with a reputation for 'wisdom'. Rather sniffily, Plutarch went on:

> This was a combination of political acumen and practical intelligence, which had been formulated and handed down since Solon's day, as though it were a set of philosophical principles. His successors combined it with various forensic techniques and transferred its application from public affairs to the use of language. They were termed 'sophists'.

The term usually carried with it something of a hint of the value-free charlatan, teaching unprincipled self-advantage for a fee. Socrates and Plato were to set their faces sternly against them; but many of them were very considerable thinkers. Themistocles was certainly admired for his far-sightedness, inventiveness and desire to win at all costs. The Athenian historian Thucydides commented that Themistocles

> had been the first to propose that the Athenians should take to the sea... he considered the harbour Piraeus more important than the city, and would advise the Athenians that, if they ever had their backs to the wall, they should retreat to the Piraeus and take on the world with their ships.

TRIREME$: POWER TO THE PEOPLE

Piraeus was originally an island, and even in classical times it was connected to Attica only by a thin strip of land. An Athenian deme (see p. 139), it had three harbours, not one. Themistocles' visionary proposal in 493 BC was presumably to fortify it against attack and build dockyards, mooring sheds and other such facilities.

The political significance of Piraeus, however, became enormous. If Athens was to become a naval power, it would depend on the ability of its rowers. Rowers, unlike hoplite fighters, did not need expensive armour. So the ships would be manned by the poorest section of Athenian society. At the same time, Cleisthenes' democratic reforms had handed the power to decide political issues to the people's Assembly (see p. 139), which consisted of *all* the citizens – and in which the poor would far outnumber the wealthy.

Whether intentional or not, this move entrenched power in those who rowed the ships, moving people to charge Themistocles with 'depriving Athenians of spear and shield and degrading them to the rowing bench and oar' (Plutarch). Piraeus would remain a hot-bed of democracy. Between 462 and 458 BC the importance of Piraeus was confirmed when Athens built the Long Walls from the city to Piraeus, enclosing the whole 4.5-mile (7-km) stretch against attack by land. In time it developed commercial facilities as well so that, as the Athenian leader Pericles put it, 'the products of the whole world flow into us... and we enjoy them just as naturally as we do our own'.

KIN⟨S, ⟨ODS, WHORES AND NUTTERS

As in every great port, all human life could be found in Piraeus. Alongside Athenians and slaves, foreigners on trade missions abounded there, especially (we are told) from Lydia, Syria and Phrygia. There were also plenty of metics (non-Athenian residents; see below) – funeral inscriptions alone list metics from sixty different states in the fourth century BC. No fewer than fifteen foreign deities were worshipped in Piraeus, one of which – Bendis from Thrace – was granted an official public cult. As well as passing statesmen, kings, tourists and gods(!), merchants, ship-owners, dealers, bankers and accountants thronged the area alongside sailors, fishermen, porters and others looking to make a living or a deal, shady or otherwise, including male and female prostitutes. And then there were the nutters. We hear of one Thrasyllus, who went down there every day holding a register, in the belief that he owned the ships and was set to make a meaty profit from them. His brother arrived and sent him off to the doctor. Cured, Thrasyllus commented that he had never been happier than when watching his ships come in.

FROM PERSIAN EMPIRE TO ATHENIAN - TYRANNY? 151

METICS: ATHENS' RESIDENT ALIENS

'Metic' derives from the Greek *metoikos*, meaning 'one who changes residence'. Anyone non-Athenian who was free-born – whether Greek or not – and who took up residence in Athens had to register as a metic within one month and pay a tax of one drachma a month (half for a woman). Further, they had to have an Athenian patron (who would vouch for them) and be willing to serve in battle, but they were not allowed to own property. They did, however, have access to the courts, festivals and theatre. Athenian slaves who were freed took on metic status. We have a list of metics rewarded for service to Athens, with their occupations; they include farm worker, butcher/cook, carpenter, muleteer, builder, gardener, olive-seller, bread-seller, fuller, labourer and sculptor. Clearly, Athens was a city of opportunity. Examples of famous metics include Lysias (p. 369) and Pasion (p. 261).

MAN-FOOTED THINGS

Greeks described slaves as *andrapoda*, 'man-footed things'. Aristotle called them 'living objects', explaining that 'the use made of slaves and of tame animals is not very different; for both with their bodies minister to the needs of life'. Homer understood the dehumanizing effects of slavery: 'Zeus takes half the goodness out of a man when he makes a slave of him.'

Perhaps about 60,000 Athenians owned up to 120,000 slaves. They were valuable. One would not routinely kick them for fun before breakfast any more than we would set about the washing machine or car, today's slave and animal substitutes. Such slaves needed looking after, and they required clothing, feeding, watering and housing (we even hear of people volunteering to become slaves for the chance of a regular meal). There were dedicated slave doctors. Some were people with high skills captured by pirates or in war – fancy coming across an Alfred Brendel or Warren Buffett. We hear of slaves who were teachers, traders, financiers, craftsmen, builders and farmers. We hear of some, especially wet-nurses, who became a welcome part of the family. That said, if they worked the silver mines in Laurium (for example), their lot was indeed a ghastly one; but there were no Roman-style mass slave revolts because there were no institutions that needed vast numbers of slaves to function.

The idea, however, that ancient Athenian democracy 'depended on' slavery is not true. As Aristotle pointed out, the state actually *paid* citizens to participate in the democracy: they needed incentives.

SLAVE SOURCES

Some slaves were home-bred, some captured by pirates, others enslaved in war. Most came from the north – Thrace, the Danube, the Balkans – and Asia Minor. Since Greeks tended not to enslave Greeks, where Greeks were sold into slavery it probably means they were pretty soon ransomed out of it. A document listing the sale of property of men convicted of sacrilege in 415 BC (see p. 237) reveals where their slaves came from and their prices. Since a drachma (*drakhmē*) was then the daily wage of a skilled worker, they were not hugely expensive:

> The property of Cephisodoros, metic [see above], living in Piraeus: slaves – Thracian female, 165 *drakhmai*; Thracian female, 135; Thracian male, 170; Syrian male, 240; Carian

male, 105; Illyrian male, 161; Thracian female, 220; Thracian male, 115; Scythian male, 144; Illyrian male, 121; Colchian male, 153; Carian boy, 174; little Carian boy, 72; Syrian male, 301; Maltese(?) male, 151; Lydian female, 85.

SLAVERY AND DEPENDENCE

Slaves were the ultimate dependent humans – dependent on their masters for their lives and livelihood, with no option but to dance to someone else's tune. That, to a Greek, was the worst conceivable humiliation. That is one reason why our concept of a 'job' would not have appealed to ancient Greeks. Slavery meant suffering the humiliation of earning a living by doing what someone else required you to do. No free Greek would willingly stoop to that.

DREAMING SLAVES

Ancients were fascinated by dreams and much thought was devoted to how they could be explained. Empedocles (see p. 172) got close to modern ideas by proposing that dreams dealt with 'the day's residue'. In his *Interpretation of Dreams*, Artemidorus from Ephesus (second century AD) examined slaves' dreams and found that they commonly featured fear of losing a master's trust, or hopes of freedom.

THE PERSIAN POSTAL SERVICE

The Persian empire had been formed by the coalition of the Medes, a powerful force in the seventh century BC, and the Persians under their king Cyrus the Great (*c.* 550 BC). The king was known in Persian as the Shahanshah, 'King of Kings', and in Greek as the 'Great King' – or simply 'the king'. Everyone knew who was meant. Under King Darius, the empire ruled some 70 million people and stretched from western Turkey down into Egypt and across to India. It was the world's first superpower. Darius reorganized and rebuilt the 1,677-mile (2,699-km) Royal Road from Susa, Persia's capital, to Sardis – a journey of seven days by royal courier, three months on foot. Herodotus said nothing travelled faster than these couriers: 'Neither snow nor rain nor heat nor gloom of night stays these couriers from the swift completion of their appointed rounds' – a sentiment inscribed on the James Farley Post Office in New York.

DRUNKEN DEBATES

Herodotus was fascinated by what made people tick and describes in great detail the habits, customs and institutions of the people he met. Here is his take on Persians and alcohol:

> The Persians have a particular passion for wine, though they regard it as the height of bad manners to vomit or urinate in the presence of others. Whenever they are drunk, it is their practice to debate some weighty issue. Next day, when they have sobered up, they will debate it all over again. If the same decision is arrived at sober, then it will be approved; if not, it is abandoned. Conversely, any sober debate will be re-engaged when the participants are roaring drunk.

Observe that Herodotus tells us as much about Greeks as about Persians: Greek pots are full of depictions of people vomiting and urinating in public. But he simply records the facts: he does not add a derogatory comment.

THE GIFT OF EARTH AND WATER

In 492 BC the Persian general Mardonius conquered Thrace and made Macedon a client kingdom. Greece was now open to attack from the north. In 491 BC Darius sent ambassadors to all Greek *poleis*, demanding a gift of 'earth and water' to signify submission (these were tokens for land, sea and everything else). Most obliged, but the Athenians put the ambassadors on trial and executed them, and the Spartans threw them down a well. So both Athens and Sparta were now at war with Persia.

MARATHON: THE BATTLE

Darius charged his general Datis to bring back the Athenians in chains. In 490 BC, a fleet of 600 ships crossed the Aegean, took and burned Eretria (which had also sent ships to help the Ionians). Then, guided by the ageing ex-tyrant Hippias, it landed at the bay of Marathon. Probably around 9,000 Athenian hoplites and 1,000 allies from Plataea, though outnumbered perhaps two to one, decided to engage the enemy there, rather than wait for the Persians to advance towards Athens. Arriving at Marathon, the Greeks had waited a few days when Miltiades (one of the ten military leaders, or *stratêgoi*) persuaded them to attack – but at speed (this, evidently, had never been done before), probably to prevent the deployment of the feared Persian cavalry. So they ran nearly a mile before launching the assault. A jog at 4.5 mph (7 km/h) would not have left them exhausted if their hoplite gear weighed 40 lb (18 kg) and not 60 lb (27 kg), as has been argued. The Athenian centre yielded to the Persian onslaught, but their wings (which had been specially extended) broke Persian resistance and forced them to flee back to the ships. On that late summer morning, 6,400 Persians were killed and 192 Greeks;

the latter were all buried in a mound there and treated from then on as 'heroes', i.e. semi-divine beings.

MARATHON MAN

As soon as the Athenians decided to fight at Marathon, they sent a professional runner to Sparta to invite their help. Named Pheidippides or Philippides, he reached Sparta – a distance of 150 miles (240 km) – the next day (in 1990 a Greek runner did it in 20 hours). The Spartans replied that they could not leave Sparta until the full moon, presumably for religious reasons. True to their word, they sent a force of 2,000 Spartans that reached Marathon three days after the full moon. They observed the dead Persians, congratulated the Athenians and returned home.

Further, we are told by a much later source (the story is not in Herodotus) that news of the victory was immediately taken to Athens by the same, or a different, runner *in full armour*, the other candidates being Eucles or Thersippos (in modern times the run has been completed with a weighted back-pack in just over four hours). He blurted out 'Rejoice! We won!' and dropped dead.

THE MODERN MARATHON

Two ancient roads led from Marathon to Athens, one 21.4 miles (34.5 km), the other 25.4 miles (40.8 km). The former is the more difficult route, but more likely, since the Persians would still have been in the region of the latter. There was no such thing as a marathon in ancient Greek games. The marathon we know today is an invention of a friend of Pierre de Coubertin, the father of the modern Olympics (see

p. 273). The first marathon, run in 1896, was set at 40 km (24 miles 1,054 yards). In 1908 the London marathon was run from Windsor Castle to White City Stadium, a distance of 42.195 km (26 miles 385 yards). In 1924 this became the official marathon distance.

487 BC: POT LUCK

How did you clear the air when political decision-making in the Assembly became deadlocked between two proposals? Answer: you 'ostracized' one of the proposers.

Once a year Athenian citizens in the Assembly were asked if they wanted to remove someone from the political arena and send him into honourable exile for ten years. If the Assembly voted for it, an 'ostracism' was staged two months later. This gave Athenians plenty of time to debate among themselves the pros and cons of getting rid of one or other turbulent speaker. On the day of the ostracism, there was no debate on the matter; each citizen simply scratched the name of his chosen candidate on an *ostrakon* – a piece of broken pottery, which was both cheap and readily available. As long as 6,000 *ostraka* were cast, the man with the most votes was given the order of the pot.

VOTING TO DEFER PLEASURE

By 483 BC the mines at Laurium on the southern tip of Attica (Athens' hinterland) had produced an over-abundance of silver to the tune of 200 talents. The people's Assembly debated a motion to copy the citizens of the fabulously gold-rich island of Siphnos and divide it up among themselves. But the statesman Themistocles seems to have had a grander vision: an Athens with total dominance of the sea. So he proposed the

Assembly should forego short-term pleasure for long-term advantage and use the money to construct a huge fleet. The motion was passed, with significant implications for the democratic power of the poor (see p. 149). These were the ships that would repel the Persian invaders at Salamis in 480 BC and subsequently realize a maritime empire, bringing the Athenians dominance of the Greek world and greater prosperity than they could ever have imagined. This rather gives the lie to those who imagine that the Greeks in Assembly were a greedy, self-seeking, uncontrollable mob (see p. 192).

A TIMELY WINDFALL

The ancients had no concept of a 'national debt', because minted coin was the sole monetary instrument, and there was no machinery for *creating* credit. So there were no banks in our sense (see p. 260), and only two sources of wealth: agricultural and mineral – the former far more important, but the latter having more dramatic instant consequences. So in 483 BC it would never have occurred to the Athenians to borrow money from somewhere to build a Persia-defeating fleet. But the mines at Laurium had come up with fabulous seams of silver, and – bingo! – there was the money.

TAMPERING WITH NATURE

The Persian king Darius died in 486 BC, to be succeeded by one of his younger sons, Xerxes (Persian: Khshayarsha, 'Ruler of Heroes'). It was he who planned the gigantic combined land/sea operation to punish Athens for the Persian defeat at Marathon. Not a man to do things by halves, he cut a canal for the fleet through the Mount Athos peninsula

(Herodotus described how it was done) because an earlier fleet has been wrecked going round it; and lashed together a bridge of boats with flax and paprus cables for his army to cross the Hellespont (a distance of 220 yards/650 metres). When a storm wrecked the bridge, Xerxes ordered the Hellespont to be flogged with 300 lashes and branded with hot irons, and the constructors to be decapitated. Herodotus details the building of the second bridge and hints at Xerxes' fatal megalomania at wishing to marry two continents, Asia and Europe, which should have been kept asunder.

POLIS BEFORE NATION

Much of Xerxes' army consisted of Greeks who had submitted to Persian rule (see p. 155) or volunteered as mercenaries (p. 248). In fact, only 31 *poleis*, out of about 700, decided to unite against the Persians. Powerful Greek cities like Thebes actually went over to the Persians, while Argos stayed out completely. As ever, independence and perceived self-interest were the name of the game for the *poleis*. If the Persians offered a better deal, over to the Persians they would go. The nature of 'international relationships' has not changed greatly.

THE WOODEN WALLS

The Athenians consulted the oracle at Delphi about how best to defend themselves against the Persian menace. Before the consultation even began, the priestess told them to run for it. Dismayed, they decided to try again: could the oracle do a bit better this time, please? Accordingly it advised them not to engage on land, but to put their trust in 'wooden walls'. Did that mean the hedge that surrounded the Acropolis? Or, metaphorically, the fleet? The matter was discussed in the Assembly, which was persuaded by Themistocles – who had urged the building of 200 triremes (see p. 157) – that the oracle meant the fleet. It was agreed, therefore, to abandon Attica. The final decision was, of course, taken by the Assembly, not by the oracle, but it is easy to see why, after the event, the oracle might take centre stage (whether or not there actually was one – we only have the Athenian consultants' word for it). The fact is that it added greatly to the drama of the story.

THE POLIS AND RELIGION

Greek priests did not run churches, preach, teach, meet in synods, or claim moral or theological authority, let alone demand adherence to Thirty-nine Articles. All they did was serve one of the gods with the appropriate cult. Many held the office merely because their families had held it from time immemorial. Further, though priests were experts on their own cults, secular experts called *exêgêtai* were also regularly consulted for advice. It was, in fact, the *polis* via its Assembly that ran state religion.

So, if any controversial problem of religious importance emerged, it was submitted not to priests but to the Athenian democratic Assembly. After due consideration, the Assembly would use its democratic vote to agree either to a solution to the problem suggested by one of its members, or to a proposal to submit the problem to the oracle at Delphi. In the latter case, a question would be framed and a deputation sent to Delphi to pose it. The Assembly would then act in light of the reply. In other words, the priesthood and Athens' religious life were under full state control. It was the Assembly that told the priests what to do, not the other way round.

DELPHIC FRENZY

Geologists recently claimed to have found the explanation for the ancient Greek oracle at Delphi and for its (apparently) moaning, howling female priestess (the Pythia). They argued that ethane, methane and ethylene issued from the spring which once flowed under the oracle; and since the first stages of ethylene inhalation (widely used as an anaesthetic in the past) induce in patients a Pythia-like 'frenzy', this was how the Pythia got into her state and generated her prophecies.

The facts. First, it would be impossible for enough ethylene to be produced along the length of a stream to have a noticeable effect on a single human being at any point along it. The essayist Plutarch, writing in the second century AD, knew about the oracle's spring and pointed out that, if trance-inducing vapours were naturally present along it, why didn't everyone who came into contact with them start prophesying?

Second, there is an assumption that religious experience is inseparable from irrational frenzy. But the ancient sources make it abundantly clear that the Pythia no more foamed hysterically at the mouth than the vicar does announcing the hymns. She gave coherent answers which were written down by her attendants or interpreters and handed over to the questioners.

The 'madness' theory arises from a misunderstanding of the Greek word *mania*. Plato said the lover, the artist and the prophet were all subject to it. Clearly it did not mean 'madness' of the foaming-at-the-mouth variety. It meant 'inspiration'. The Pythia knew all about it, in her terms; so did J. S. Bach, in his. None of it had anything to do with ethylene.

THERMOPYLAE NIGHTMARE

There were not 300 Spartans at Thermopylae (as the film of that name suggested) but 301: 300 plus the Spartan leader Leonidas. Further, these were the elite Spartiates: the cream of the Spartan army. They all died there, with perhaps 700 other Spartans and about 1,000 other Greeks.

The scheme, proposed by Themistocles, was to hold up the Persian advance at a place where there was only a narrow pass between cliffs and sea, diminishing the effect of Persian numbers. There was another, difficult pass running round *behind* the mountains, but 1,000 Greeks from Phocis were posted to guard it. When the Persian spies saw the Greek numbers, they told them to lay down their arms. 'Come and get them,' replied the Spartans. After two days of stout defence, a Greek traitor Ephialtes showed the crack Persian 'Immortals' regiment the route behind the mountains. At the sight of the Persians, the Phocians abandoned their position, and the Greeks were trapped back and front. It was all over. Both then and now, *ephialtês* in Greek has meant 'nightmare'.

Meanwhile, the Greek fleet had the better of the Persians (or rather Phoenicians, who made up the Persian fleet) off Artemisium. The Phoenicians were among the finest seamen in the ancient world – the Greek success was partly due to a gale which wrecked many of the enemy ships. This engagement would serve as a considerable morale-booster for the Athenian fleet at Salamis.

The poet Simonides celebrated the heroic stand at Thermopylae in a famous couplet:

Go tell the Spartans, passer-by,
We followed orders. Here we lie.

SALAMIS-SLICING THE PERSIANS

Since the Athenians had already abandoned Attica (see p. 160), the Persians sacked Athens, with special attention given to destroying Athena's temple on the Acropolis. At this, the Greek allies, led by the Spartan Eurybiades, agreed to abandon central Greece entirely and make their stand at the isthmus of Corinth. This, like Thermopylae, was a narrow space where the effect of Persian numbers would be diminished. But Themistocles saw that it would be fatal to allow the Persian army *and* fleet to fight in combination at the isthmus; the wide open waters would give the Persian fleet too much of an advantage. So he argued that the Greeks should lure the Persian fleet into fighting opposite Athens, in the narrow, confined waters between the nearby island of Salamis and the mainland. Xerxes, who could simply have sailed directly for the isthmus, also seemed to think it worthwhile taking on the Greeks there and then, because he proceeded to trap their fleet by blocking either end of the narrows. As a result, the Greeks had no option: they had to fight it out. Battle was engaged – and the Persian fleet destroyed.

ROLE REVERSAL

Artemisia was a Greek from Halicarnassus (where Herodotus came from). Her husband had been made tyrant of Halicarnassus by the Persians, and when he died, she took over. Herodotus tells how she was in charge of five Persian ships at Salamis, and when the Persian fleet was in retreat, she was in danger of being rammed by an Athenian. So she rammed one of her own ships and sank it. This persuaded the Athenians, in the fog of war, that she must be a Greek ship, or a Persian deserter. Xerxes too saw the incident and assumed that she had rammed an Athenian ship! Given the dreadful showing his men had put on in the battle, he commented: 'My men have turned into women, my women into men.'

HISTORICAL TRAGEDY (2)

Themistocles was never one to give up the chance of hymning his own achievements. So when in 476 BC Phrynichus decided to write a tragedy about the Athenian victory at Salamis, he funded it (see p. 142). The play was called *Phoenician Women*, but it does not survive. Its title probably refers to the widows of the Phoenician sailors who formed the bulk of Xerxes' fleet. We know that the play opened with a eunuch announcing the disaster to the king's counsellors.

THE TIMES TRIREME DEBATE

Question: what was the subject of the longest correspondence in the history of *The Times*? Answer: the workings of the ancient Greek trireme. The correspondence was triggered by an article of 30 August 1975 on its use of sail. On 6 September the first letter of reply was printed, sent by the Cambridge authority on Greek oared ships, Professor John Morrison. Others followed, mathematicians in particular. Scornful of mere classicists' calculations, they wielded computers, slide-rules and envelopes to predict with sublime confidence the absolute maximum speed of such a vessel; their answers ranged from 7 to 13.5 knots. After five weeks, thirty-one letters, one fourth leader, two Latin elegiac couplets and with many theories now sunk, listing badly or completely abandoned, it became clear that the problem would be solved only by actually building a trireme and putting it through its paces. In 1981 John

Morrison was joined by John Coates, the retired chief naval architect for the Ministry of Defence, and a team of financial backers. Agreement was reached to build the boat by traditional methods in the harbour of Piraeus in Athens, and the project was on. In 1987 the trireme, named *Olympias* after the mother of Alexander the Great (all ships are feminine), was launched.

Trials of *Olympias* demonstrated what a superb fighting machine the low-in-the-water, sturdily built Greek trireme was. The key factor at Salamis was its manoeuvrability. The trireme could reduce speed from 5.7 to 1.1 knots in less than one ship's length; at 6 knots it could turn 360 degrees in under two ship's length and two minutes. This capacity enabled the trireme to dodge, back water, turn and ram in a very tight space indeed. It was all too much for the less manoeuvrable Persians.

A SPARTAN TRIUMPH

Having achieved what he had set out to do – ravage Athens and destroy its temples – Xerxes and the remains of his fleet returned to Persia, leaving his general Mardonius to winter in Greece with his formidable army and to sort the Greeks out at his own convenience.

At the battle of Plataea, after preliminary skirmishes and much tactical manoeuvring, a lengthy encounter ensued. The result, according to Herodotus, was 'the most brilliant victory of all those we know about', in which Mardonius was killed and the starring role went to the Spartans. Doubtless the Athenians on the left wing too enjoyed their success against those Greeks facing them who had 'medized' (i.e. joined the Persians) – Thessalians, Boeotians and Thebans – though many of the medizing Ionians had deserted back to the Greeks. That said, the effect on Sparta was severe. The number of Spartiates available to them was being dramatically reduced – a trend that would continue, with disastrous consequences (see p. 270).

A <OMMON HERITA<E?

At one stage Mardonius had attempted diplomacy to wean the Athenians away from their Greek alliance, but failed. Challenged about this by the Spartans, the Athenians replied that the Persians had burnt their temples and images of the gods: that required revenge; second, the Greek nation was 'a community of blood and language, temples and rituals, and common customs – if we Athenians were to betray all this, it would not be well done'. The many 'medizing' Greeks might have offered a different analysis.

RAMMIN< THE POINT HOME

A Greek pot datable to the early 460s BC shows on one side a Persian, bending over in the position of a woman about to be entered from behind; on the other, a naked Greek male advancing towards him, erect penis in hand. It is hard to resist the conclusion: we buggered the Persians.

PRO/E<UTIN< A /TATUE

Theagenes from Thasos, living in the fifth century BC, was one of the greatest athletes of all time. He won with embarrassing regularity at games all round Greece, in boxing, the *pankration* and (amazingly) a distance running event. In all, we are told, he had 1,400 victories. When he died, the people of Thasos proudly erected a bronze statue of the great man in their town. But he had made enemies, and one of them took to coming every night and flogging the statue. The statue eventually lost patience with this treatment, fell on his attacker and killed him. So the sons of the deceased prosecuted the statue for murder. It was found guilty, 'exiled' out to sea and dumped. Next year, however, the crops failed. The Thasians consulted the oracle at Delphi, which replied: 'You have forgotten your great Theagenes.' By a stroke of good fortune a fisherman netted the statue. The Thasians immediately re-erected it in its original position and sacrificed to it as to a god regularly for at least the next 650 years (i.e. up to the time this story was told in the second century AD).

TRAGEDY AND COMEDY

There were two main dramatic festivals in Athens, both in honour of the god Dionysus: the Lenaea in January (the comic festival) and the City Dionysia in April (tragedy and comedy). They were funded as a state duty by rich individuals. To generalize:

- in tragedy, the hero(ine) – a self-assertive aristocrat, of high status and some ethical greatness of spirit – grapples with ancient (mythical) problems, featuring gods in the background, usually centred round the household, with disastrous outcomes for him/herself and/or family, and no resolution of problems;
- in comedy, the hero(ine) – a self-assertive nobody, of no status, but blessed with usually quite unethical bravado, cunning and trickery – grapples with modern problems concerning life in Athens, with gods joining in the fun, finally emerging triumphant, problems solved.

Further, while tragedy never acknowledged the presence of an audience or a stage, comedy constantly involved audience and stage machinery in the action: anything for a laugh.

HISTORICAL TRAGEDY (3)

In 472 BC, at about the age of fifty and after military service himself, the tragedian Aeschylus staged *Persians* at the Dionysia in Athens. Like Phrynichus' earlier effort of 476 BC (see p. 164), it took as its subject a known historical event rather than a story from the deep past (what we would call a myth): the battle of Salamis in 480 BC. The title refers to the chorus of Persian counsellors at Xerxes' palace in Susa, awaiting the news. The queen Atossa is full of fears about the outcome of the battle because of her dreams – and she is proved right. A messenger arrives to describe the course of the battle (some of what he says must surely have rung true with the watching Athenian audience). Lamentation takes over; the ghost of King Darius emerges to say the calamity was the result of insolently destroying the statues of temples and gods; and finally Xerxes appears, clothed in rags to lament yet further. So the gods ensured that the Persians got what they deserved. It is terrific, xenophobic, chauvinistic, tub-thumping stuff, though not without sympathy for Persians like Atossa and Darius. How the Athenians must have loved it! It won first prize at the festival. It was paid for by Pericles, who was to become the leading man in Athens in a critical phase of its imperial development (see pp. 191, 205).

THE SURVIVING FEW

Six plays by Aeschylus (525–456 BC) survive in full (another, *Prometheus*, is probably not by him), seven by Sophocles (496–406 BC) and nineteen by Euripides (485–406 BC). But we have records of the titles of about 80 plays by Aeschylus, 123 by Sophocles and 92 by Euripides. This represents a phenomenal lifetime's output (by way of comparison, Shakespeare racked up 38 plays and 154 sonnets; Alan Ayckbourn has more than 70 to his credit). We also have records of who was victorious, and when: Sophocles came first on twenty-four occasions, Euripides on just six. There were many other playwrights too, of course. Since the drama festivals were paid for by the wealthy, this added up to quite a benefaction (see pp. 219–20).

POTTED THEMISTOCLES

Thousands of *ostraka* with names of famous Greeks have been dug up (see p. 157), but the most notable are a batch of 191 relating to Themistocles' ostracism in the 470s BC. They all had Themistocles' name inscribed on them, but by only four separate hands – either a case of deliberate fraud or the work of an anti-Themistocles hit squad ensuring that the illiterate did not miss the chance to vote. Still, Themistocles would have expected nothing else. His father had warned him of the fate of politicians: he had taken his son to the beach when he was a young man, pointed to the trireme hulks rotting on the shore, and said: 'That is how the people treat unwanted leaders.' He fled to Persia – surprise, surprise – where, decked with honours by a king elated to have so dangerous an old enemy on board, he served out his time as governor of Magnesia in Asia Minor.

THERE'S NO PLEASING SOME PEOPLE...

A friend of Cleisthenes who fought at Marathon (see p. 155), Aristides had suffered ostracism in the late 480s BC, but he had been recalled in time for Salamis, where again he did sterling service. He was known as 'the Just'. It was said that an Athenian who could not write came up to him, not knowing who he was, and asked him to write 'Aristides' on an *ostrakon*. Aristides enquired what harm 'Aristides' had done him. 'None at all,' came the reply, 'I'm just sick and tired of hearing this bloke being called "the Just".' Aristides shrugged and obliged.

LIMBERING UP FOR WAR

Ever since the formation of the Delian League, Athens and Sparta had been worrying away at each other. Athens' confidence after the Persian wars and leadership of the League was beginning to give it thoughts of increasing its power in the Aegean; Sparta and its allies looked on suspiciously. When Athens forced the island of Thasos back into the Delian League in 465 BC, Sparta contemplated invading Attica; an earthquake – a bad omen – prevented them, but stirred the helots to a serious revolt (see p. 79). Athens sent 4,000 men to help, but Sparta rejected them. The Athenians were not pleased at this insult, and, over the next fifteen years, a series of battles was fought between the two powers and their allies. In 445 BC a thirty-year truce was called. All this was a taste of things to come.

POWER TO THE PEOPLE

In 461 BC the Athenian Ephialtes, who had been a commander in the Aegean in 465 BC, began a series of reforms that marked radical democratic development in Athens. Essentially, he took away many of the legal powers lodged up to that time with the Areopagus (see p. 92) and divided them up between the Steering Committee, the Assembly and the people's courts. Ephialtes was assassinated for his pains, but his work of democratization was continued by his associate Pericles in the 450s BC, in particular: pay for jurors in the people's courts, the right of Solon's third financial class of citizens (see p. 104) to stand for the *arkhón*ship, and the law that to qualify as a citizen one needed both an Athenian father and an Athenian mother (previously the former had sufficed).

HORNS OF A DILEMMA

When Pericles was making his mark in politics, he was sent from his country estates the head of a one-horned ram. The prophet Lampon noted how strongly and solidly the horn grew out of the middle of its forehead. So he interpreted it to mean that, of the two people currently fighting for the ear of the people in Athens (Pericles and Thucydides – not the historian), one would emerge victorious: Pericles.

Pericles' mentor, however, was the natural scientist Anaxagoras (*c.* 510–428 BC), whose influence had caused Pericles to take a great interest in abstract speculation. Anaxagoras had the skull dissected and showed how the growth of the single horn had occurred quite naturally as a result of a skull deformity. Down with Lampon! But not long after, Thucydides was ostracized, leaving Pericles as the most influential man in Athens, and Lampon's view of the matter returned to favour.

The essayist Plutarch, who reports this story in the second century AD, went on to say that both men were right: Anaxagoras, whose job it was to explain how something had come about, had correctly diagnosed the *cause* of the prodigy; but Lampon, who was concerned with purpose and significance, had understood its *meaning*. Plutarch continues:

Those who proclaim that the discovery of the *cause* of any phenomenon automatically does away with its *meaning* fail to observe that such reasoning also dispenses with artificially created human (as well as divine) signification. Take, for example, sundials. Their shadows have particular *causes*, but the dials have been constructed so as to *signify* something else.

<LOAK JOKE

Ancient eclipses were the subject of much scientific debate. Anaxagoras explained accurately how they were caused, and Pericles put this information to excellent use. A solar eclipse occurred as he was about to set off with his navy, and panic broke out at the 'omen'. Pericles at once wrapped a cloak around his helmsman's eyes and asked whether he thought that was an omen. 'Of course not,' replied the helmsman. 'Same difference, then,' said Pericles. 'The eclipse has just been caused by something bigger than this cloak.'

THE FOUR-ELEMENT THEORY

When it came to explaining the nature of the world, no one at this time was more influential than Empedocles (*c.* 490–430 BC), a Greek from Acragas in Sicily. He believed that there were four primary substances, not one, out of which the cosmos was constructed – earth, air, fire and water – and this theory became adapted to account for everything (for its role in medicine, see p. 174). Even the great Aristotle swallowed this, and his authority was so great among intellectuals and the church fathers that the theory was simply assumed to be true for nearly 2,000 years, till the experimental method – the foundation of all modern science

– was invented in the sixteenth century AD (it is strongly associated with Francis Bacon, AD 1561–1626). Ancient Greeks did, of course, *test* to see what worked best: they could not otherwise have sailed a ship, drained a mine, blown glass, fired a pot, ploughed a field, built a temple or produced tools and fine tableware. But that is not the same as testing, rejecting and retesting *hypotheses* on the basis of experiment, till an answer, whatever it may be, emerges.

BRAINY DOCTOR

Alcmaeon from Croton in southern Italy, active around 450 BC, was the first person we know of to identify the brain as the seat of understanding and to distinguish understanding from simple perception. He also argued that the body remained healthy because of the equal balance of certain powers within it – moist and dry, cold and hot, bitter and sweet and the rest. The abundance of one over others caused disease. Health was the harmonious blending of these powers.

HIPPOCRATIC MEDICINE

Hippocrates was perhaps the most famous ancient doctor of all and the founder of 'rational' medicine. He came from Cos and lived in the fifth century BC. That is all we can say about him for sure: he is 'a name without a work'; or rather, a name with thousands of works. It was not till the time of the emperor Hadrian in the second century AD, 500 years after Hippocrates' death, that the complete collection of his work became finally agreed. So any medical treatise written during that 500-year period had a good chance of being called 'Hippocratic' – such was his reputation!

HUMOROUS MEDICINE

Hippocrates is associated with the famous theory of the four humours (i.e. liquids). From observation of what came out of bodies and how a person's health seemed to respond to it, he argued that the body of man 'had in itself blood, phlegm, yellow bile and black bile' and concluded that it was healthy when these constituents were perfectly balanced and mixed.

Over more than a thousand years, this developed into a theory of almost everything. The four humours became associated with Empedocles' four elements, the four seasons, Alcmaeon's four powers (hot, dry, cold, wet), four body parts, and the four basic character types, as follows:

BLOOD	air	spring	liver	warm/ moist	sanguine (hopeful)
PHLEGM	water	winter	gall bladder	cold/ moist	phlegmatic (calm)
YELLOW BILE	fire	summer	spleen	warm/ dry	choleric (bad-tempered)
BLACK BILE	earth	autumn	brain/ lungs	cold/dry	melancholic (despondent)

In the Middle Ages this pattern became enormously enlarged – apparently, it embraced even the four gospels! Medicine was dominated by this theory till well into the eighteenth century.

DIETARY HUMOUR

One of Hippocrates' treatises illustrates how this system of keeping the 'humours' in balance worked: one had to eat foods which were opposite to the weather. Given that winter corresponds with cold and moist, at this time one should eat as much 'hot' food as possible (but only a few vegetables) and drink as little as possible; all meat and fish should be roasted. This will keep the body warm and dry. When spring comes (warm/moist), take more drink, increasing the quantity; meat should be cut down, boiled meat replacing roast, and a few vegetables should be eaten. Towards the summer (warm/dry) take a diet consisting entirely of soft cereals, boiled meat and vegetables both raw and boiled, and a lot of very diluted wine (but make the change gradual).

RATIONAL MEDICINE?

Given that dead bodies were sacred and not to be cut up, and technology of the sort we have today, from X-rays to blood tests, was non-existent, Greek doctors were severely limited in what they could learn about the body from the living (though wounds on the battlefield were helpful). All they could do was observe the externals and try to draw conclusions. In one of his most important works, Hippocrates emphasized the point:

> Internal diseases have not been mastered, but they have been mastered as far as possible for the present. The future depends on how far the intelligence of the patients permits the drawing of conclusions, and how far the abilities of future investigators are fitted for the task. If the nature of a disease cannot be perceived by the eye, its diagnosis will involve more trouble and

certainly more time than if it can. What escapes our vision we must grasp by mental sight, and the doctor, being unable to see the nature of the disease nor to be told of it, must have recourse to reasoning from the symptoms with which he is presented.

Note the rational approach; but given the premise that the 'four humours' explained health, no wonder the results were not encouraging. At least Greek doctors were good at one thing: prognosis – they observed and could therefore predict the courses of many illnesses quite accurately. They could just do little about them. But then no one could; it was not till the 1880s that germs and viruses were understood.

TEMPER, TEMPER

Given the four humour theory, it is not surprising that we are 'good-humoured' if the balance is right. Absurd behaviour indicated that you had too much of one of these humours – hence 'humorous'. One's temperament – from Latin *temperare*, 'to mix', hence *temperamentum* – was one's personal 'mixture' of these humours. 'Temper' originally meant the same as temperament, before it became associated with anger, which is the same as 'distemper', meaning the mixture had become unbalanced (*dis-*, apart, separate). 'Complexion' derives from Latin *cum* ('together') and *plectere* ('to weave') – one's temperament, it was believed, was shown by the 'weaving together' of colours in the face.

NO SEPARATION OF POWERS

Solon had already established people's courts of appeal (see p. 104). Thanks to Ephialtes, in 461 BC they became courts of 'first instance', i.e. courts which could actually hear original cases as well as appeals.

This one development handed enormous legal and *political* power to the citizens (males over thirty) who sat on them. After all, these males also made the laws in the Assembly. If they also sat in the people's courts, they took the laws they had made for granted. So there was *no* separation of powers – a key concept for us – in the ancient world, because while our parliament makes the laws, quite independent judges test their legality. Athenian citizens in the Assembly and people's courts were sovereign and could – in theory – make or scrap law, on the spot, as they saw fit. 'Legality' did not necessarily come into it (see pp. 244–5).

SWIFT AND OPEN JUSTICE

Athenian courts knew nothing of judges, barristers, solicitors, clerks or reference books, and certainly no conventions of legal precedence. The people's courts sat around 150 to 200 days a year, and the proceedings were in a space open to the public. Each court was overseen by officials whose duty was simply to ensure that procedures were followed and order kept. Litigants pleaded their cases themselves – though they hired professionals to write speeches for them and even someone else to deliver the speech, if they so chose. Both parties gave one speech, the same period of time for each. Witnesses were not called or cross-questioned; their evidence was simply read out. Most cases probably lasted one day.

TWO THOUSAND FIVE HUNDRED AND ONE GOOD MEN AND TRUE

Dikasts (*dikastai* in Greek) were the 'jurors' of the people's courts. But they bore no relation to modern jurors at all. Those who wanted to serve as dikasts turned up each day, hoping to be selected; they were paid about half a day's wage per day (later increased by Cleon from 2 to 3 obols). Juries ranged in number from 201 to 2,501, depending on the case. All they did was sit and listen; and when the speeches were over, without any discussion, they passed their verdict by simple majority, guilty or innocent. For most cases, a fixed penalty was triggered by the guilty verdict. Sometimes there was no standard penalty laid down. In that case, defence and prosecution could then put before the jury their own proposals for the penalty, which the jury then voted on (see p. 251).

CAST YOUR PEBBLE

Each dikast came with a pebble (*psêphos*). When the speeches were over, the dikasts filed past two urns, the first for acquittal, the second for condemnation. They dropped their pebble into the urn of their choice. The urns were then tipped out and the votes counted. Our word 'psephology', the study of voting, derives from *psêphos*.

TORTURED EVIDENCE

Women and children could not give evidence, and slaves could do so only under torture. The theory was that this would prevent slaves being unduly partial or hostile to their owner. In fact, we hear of very few uses of slave evidence, presumably because no owner wanted a valuable resource crippled, and if an owner knew a slave was hostile, he would not want the slave's evidence to be heard. So the probable effect of the practice was to prevent evidence from such an 'unreliable' source being heard at all.

WATER-BORED

The length of the speeches in court were controlled by a water-clock (*klepsudra*), the same for both sides. This was an amphora – a clay jar – filled with water, with a stopper at the bottom. The stopper was removed, and when the water had run out, the speech had to end. The stopper was replaced only during witness statements, oaths, etc. A small klepsydra has been found – it is one-sixth of an amphora and drains in six minutes. So an amphora would drain in thirty-six minutes. We are told that a case lasted eleven amphoras – i.e. six hours and thirty-six minutes – but it is not clear whether that meant one speech or both.

JUDICIAL HEDGEHOGS

Since Athenians were keen to prevent cases coming to court, they had systems for both private and public arbitration to try to nip the problem in the bud. If the parties could not reach some settlement themselves, they would privately agree on arbitrators and their terms of reference, and contract to stand by the decision. If that did not work, they would take their case to the legal *arkhôn*, who would invite his choice of public arbitrator to settle matters. If that failed, all the evidence gathered so far was sealed up in a box (*ekhinos*, literally 'hedgehog' or 'sea urchin'), to be read out in court when the time came. At any time, the parties could agree to revert to private arbitration.

FROM VENDETTA TO JUSTICE

Tragedies at the Dionysia (see p. 125) were put on in trilogies. Of these, Aeschylus' *Oresteia* (458 BC) is the only one to survive in full. The trilogy is dominated by the curse placed on the house of Pelops

(Agamemnon's ancestor) many generations earlier by Myrtilos (see p. 38), and the series of murderous family vendettas that resulted:

- in *Agamemnôn*, Agamemnon, who had sacrificed his own daughter Iphigeneia to raise the wind so that the Greek fleet could sail for Troy, returns from Troy to be murdered in revenge by his wife Clytemnestra;
- in *Khoêphoroi*, she is murdered in turn by their son Orestes;
- in *Eumenides*, Orestes is pursued by the Furies of vengeance to Athens, where he is put on trial. The case is judged by the Areopagus under the guidance of Athena, and he is found innocent. Since the Areopagus had been reformed a few years earlier (see p. 170), this is one of the very rare surviving instances in which politics *openly* rears its head on the tragic stage. Given that the myth originally had nothing to do with Athens, Aeschylus was presumably making a point about the historical importance of the Areopagus by connecting it to this famous story of vendetta, and showing how Athena and the Areopagus turned vendetta into justice. The *Oresteia* won the prize for tragedy that year.

VII

450–421 BC

TIMELINE

447 BC	Parthenon begun
445 BC	Thirty-year truce between Athens and Sparta
442 BC	Sophocles' *Antigone*
440 BC	Samos revolts from Athens
438–432 BC	Rising tensions at new Athenian interventions
431 BC	The (second) Peloponnesian War begins: the attack on Plataea
430–429 BC	Athenian plague: death of Pericles, rise of Cleon
427 BC	Mytilene revolts
427 BC	Civil war in Corcyra
425 BC	Major Athenian success at Pylos
425–421 BC	Further conflicts; fifty-year Peace of Nicias signed

ATHENS V. SPARTA:

THE PELOPONNESIAN WAR

At the outbreak of *the* Peloponnesian War in 431 BC, roughly the whole of the Peloponnese, continuing over the Isthmus of Corinth north to Thermopylae, was allied with Sparta; allied with Athens were Thessaly, Euboea, all the islands and the northern and eastern coastal regions of the Aegean, and some islands in the Adriatic west of the Greek mainland, including Corcyra (modern Corfu). At a rough calculation, Sparta had a three-to-one advantage in hoplites, Athens the same in triremes.

War was nothing new to the quarrelling *poleis* (city-states), but this war was different: it was not *polis* against *polis* over (say) local boundaries, but alliance against alliance, something approaching total war, involving citizen hoplites and mercenaries, and guerrilla tactics alongside set battles. The aim was to shore up one's own allies, and weaken the allies of the other side or get them to defect. So the theatre of battle switched piecemeal from land to sea and back again, all over Greece and the Aegean.

The Alcmaeonid Pericles was now Athens' leading light, responsible for the building of the Parthenon (finished with full decorations in 432 BC). This sign of Athens' cultural prowess was one among many other aspects of their growing power which so worried Sparta. In 440 BC Athens put down a revolt in Samos, with a fleet under all ten *stratêgoi* (military commanders) including Pericles. Sparta considered helping Samos, but its allies refused.

Athens now settled colonies and created allies in the north Aegean and Black Sea, and also made a defensive alliance with Corcyra, a colony of Sparta's close ally Corinth. The crunch came in 432 BC when Athens interfered in the business of Potidaea, a city in northern Greece and ally of Corinth. Corinth, joined by other Spartan allies, appealed to Sparta – why are you not supporting us? Do you want us to join a different alliance? Sparta had no option: it was war – against Athens. It took a year before their preparations were over. The pro-Spartan Theban attack on Plataea in 431 BC launched it.

Pericles' policy was to fight Sparta not by land, but by sea. The whole of Attica retreated into the security of Athens' Long Walls (see p. 150), while the fleet harassed Sparta's allies. In 430 BC a plague swept a crowded Athens, killing Pericles – and his policy. Some Athenian successes put Sparta on the back foot, and Athens quashed a revolt in Mytilene. In 427 BC a bloody civil war between democrats and oligarchs developed in Corcyra, now Athens' ally, once Sparta's. In 425 BC Athens struck lucky, trapping and (thanks to Cleon) taking hostages including 120 Spartiates on the island of Sphacteria. This emboldened the Athenians to carry on the war and expand by land into the north, but the Spartan general Brasidas got the better of them there, and in 421 BC a peace treaty engineered by the Athenian Nicias was signed.

The major source for these events is the superb contemporary Athenian historian Thucydides.

THE FIGHT FOR CONTROL

The interests of both Sparta and Athens lay in 'hegemony' over their allies – ensuring they remained allies and did not defect. Since Greek *poleis* were fiercely independent, there was a delicate balance to be maintained between assuring allies that they were not being bossed about, while at the same time ensuring they stayed loyal to the alliance. As we have seen, Greeks had no problems about switching sides if they thought it was in their interests to do so. Any threat by an ally to change sides was taken extremely seriously.

SOPHOCLES' ANTIGONE

In 441 BC the tragedian Sophocles was elected *stratêgos* (military commander) with Pericles on the strength of composing *Antigone* (one could not have imagined Harold Pinter being appointed to lead a military expedition as a result of his latest masterpiece). So our best guess at the date of *Antigone* is around 442 BC.

Antigone's two brothers have killed each other in a civil war. Their uncle Creon, the king, decrees that one will be buried with full honours; the other is a traitor and anyone who attempts to bury him will face the death penalty. Against the advice of her sister Ismene, Antigone decides to bury him. She is caught by the guards and confronts Creon, who asks why she broke the law. She replies:

> It was not Zeus that made me this proclamation;
> not such are the laws established among men by the Justice
> that dwells with the gods below; nor did I consider
> that your decrees, mortal as they were, had the authority

to override the unwritten and unfailing ordinances of the gods.
For their life is not of today or yesterday, but from all time,
and no man knows when they were first put forth.

But Creon is adamant that she will pay the penalty. It then emerges
that Creon's son Haemon is engaged to Antigone. He pleads with
his father for Antigone's life: in vain. She is buried alive in a cave, at
which point the prophet Tiresias announces that none of his auguries
are working. Something has gone badly wrong. Creon realizes he is to
blame, and calls his men to release Antigone. A messenger reports what
happens next: Creon finds Antigone dead and Haemon clinging to her
body. They grapple, and Haemon stabs himself to death. When Creon's
wife hears the news, she commits suicide. The play ends with Creon a
broken man.

The great themes of tragedy are all here in one play: young against
old, male against female, man against gods, family against state, the
living against the dead. There were no winners there.

AN ACTOR'S LOT

Playwrights were allowed only three actors (all males) with speaking
parts (actors also sang when required). This is why it is very rare for
anyone to be killed on stage: you at once lose one of the speakers. So
deaths happen only off-stage and are reported on-stage by a messenger
(as in *Antigone* above). To get some idea of what range the ancient actor
must have had: in *Antigone*, one actor probably played both Antigone
and her fiancé Haemon. The second may well have played the part of
Creon, who is on-stage most of the time. If so, the poor old third actor

had to play Antigone's sister Ismene, a guard, the messenger, the blind prophet Tiresias, and Creon's wife Eurydice. In Aeschylus' trilogy *Oresteia*, the three actors needed to play nineteen parts in all. In some plays, indeed, it is impossible to distribute the parts among three actors without two different actors playing the same role at different times! The fact that all actors wore masks to help establish their identity must have been some comfort.

THE GREEK CHORUS

Tragedies had a chorus of fifteen, comedies a chorus of twenty-four, all males, playing the parts of men and women, free and foreign, captive and slave, old or of indeterminate age, nearly always of lower social standing than the main characters. The choruses often gave their names to the plays concerned – for instance, *Persians*, *Trojan Women* and *Bacchae* in tragedy, *Acharnians*, *Clouds* and *Frogs* in comedy. They were on-stage virtually all the time, singing and dancing (Greek theatre was very balletic and operatic), moving in and out of the action, and collectively responding to it or trying to come to terms with it, as the poet saw fit.

THUCYDIDES: HISTORIAN OF FOCUS AND PRECISION

The great Athenian historian Thucydides (*c.* 460–400 BC) began his history of the war between Athens and Sparta known as the Peloponnesian War (431–404 BC) where Herodotus ended, in 479 BC, with the defeat of Persia. But while for Herodotus all human life was there, Thucydides:

- focused exclusively on politics and fighting;
- set a highly influential precedent, describing events – with occasional digressions – in strict chronological sequence year by year;
- absolutely excluded the gods as drivers of events (naturally, he was well aware that humans acted out of religious conviction, but that did not bind him to do anything other than record the fact);
- stated that he composed his history as 'a possession for all time' (he believed, not that events came in cycles, but that situations similar to the Peloponnesian War would recur, and that his history would help people understand them);
- proclaimed a passion for exactness, judging Herodotus' work 'mere romance'.

Herodotus' broad vision of history and Thucydides' narrow vision have been in competition ever since.

WHEN CITIZENS ARE SOVEREIGN: THE PRIN-CIPLES OF RADICAL DEMOCRACY

The word 'democracy' derives from the ancient Greek *dêmos*, 'citizen body', and *kratos*, 'power'. Invented in Athens in 508 BC by Cleisthenes (see p. 139), it lasted a mere 180 years and never strayed from its central principle: that the Athenian *dêmos* was sovereign. Athenian citizen males over eighteen would meet in Assembly (*ekklêsia*) on the Pnyx every eight days and make every sort of decision that our politicians make for us; while members of the *dêmos* over thirty, sitting on judge-free juries, would make every legal decision – in both political and criminal trials – without oversight from any higher authority. In 322 BC Macedonian Greeks killed democracy, in a campaign begun originally by Philip II, father of Alexander the Great.

CITIZEN POWER

It is commonly said of Athens that it was not a democracy because women and slaves did not get the vote. But 2,500 years ago, uniquely among all nations then *and since*, it established the principle that those qualifying as citizens, irrespective of wealth, status or connections, had the right to determine, in Assembly, their own political fate. Governments have always resisted the principle. In the UK it was not till 1918 that all male and female citizens even got the vote; but even then, a Greek would not have thought that enough to qualify us as a democracy. No society ever gave the vote to slaves. Only in Switzerland is there a system which in certain cases – mainly at local level – resembles real democracy, in which citizens can force debate, referenda and changes in laws. Swiss politicians, naturally, are doing all they can to destroy it.

MERITOCRATS? NO, DEMOCRATS

The power of the *dêmos* meant what it said in another sense: it had the power to ensure that office was open, in rotation, to any citizen who wanted to hold it. The only truly democratic way to ensure that a person could be so appointed was not by voting him into office (that is, on merit, or meritocratically), but by lot. To caricature the system, if you wanted to be minister in charge of the dockyards, you put your name into a hat, and if your name was pulled out, you got the job.

Running the Assembly

The decisions of the Assembly had to be overseen. To this end, Athenians appointed annually the *boulê* – a steering committee of 500 meeting in the *bouleutêrion* – to serve for one year (and no citizen could serve more than twice, or in succession). Its members (male citizens over thirty) put themselves forward at local level, but the final selection was made by lot. They met every day to receive business and to report to and prepare the agenda for the Assembly; and they saw to it that the decisions of the Assembly were put into effect and kept to budget. Finance was their major concern.

State officials

State officials who enacted Assembly decisions were mostly appointed by lot to positions that could be held for one year only and never again: budget controllers, architects, market inspectors, and so on (there were about 400 posts in all). The top jobs were those of the ten *stratêgoi* (whence our 'strategy'), or military commanders. These appointments, together with those of the top financial officials, were the only ones that could be held in succession, without limit, and were made by vote, not lot.

In our system, the majority party has only about 400 members, many of unknown quality, and from their number those who will run the great offices of state are appointed. In Athens the whole citizen population was available.

UNDER THE BEADY EYE OF THE PEOPLE

Surely the Athenian way of making appointments – drawing a name out of a hat – was likely to produce a grotesquely incompetent officialdom?

No more, one might say, than our current system, which hands high office to someone simply for having been elected.

Athenians were not that stupid. Candidates were closely scrutinized before being permitted to put their names forward; and the job came at a potentially very high price indeed, because the *dêmos* kept the closest eye on an official's performance throughout his term of office. Accusations of incompetence could be laid before the Assembly every month; and at the end of an official's term, performance was assessed by auditors and debated in Assembly. Officials proved to have been incompetent could be fined, exiled or (in extreme cases) executed. Among the ten annually elected *stratêgoi* (military commanders), on average *two a year* were condemned to death. Even the great Pericles was on one occasion successfully prosecuted.

The Greeks would have found nothing democratic about our parliament, which fights popular scrutiny tooth and nail and where failed ministers, at the end of their term of office, far from being held to public account, are waved off to the House of Lords.

PERICLES AND THE POWER OF PERSUASION

In a system such as that of the Athenians, it seems hard to see much of a role for supreme leaders. What role could a man have when the *dêmos* meeting in Assembly made all the decisions by majority show of hands, and the *boulê*, the steering committee, put everything into effect? The fact is that in Assembly Pericles had no more voting power than any other Athenian, nor any executive power to impose decisions. He was, in other words, subject to Assembly decisions like everyone else. All he had was the power of *persuasion*, and it was here that his authority lay.

The Athenians rated Pericles. They voted him *stratêgo*s fifteen years in succession. When he spoke in Assembly, they listened, and they must have liked what they heard. Indeed, so dominant a figure was he that the contemporary historian Thucydides approvingly described Athens at that time as 'nominally a democracy, but in fact the empire of the first man' – Pericles. But he was first among equals, and at all times subject to the will of the *dêmos*.

FEAR OF DEMOCRACY

For hundreds of years the very name 'democracy' was regarded by Western governments with terror and loathing: it was for them synonymous with rabble-rousing. They much preferred monarchy or an elective oligarchic system, which they called 'republicanism' (Romans were perceived as more responsible than 'fickle' Greeks). But from the late eighteenth century 'democrat' came back into fashion, meaning an anti-aristocratic revolutionary, demanding equality for the people. 'Democracy' is now sacred, untouchable, and almost meaningless, covering every form of government from Zimbabwe through Yemen to Switzerland and China.

DEMOCRACY AND RHETORIC

Greeks were aware that if radical democracy was to work, the means of persuasion had to be in the hands of *everyone*. If that were not the case, open, radical democracy of the sort they developed would be nothing but a façade, since the few citizens who possessed the means of persuasion were bound to hold an overwhelming advantage over everyone else. It is therefore no coincidence that the rules of persuasive public speaking – otherwise known as rhetoric (we would call it 'communication skills') – were said to have been invented shortly after Cleisthenes' invention of radical democracy. Aristotle composed a whole treatise entitled *The Art of Rhetoric*. It was here that the sophists came to play such an important part in Athenian life (see p. 148).

VIRTUE REDEFINED

Once upon a time, virtue (Greek *aretê*) meant heroic manliness; in fifth-century BC Athens, it came to mean 'success in public life', a success taught by sophists. We associate 'sophistry' with tricky, fallacious arguments (Greek *sophos*, 'ingenious, inventive, accomplished'; *philo-sophos*, 'lover of ingeniousness'). In fact the sophists were freelance professional educators, most coming from outside Athens, with a commitment to teaching pupils to make a successful public career for themselves by becoming great 'communicators' in the Assembly and people's courts. Sophists charged hefty fees both for this and for giving seminars and displays of public eloquence. This was all part of the process of democratization and giving men the skill they needed to speak effectively and become aware of the various tricks of the oratorical trade (*orator* is the Latin form of the Greek *rhêtor*).

DOUBLE-SPEAK

Probably in the late fifth century BC, a booklet was produced which demonstrated that any case could be argued equally effectively on both sides, depending on your point of view. Here is an extract:

So sickness is bad for the sick, but good for the doctor:
death is bad for the dead, but good for the undertakers and
monumental masons: a good harvest is good for the farmers,
but bad for the grain-traders: shipwrecks are bad for the ship-
owners, but good for the shipbuilder.

And so on. This raised a broader, general question which had
been troubling Greeks for a long time: is anything *objectively* good or
bad, right or wrong? Or is it all relative, depending on your point of
view? Protagoras, a sophist from Abdera, summed up the basic sophist
principle:

Man is the measure of all things, of things that are, that they
are, and of things that are not, that they are not.

Plato makes Protagoras say:

Whatever in any particular city is considered just and
admirable is just and admirable in that city, for so long as the
convention remains in place.

DO GODS EXIST?

Claiming to be able to teach men how to make a success of their careers,
sophists encouraged them not to be constrained by normal social
conventions but to use *logos* ('reason, argument', as in our 'logic') to
advance their cause, whatever the implications for traditional belief
(*nomos*). This had effects elsewhere in the intellectual life of Athens.
Religion, in particular, which Greeks acknowledged rested entirely on
traditional beliefs, came under attack. For example, Protagoras stated

that one could not *know* whether the gods existed or not: 'for there is much that prevents knowledge – the subject's obscurity and human life being so short.'

So the case against the gods was the agnostic, not the atheistic, one. Nor is there anything to suggest that Protagoras' sentiment was designed to subvert religious worship and cult according to ancestral beliefs.

EXPLAINING THE GODS

The sophist Prodicus from Ceos speculated that early man invented gods by giving the name 'god' to natural phenomena that were useful, like the sun and water, and then came to revere men who invented useful things, like wine and agriculture, as gods. Democritus thought that people imagined the existence of higher powers because of phenomena like thunder and eclipses, and the laws controlling such things as the succession of the seasons. Critias argued that the gods were invented by an unscrupulous individual to control people by making them afraid of unseen forces.

ZEUS THE WEATHERMAN

Greeks were well aware of the paradoxes inherent in Homer's view of the gods. The brilliant satirist Lucian, writing in the second century AD, described how Zeus sat up in heaven in front of a collection of what looked like wells, each with a cover. He lifted the lid off each well to hear what prayers, covenants, oaths, omens and sacrifices in his name were coming through to him. One man asked to become king, another that his onions and garlic should grow, another that his father should soon die. Some sailors prayed that the north wind should blow, others the south; farmers prayed for rain, people doing the washing for sun. When Zeus had listened to them all (groaning, as he did so, at the impossibility of keeping everyone happy), he left his orders, sounding rather like a BBC weatherman: 'Rain today in Scythia, lightning in Libya, snow in Greece; north wind in Lydia, south wind, take a rest, west wind, raise a storm over the Adriatic; and a few large baskets of hailstones, fall on Cappadocia.'

EURIPIDES' MEDEA

In 431 BC the controversial playwright Euripides staged *Medea*. A witch from Colchis, Medea had fallen in love with the Greek hero Jason and helped him win the Golden Fleece. He had brought her back to Corinth, where they had two children; but as the play starts, his love has turned cold and he has divorced her to marry Glauce, daughter of the Corinthian king Creon. Medea plots revenge. She sends a wedding dress to Glauce, which burns both her and Creon to death as he tries to help her; and she slaughters her two children by Jason. She flies off in her airborne chariot to safety, leaving a despairing Jason to curse his fate.

THE TRENDY TRAGEDIAN

Euripides did not win many first places at the tragic festivals (see p. 167). *Medea* came third. One reason may be that he was associated with the sophistic movement. In Aristophanes' comedy *Frogs* (405 BC), he is depicted as a trendy poet, praying to the gods as follows:

> O Air, my food, O Pivot of my Tongue, O Mother-wit, O Nostrils, keen of scent.

Reasonable enough for a laugh; after all, Hecabe in Euripides' *Trojan Women* prayed to the gods as follows:

> O you who support the earth, and are supported by it,
> whoever you are, power beyond our knowledge, Zeus,
> whether you are a stern law of nature, or intelligence in man...

In fact Euripides was simply integrating contemporary thought on contentious issues with ancient myth. After all, tragedy was fundamentally about responsibility, guilt, choice, motivation, and gods – all big human issues, on which the sophists had much of interest to say. Some of the things that Euripides' characters say might well have seemed out of place on the grand tragic stage. For example, here is Medea unfolding her thoughts on marriage:

> Of all creatures that have life and reason, we women are the
> most miserable! In the first place, at great expense we must
> buy a husband [i.e. by means of the dowry], taking a master
> to play the tyrant with our bodies (this is an injustice that
> crowns the other one). And here lies the crucial issue for
> us, whether we get a good man or a bad. For divorce brings
> disgrace on a woman, and in the interval she cannot refuse
> her husband. Once she finds herself among customs and
> laws that are unfamiliar, a woman must turn prophet to
> know what sort of man she will be dealing with as husband
> – not information gained at home. Now if we manage this
> task successfully, and share our home with a husband who
> finds marriage an easy yoke to bear, our lives are enviable.

But if not, we'd be better off dead. When a man becomes dissatisfied with married life, he relieves his frustrations by playing away. But we are bound to love one partner and look no further. They say we live sheltered lives in the home, free from danger, while they wield their spears in battle – what fools they are! I would rather face the enemy three times over than bear a child once.

HISSED OFF

Since Greek plays were staged in competition with one another for prizes, the crowd often tried to influence the judges by indicating how it felt about the performances, often while they were still going on. The most common form of abuse was hissing and hooting, accompanied by heels kicking against the seats. Actors could be hissed off in mid-performance (we hear of an occasion when one comedy after another was brought to a halt as a result of this treatment) or forcibly thrown out of the theatre. Plato complained that things had got so bad that the crowd had established a sort of 'boxoffice-ocracy'. The essayist Plutarch tells us that by his time, around AD 100, actors needed claques to support them, in case the crowd did not like their interpretation.

TRAPPED IN A MAZE OF STREETS

The flash-point of the Athens–Sparta conflict was the attack by Thebes, allied to Sparta, on its close neighbour and age-old rival Plataea, an ally of Athens. Thucydides gives a brilliant sense of urban battle in an ancient town. Note in particular the difficulty of finding your way about the winding, narrow, confusing streets and dead ends. Anyone who has visited a Greek island will recognize the layout. There was defensive method in this apparent madness, on islands especially: pirates raiding for human booty knew what would happen to anyone who got lost in the maze of streets.

> The Thebans, finding themselves outwitted, immediately closed up to repel all attacks made upon them. Two or three times they beat back their assailants. But the Plataeans raised a shout and charged them, while the women and slaves, screaming and yelling from the houses, pelted them with stones and tiles. On top of that, it had been raining hard all night; so at last their courage gave way, and they turned and ran for it through the town. Most of them had no idea how to get out, and this, combined with the mud, and the darkness (the moon was in her last quarter), and the fact that their pursuers knew their way about and could easily stop their escape, proved fatal to many... The biggest Theban group rushed into a large building next to the city wall. Its doors happened to be open, and they thought that they were the town gates, leading through to the outside.

LOGIC OVER EMOTIONS

Pericles' policy of moving the *whole population* of Attica from their villages and farms inside the walls that led from Athens down to the Piraeus seems extraordinary, but if the Spartan army was unbeatable on land, it was the logical thing to do. Thucydides movingly records how difficult it was:

They found it hard to move, as most of them had been always used to living in the country... and had only just restored their households after the Persian invasions. Heartfelt was their anguish and misery at abandoning their houses and their ancient shrines, and having to change their way of life and bid farewell to what each thought of as his native city.

But the point is that the *démos* had voted to do it. No one had forced this policy on them. It was Pericles who had *persuaded* them into this course of action. All they could do was watch the Spartans destroying their crops and farms, unhindered.

PERICLES' FUNERAL SPEECH: PRAISE OF THE LIVING

Every year the Athenians held a state funeral for those who had died in the war. The bones of the dead were carried in a coffin, one coffin for each of the ten tribes. One dressed, but empty, bier was carried for those missing or whose body could not be recovered.

Pericles had been the speaker on a similar occasion after the war against Samos (see p.184), where perhaps he made his famous remark, 'The spring has been taken out of the year.' The famous Funeral Speech of 430 BC is notable for the fact that Pericles does not dwell on past glories so much as eulogize the way of life of contemporary Athens, contrasting its openness and versatility with that of Sparta. Here are some extracts:

Our constitution does not copy the laws of neighbouring states; we are rather a pattern to others than imitators

ourselves. Its administration favours the many instead of
the few. This is why it is called a democracy. If we look
to the laws, they afford equal justice to all in their private
differences. Advance in public life falls to reputation for
capacity, not social standing. Class considerations are not
allowed to interfere with merit. Nor again does poverty bar
the way. If a man is able to serve the state, he is not hindered
by the obscurity of his condition.

We throw open our city to the world, and never by alien
acts exclude foreigners from any opportunity of learning or
observing, although the eyes of an enemy may occasionally
profit from our liberality. We put less trust in system and
policy, more in the native spirit of our citizens; while in
education, where our rivals from their very cradles train
for manliness under rigorous discipline, at Athens we live
exactly as we please, and yet are just as ready to encounter
every legitimate danger.

We value beauty, but without extravagance, and knowledge,
without effeminacy; we use wealth rather than show it off,
and place the real disgrace of poverty not in owning up to
the fact, but in refusing to take active measures against
it. Our politicians combine their private affairs with state
business, and our ordinary citizens, even though committed
to their own work, are still fair judges of political matters.
For, unlike any other nation, we regard the man who takes
no part in these duties not as unambitious, but as useless.

> We Athenians are involved in discussing policy, even
> if we cannot all formulate it, and, instead of looking on
> discussion as a stumbling-block to action, we think of it as an
> indispensable preliminary to any wise action at all... in short,
> as a city we are the educators of Greece.

This is, of course, Thucydides' account of his speech. He tells us that his principle with speeches is to report what the occasion demanded, but always to keep as close as possible to the general sense of what was really said.

THE WORLD'S FIRST DETECTIVE STORY

We have no idea when Sophocles' *Oedipus Turannos* was performed (see p. 91). But we do know that, even though Aristotle made it his 'perfect' example of a tragedy, it did not in fact win the first prize.

The story centres on the uncovering by Oedipus of the true nature of events occurring many years earlier. The play opens with a plague that has struck the city of Thebes, and the Delphic oracle tells Oedipus that he must find the killer of Laius, king of Thebes before Oedipus was made king (Oedipus was now married to the bereaved queen Jocasta).

Oedipus sets about the task with a will, but as the truth slowly emerges, two things become clear: not only did Oedipus kill Laius, but in doing so he had killed his own father and then married his own mother, in the process fulfilling oracles of long ago. Jocasta commits suicide and Oedipus blinds himself. The play ends with Oedipus being led away into the palace.

However unlikely the actual plot, it is so masterfully constructed by Sophocles that one is swept away by it – a great man, determined to reveal the guilty man behind an event happening long ago, finding that every move he makes points the finger of guilt more and more clearly at *himself*, with even more horrific consequences for his mother and for his surviving daughters by her, Antigone and Ismene.

It is Oedipus' determination not to flinch from facing this increasingly dreadful truth about *himself* that makes him such a powerfully tragic figure.

TRAGEDY: REAL-TIME PLOTS IN THE FRONT GARDEN

Homer restricted his plots to action over a few days, using flashbacks and reminiscences to make it appear that they covered many years (see p. 59). Greek tragedians did just the same: everything had to happen in 'real time', the 120 minutes or so that the stage production took. But the *mise-en-scène* could not be changed: so how do you write a tragedy on matters of life and death, chance and fate, gods and heroes, when characters come and go in the same location – out of doors, usually in front of a palace?

The poet had to focus on the crucial two hours in the *real time* of the play in which the characters could grapple with the consequences of their behaviour. As a result, much of the story – deaths, armies fighting, naval battles – happens off-stage and is reported on-stage by messengers, or on-stage between characters reminiscing about *past* events many years ago. So even before he picked up his quill, the poet had to decide: whose tragedy? Where does it happen? Which two hours? What happens on-stage, what off? And who should the chorus be? *Oedipus Turannos* offers a masterclass in the art.

FREUD FRAUD

Sigmund Freud used the term 'Oedipus complex' to describe feelings about our parents that we wish to repress. He said:

> It is the fate of all of us, perhaps, to direct our first sexual impulse towards our mother and our first hatred and our first murderous wish against our father. Our dreams convince us that this is so.

Unfortunately for Freud, this is the precise *opposite* of what Oedipus desired. He was brought up by people in Corinth who were *not* his parents (he did not know this). When he heard the Delphic oracle say that he would marry his mother and kill his father, he fled in horror to get away from them – to Thebes. En route, he got into a fight and killed the king of Thebes, his father Laius; found Thebes mourning their king's death; answered the riddle of the Sphinx, which was spreading a plague over the city; and then became king and married his mother Jocasta at the request of the grateful citizens.

430 BC: THE PLAGUE

The plague that struck Athens in 430 BC, carrying off about a third of the population in the overcrowded shanty town that Athens had become, is brilliantly described by Thucydides – how it manifested itself and the stages it went through. He reports that the plague was *said* to have come from Ethiopia via Egypt and Libya. He describes its sudden attack on brain, eyes, throat and tongue, followed by retching and vomiting. Blisters and sores broke out, he tells us, and most sufferers succumbed after seven to nine days. Those who survived that period, he goes on, found the disease attacking the bowels, and diarrhoea and ulceration ensued. The extremities were attacked – fingers, genitals, toes – and memory loss was common among survivors.

We cannot identify the disease. Smallpox, typhus, ebola virus and others have all been proposed. What is significant is that Thucydides, clearly influenced by contemporary medical thought, was laying the groundwork for a cool, rational analysis of what caused it, pointing out, tartly, that prayers and oracles were helpless to stop it and that 'it seemed to be all the same whether you worshipped gods or not, when one saw the good and the bad dying indiscriminately'.

THE DEMOCRATIC TYRANNY

Pericles admitted that, in the eyes of its empire, Athens was a tyranny and therefore (as he said to the Assembly) in danger 'from those whose hatred you have incurred in gaining it'. But 'while it may be thought wrong to have acquired it, to let it go would be extremely perilous'. Thucydides was full of admiration for Pericles. He was a man who 'knew what needed to be done'. He was passionate about Athens but never played up to the Assembly. He restricted his performances there to matters of importance, and was as good at raising Athenians' spirits when they were down as at dampening them when they became too bullish. He was elected *stratêgos* (military commander) fifteen years in succession. Thucydides judged that Athens at that time was 'nominally a democracy but in fact the empire of the leading man'.

NEARLY THE PERICLEION

Perhaps Pericles' most famous achievement was cultural: persuading the Assembly to throw an incredible 9,000 talents from the Delian League treasury into glorifying Athens with many magnificent buildings, including the Parthenon, dedicated to Athena. At one stage the *dêmos* said Pericles should stop spending so excessively. He said 'Fine: charge the cost to me and I shall dedicate all the public buildings in my own name.' They promptly changed their mind and told him to continue.

A VERY STRANGE TEMPLE

Parthenôn in Greek means 'virgins' quarters' – an odd name for a temple anyway, and a word very rarely used of the building by Greeks: they called it 'the temple' or 'the hundred-footer'. Astonishingly, given how famous it is to us, only one description survives in the whole of ancient literature: that of the travel writer Pausanias, writing around AD 150. However, his interest was not in the building itself! It was centred on the 40-foot-high, brightly shining gold and ivory statue of Athena inside it (the gold and ivory were not solid but covered a wooden frame; ancients laughed about the mice that lived inside such structures).

Further, the temple did not even have an altar outside, where worship of the god involved would take place (the interior of the temple was for the god's statue, not for worshippers). And if it was dedicated to Athena Parthenos ('the virgin') – it did not have any body of priests serving her cult there.

PLANK WORSHIP

The grandeur of the Parthenon's gold and ivory statue of Athena must have made an interesting contrast with another image of Athena in the much more ancient temple of Erechtheus next to it. This 'statue' was not much more than an olive-wood plank of great antiquity, said to have fallen from the skies, redolent of awesome mystery. It was this that was robed every four years in the Panathenaic festival (see p. 125).

TEMPLE WORKS

Building accounts give a clear picture of the typical sequence involved in constructing a temple:

year 1 – foundations for the columns

year 2 – columns and foundations for interior room (cella)

year 3 – cella

year 4 – internal ceilings over cella, etc.

year 5 – main roof

The Parthenon, being very large and heavily decorated with sculptures, took much longer. The sculptures were begun almost last of all in 440 BC and finished only in 432 BC.

ART V. INTELLECT

Parthenon accounts for one year reveal that the wages bill for work on the superb sculptures came to 16,392 drachmas. On the assumption that twenty sculptors were at work for 300 days in the year, that works out at wages of two to three drachmas a day. So much for artists: Greeks thought of them basically as manual workers, though exceptional technical skill (*tekhnê*) was rewarded. A sophist, however, could earn fifty drachmas for just one lecture.

Incidentally, Aristotle defined art as *tekhnê* combined with *logos*, 'reason'.

UNDER THE BEADY EYE OF THE ACCOUNTANT

Accountants kept very detailed records of what was in the Parthenon, and its general state of repair. In 434 BC the contents included a gold wreath; two gilded silver nails; twelve stalks of golden wheat; three ivory and four wooden lyres, both gilded; thirteen bronze feet for couches; and 'eight and a half boxes of rotten and useless arrows'. The doors leading into the temple's interior room (cella) had the leaves around a lion's head and a strip of moulding missing, while three nails lacked poppy heads.

DONKEY WORK

Plutarch tells us that among those animals moving the Parthenon's 22,000 tons of marble – flawless white with a faint yellow tint from iron oxide – from Mount Pentelikon to Athens (about 15 miles/24 km) was a very diligent donkey. It had been put out to grass, but still met the donkeys coming down with the stones, urging them on. The Athenians ordered it to be looked after at public expense and given free meals for life 'like athletes receiving a pension'.

ATOMIC THEORY

Early thinkers speculated that the cosmos was made of a single basic stuff which changed to produce the variety we see around us (see p. 96). But what was that stuff? And how precisely did it change? Then the thinker

Parmenides put the cat among the pigeons by proposing that change was impossible! (see p. 134). Leucippus of the fifth century BC and his disciple Democritus made the radical breakthrough. They invented the atomic theory of the universe, arguing that the basic stuff was an *atomos* (meaning 'uncuttable'), so small as to be below the level of perception; and that these immutable, indivisible, everlasting, indestructible *atomoi* combined in different ways to produce the world about us. How did they combine? They were in a constant state of motion, colliding and rebounding to produce compounds which lasted only so long before breaking up. By this score the world was the subject of *random* forces.

MANY ATOMS, MANY WORLDS

One fascinating point the atomists made was that the universe must consist of an infinite number of atoms in an endless extent of emptiness ('the void', akin to Hesiod's chasm; see p. 40). Under these circumstances, they argued, the idea of a single world system – i.e. *our* world – was an absurdity. There must be an innumerable, possibly even infinite, number of them:

> There are innumerable cosmoses differing in size... some are growing, others are fully grown, others again are dying.

All well in tune with modern cosmological theory.

THE SMALL MATTER OF GOODNESS

The 'pre-Socratic' philosophers, as all these early thinkers have been called, were mainly interested in what the world was made of and how it worked. The sophists were interested in a whole range of different intellectual topics, particularly being 'successful' (see p. 148). It was the Athenian Socrates (469–399 BC) who changed the terms of the debate away from all this to the function and purpose of *man* on this earth. The big question he raised was: how could we decide, and define accurately, what was good? And then how could we lead our lives in accordance with it? Because, he claimed, that was our only route to true happiness. The agenda could not be more different from that of the sophists.

Incidentally, one Zopyrus, who claimed to read the character of a man in his face, said that Socrates was dull, thick-witted and a womanizer. Alcibiades fell about laughing at the last assertion (see p. 253).

CRAFTY QUESTIONS

Socrates did not know what goodness was, but was determined to find out. So he went around Athens asking people. One favourite tactic was to argue by analogy with crafts, such as carpentry and shoe-making. In these cases, he said, it is possible to define exactly what (for instance) a shoe is and how it is produced, and there are criteria for determining what a *good* shoe is. Further, such a craft can be taught and passed on. Most important of all, one can say who the expert craftsman actually is and you can get him to mend a shoe if it falls apart. So should it be with goodness (morality, virtue): what is a good citizen? How is one produced? And who produces one? And is producing good citizens a skill that can be taught? And who does one go to for help if one turns into a bad citizen?

We have been trying to answer these questions ever since.

QUESTION TIME

Socrates himself never wrote a word. It is Plato who was mainly responsible for preserving Socrates' life and teachings for us, and he depicts Socrates, not lecturing vast crowds for money (like the sophists), but with questions and answers among a few companions, trying to reach the truth about, or at least clarify, the topic under discussion. This is the 'dialectic method': 'dialogue' and 'dialectic' come from the same Greek root meaning 'converse with, work towards conclusions by discussion'.

One very typical approach was for Socrates to ask (for instance) what is courage? Companion A would offer a definition, which Socrates would shoot down; B would then try another one, taking Socrates' objection into account, and Socrates would shoot that down too; then C would try, and so on. Mostly they would be giving *examples* of courage, while Socrates would be pointing out that an *example* of courage was not enough: the question was – what was it about that example that *qualified* it as an example? And so what was the single essential property that was always present in *all* examples of courage? What Socrates was aiming for was a general definition. The dialogue would end with no ultimate conclusion, but with at least a clearer picture of what was entailed, the sort of questions that needed asking, if one wanted an answer.

WISDOM IN IGNORANCE

On one occasion, Plato tells us, Socrates' friend Chaerephon went to the oracle at Delphi and asked it if anyone was wiser than Socrates. 'No,' came the answer. This baffled Socrates, so he went around Athens trying to find someone wiser than himself. But everyone he talked to claimed they knew something, but under questioning from Socrates, turned out to know nothing. It was in this sense that Socrates claimed he was wiser than other men: they *thought* they knew what they were talking about when they transparently did not, while he at least *knew* he knew nothing. Hence Socrates' dictum: 'for a human, the unexamined life is not worth living.'

NO ONE WANTS TO DO WRONG

Socrates was one for paradoxes. Since he believed that true happiness depended above all on goodness, he asserted that 'No one goes/does wrong intentionally.' In other words, if you knew what was good, you would do it automatically. For that was the certain road to happiness – and who does not want to be happy? But surely one can know what is good and yet *not* do it? In that case, argued Socrates, you do not really *know* what is good. Your judgement has, for some reason, become clouded.

PUNISHMENT IS GOOD FOR YOU

Another Socratic paradox was that the criminal who had been punished for his crimes was happier than the criminal who had not. The argument went like this. Crime deserved punishment; therefore punishment was just. Justice was the greatest good; therefore the punished criminal was experiencing the greatest good, while the unpunished one was not. Goodness resulted in happiness; therefore the punished criminal was happier than the unpunished.

So: if you are ill, you go to your doctor. Have you committed a crime? Go to your punisher.

MEDICAL MANNERS

Greeks were well aware that doctors had to carry conviction, and three treatises were devoted to this subject. They have much to say about a doctor's appearance, bearing and attitudes. He should look healthy and plump, or his patients will not think he can look after himself. He must be serious, but kindly, not given to arrogance (though it can be useful to lay down the law) or vulgar knockabout. He must be morally impeccable and in complete self-control, given the intimacy of his relationship with his patient. Further advice follows:

Disobedient patients

Look out for your patients' misbehaviour. They often lie about taking the medicine you have prescribed. They won't take medicine they don't like, whether purges or tonics, and they sometimes die in consequence. They never confess what they have done, and the doctor gets the blame.

The importance of discretion

Carry out your treatment in a calm and orderly way, concealing most things from the patient while you are treating him. If you have to give orders, give them cheerfully and calmly, turning a deaf ear to any comments. Reproach your patient sharply and emphatically at times; at others encourage him with concern and careful attention; but do not reveal anything about his present or future condition. Statements on the subject often cause a setback.

Be prepared

Decide before you enter the sick man's room what treatment is needed.

For what is needed is often not reasoned diagnosis, but practical help. So you must predict the outcome from your previous experience; it makes a good impression and is pretty easy. When you do go in, be careful how you sit and maintain your reserve. Be careful of your dress, be authoritative in what you say, but be brief, be reassuring and sympathetic, show care and reply to objections, meet any difficulties with calm assurance, forbid noise and disturbance, be ready to do what has to be done.

JUSTIFYING EVIL

The revolt in Corcyra (modern Corfu) in 427 BC, Thucydides says, stirred up revolt all over the Greek world, as democrats fought to bring in the Athenians, and oligarchs to introduce the Spartans. His analysis of the phenomenon is quite remarkable.

Human behaviour came to be evaluated differently, he explains: 'mindless aggression' became 'the courage you would expect in a comrade'; 'moderation' disguised 'weakness'; 'fanaticism' was the 'mark of the real man'. Violent opinions could always be trusted, and anyone who objected to them was suspect. Revenge was more important even than self-preservation, while pacts were made merely to overcome temporary difficulties. A victory won by treachery was a mark of intelligence. Neither justice nor people's interests prevented men doing anything to win power by any means; those who relied on policy rather than naked force were easily destroyed. Conscience was ignored: more attention was given to the man who could justify outrages attractively.

A DEBATE ON CAPITAL PUNISHMENT

'Execute all adult males and sell the women and children into slavery': that was what an angry Assembly in 427 BC voted should happen to the people of Mytilene who had revolted against them. A trireme was sent to see to it.

But next day the debate was reopened, as Thucydides tells us, because 'people began to think how cruel and unprecedented it was to destroy everyone, not just the guilty'. Thucydides polarizes the debate around two speeches, both of which avoid issues of pity, fairness and justice, and concentrate on self-interest. First, Cleon (on whom see p. 223 below) argues that the people must not become

> guilty of weakness which is dangerous to you and will not
> make them love you any more... you will not make them obey
> you by injuring your own interests to do them a favour... it
> is fatal to pass measures and not abide by them... humans
> despise those who treat them well, but look up to those who
> make no concessions.

Then Diodotus, making his first and last entrance in history, warns:

> We are not in a court of justice, but in a political Assembly;
> and the question is not justice, but how to make the
> Mytileneans useful to Athens.

To execute the innocent Mytileneans who supported Athens, he says, will alienate those who never opposed Athens in the first place, and will ensure full turnouts for future revolts since Athens treats innocent and guilty alike. The best long-term security is so to treat others that they will not want to revolt. This is not a matter of pity or indulgence, he says, but simple self-interest.

Diodotus' motion won by a whisker. But how to stop the boat sent out the day before?

A CLOSE-RUN THING

Athens to Mytilene was 187 nautical miles (345 km). The first boat had a twenty-four-hour start. Thucydides describes how the men in the second boat rowed as they ate (barley-meal kneaded with oil and wine, provided by Mytilenean ambassadors) and took it in turns to sleep (all the opposite of normal practice: see p. 97–8). Also, 'fortunately there was no contrary wind' (typically, Thucydides does not see the hand of a god here), and the men in the first boat were in no hurry to fulfil their 'outlandish mission'. They arrived just as the decision had been read out to the Mytileneans, and they were able to prevent the general slaughter. Only the 1,000 judged guilty of revolt were executed. The first boat probably took about forty hours to reach Mytilene, the second boat twenty.

MILKING THE RICH

The Athenian tax system was genuinely 'progressive'. The only taxes were on property, and there were two such taxes in Athens. One tax was the annual *leitourgia* ('liturgy'), when the 300 wealthiest men in Athens were asked to underwrite specific public projects (see below). These men were probably drawn from families that had done one before. The other tax was irregular and levied only in war or other emergencies. But like the 'liturgy', this tax too was imposed only on a selected few – the

6,000 Athenians who had declared a certain level of property. When this class was later put into an official 'taxation partnership', the three richest members had to fork out the sum for the whole group and get it back from the others themselves!

LITURGIES: WORKING FOR THE PEOPLE

In Athens' radical democracy, the culture of liberal benefaction was slightly frowned on. The reason was that the citizens saw each other as equals and suspected any citizen who lavished benefactions on others of trying to gain political ascendancy. If benefaction, therefore, was not to dry up, it would have to be under the Assembly's direction. As a result, Athenians invented the *leitourgia* (liturgy) system, under which the 300 richest citizens in each year were ordered to subsidize a number of state activities. Those liable for it had property worth about four talents or more (equivalent to 24,000 drachmas – a skilled workman was paid about 350 drachmas a year). These activities did not come cheap. One of the cheapest liturgies was staging a choral show at 300 drachmas; putting on a dramatic production could cost 3,000 drachmas; and running a trireme for a year at least 5,000 drachmas. That said, such liturgies created goodwill, conferred high public status and could bring considerable political or personal advancement. The result was that, for many Athenians, the duty became a great honour. Many volunteered for it (see Alcibiades, p. 236).

PROPERTY SWAP

What if citizen A, appointed to carry out a liturgy, thought that B was richer? In that case A could challenge B to a property exchange. If B agreed, property was exchanged and A carried out the duty; if B refused – and the only reason can have been that B knew he really *was* richer – B carried out the duty. Problem solved! But since this duty could bring high social and political benefits, we hear of Athenians who, though officially failing to qualify, actually volunteered for it.

NOTHING IN EXCESS

Athens was a world where wealth was transient and unstable. We know of only one family from among the Athenian rich that maintained its wealth over five generations, but 357 families that went from rags to riches and back in one generation! In this situation, expensive tastes in food, drink and sex were a serious threat to the survival of the family. Further, Athens was a radical democracy. Excessive consumption was seen not as a desirable sign of membership of an élite, but as a warning: it was wealth for the benefit not of the city but of the individual, and it threatened to impoverish him too. Even more dangerously, if wealthy individuals clubbed together, who knew what damage they could inflict? Accusations of conspiracy and tyranny were never far from the surface where the spendthrift rich were concerned.

'Nothing in excess' read one famous saying over the entrance to the temple of Apollo at Delphi; 'Know yourself' another. They were two sides of the same coin: know what you can and cannot successfully hope to do. Wealth could too easily pervert one's judgement.

CARRIED AWAY BY FISH

Fish was Athens' greatest delicacy and much prized. The famous chef Archestratus from Sicily tells you what to do if you find a Rhodian boarfish available in the fish-market. It might be the death of you, he says, 'but if they won't sell it to you, seize it by force [and eat it]. Afterwards you can patiently submit to your fate.' But ancient authors also warned against allowing your better judgement to be warped by fish's almost magical allure (not to mention its ruinous cost). When Plato discussed the tripartite Athenian diet of bread, relish and wine, it was the fancy fish relishes that got frowned on.

FLEE<IN< THE RI<H

According to an ancient critic of democracy (known as the 'Old Oligarch'), the poor felt it was almost their right that the rich should pay for their pleasures. After all, the rich had their cultural activities – poetry, music, gymnasia – which the poor could not enjoy, so it was only fair for the rich to help out:

> The common people have subverted those who spend their time in gymnasia or who practise music, poetry and drama; they consider that it is not a good thing because they know that they cannot practise these pursuits themselves. In the case of providing financial support for festivals, for activities in the gymnasia and for manning triremes, they know that it is the rich who put up the money for these activities, while the common people enjoy their festivals and contests, and are provided with their triremes. The common people think that they deserve to take money for singing and running and dancing and sailing in the ships, so that they get more, and the rich become poorer.

The Dionysia alone (see p. 167) featured three tragedians, each with a chorus of 15 (45); five comedians, each with a chorus of 24 (120); and singing competitions between the ten tribes for both men and boys, 50 in each chorus (1,000). That makes 1,165 in all, trained for months on end, all subsidized by the sponsor, or *khorêgos* ('he who puts on the chorus', the title of the rich man paying for it all).

THE YOBBO AND THE CRETIN

It took all sorts to make up a theatre audience. In his *Characters*, Theophrastus, active in the fourth and third centuries BC, describes the 'Yobbo' as one who hissed while others applauded and applauded while others remained silent (unless he decided to emit a loud belch instead); and the 'Cretin' as one who slept soundly during the performance and remained asleep long after the theatre had emptied.

COMIC WAR AND PEACE

Aristophanes' comedy *Men from Acharnae*, produced in 425 BC, was written to appeal especially to the prejudices of ordinary farming people during Athens' war against Sparta. It opens with the hero farmer Dicaeopolis waiting for the democratic Assembly to begin. The war has been going on for six years now, and like everyone else he is cooped up inside Athens' impregnable walls, his farm ravaged by Spartan troops (see pp. 150, 199). All he wants is for the war to end and peace to return: 'my heart's in the fields, out there. I'm fed up with the city. I just want peace.' But when the Assembly eventually begins, no one is interested in peace, especially not the embassy newly returned from Persia with a (fraudulent) promise of money with which to continue the war. It had been dreadful, they explain: double expenses, luxury travel, drinking unmixed wine from glass-gold goblets, etc.

Thoroughly fed up, Dicaeopolis decides to take radical action. He pins a Unilateral Declaration of Independence notice up on his farm, and concludes a personal thirty-year peace treaty with the Spartans. But men from Acharnae (just north of Athens), committed to revenge on Sparta for its attacks on their land, assail him. He manages to win them round, pointing out that it is the military that get all the good jobs and top pay. And when were Acharnians ever sent on luxury embassies abroad? He drives off various creeps trying to take advantage of his treaty and mocks the *stratêgos* Lamachus, who comes in bloodied from battle. The play ends with Dicaeopolis, drunk and randy with a girl on either arm, celebrating with the Acharnians. The little man has triumphed.

FANTASY POLITICS

Aristophanes was free from the constraints of reality. Fantasy is his world, where little men of no account – like most of his audience – take on and defeat great political forces and fulfil their dreams. He combines real and fictional characters (his comedy *Clouds*, for instance, is all about Socrates), blending and confusing real and fictional worlds. Appealing to the prejudices of the common man, he gets his laughs from personal ridicule of individuals and their ideas and policies (parody is a major weapon).

Aristophanes presents no policies, no programmes, no visions of the future. The current political scene is merely the setting, the starting point, from which to draw these laughs, not an opportunity to impose some aching political manifesto – unless that manifesto is pleasure, drink, sex and peace (he can be wonderfully lyrical). Aristophanes uses any stick to beat the lunacies of the present and make people laugh. It was gales of laughter that won the prize for comedy.

Such laughter may also have served a social purpose. It was the wealthy, whether new (like Cleon) or old, who were the dominant figures in the Assembly. Perhaps comedy, by making them look fools, helped to lessen any chance that the resentment the people might feel against them turned genuinely nasty.

ORGAN EXTRAVAGANZA

Aristophanes' vocabulary is vast. He matches Shakespeare for verbal exuberance. Consider his vocabulary for male and female sexual organs, drawn largely from rustic images of agricultural instruments, plants, animals, birds and food, with military images from land and sea battles added for the male organs. Many of these terms are matching pairs (for example, 'bolt' and 'bolt-hole'). So:

Male organ

Tip, neck, finger, thing, flesh, skin, biggy, sinew, equipment, muscle, dried fig, fig petal, mallow stalk, acorn, chickpea, barleycorn, alabaster pot, spear, peg, pole, ram, oar, goad, beam, punt pole, bolt, handle, sword, spit roast, axe, club, staff, top, token, seal, drill, thong, wing, tail, sparrow, various sorts of cake, foot, rope, lump, soup-ladle.

Female organ

Box, piggy, sucking-pig, fig, pomegranate, myrtle berry, rose, garden, delphinium, meadow, thicket, grove, plain, celery, mint, fuzz, door, gate, sheath, ring, circle, hole, cave, pit, gulf, hollow, bolt-hole, venthole, sea-shell, sea-urchin, conch, hearth, brazier, hot coals, bowl, dish, boiled sausage, varieties of meat and fish, hors d'oeuvres, milk-cake, barley-cake, pancake, delta, nightingale, thrush, mousehole, bird's nest, swallow, crack, gravy-boat.

LOWERING THE TONE

Cleon is the first man we know of to be termed a demagogue: *dêm-agôg-os*, 'people-leader', as in 'leading by the nose'. Thucydides depicts him as 'very violent and most persuasive', and the comic playwright Aristophanes, rather more forcefully, portrays him as an ill-educated, foul-mouthed gutter-snipe. When speaking, Cleon was (apparently) the first to 'shout and utter abuse and gesticulate'. But Cleon was not from a noble family of the sort Athenians had come to expect to lead them. After the death of the magisterial Alcmaeonid Pericles, it was easy to stir up prejudice against people like Cleon, who were seen as 'new' men and who had made their money through commerce, not through inheritance as landowners, and were powerful simply because of their forceful, populist speaking in the Assembly.

Incidentally, ancient Greeks swore, but never in the sexual or excretory registers that we regularly use. For example, the Greek equivalent of 'fuck off' was 'go to hell' or 'get lost'.

SPARTANS AT (PYLOS) BAY

In 425 BC Athens had a great stroke of luck. Its fleet had taken the fight to Sparta's territory in Pylos and had managed to trap 420 Spartans, including 120 of their warrior elite (Spartiates), on the island of Sphacteria. Capturing these would be a tremendous coup, since the

Athenians knew the Spartans would do anything to get them back, as at this time Spartiate numbers were falling (see p. 166). But the Athenians were unable to starve the Spartans into surrender, and with their own supplies running short and winter approaching – triremes could not handle rough weather – they were getting desperate. It was proposed to use this situation to agree a peace treaty with Sparta, but Cleon argued against it in the Assembly, and nothing came of it.

The Spartans were equally desperate to get their men off Sphacteria or to delay the Athenians till the onset of winter. So they offered freedom to their helots (slaves) and financial rewards to others to get food across to the island by any means they could. Some did this by sailing at night in rough weather from the seaward side onto the island; others did it by swimming underwater.

<LEON TO THE RES<UE

In Athens the *dêmos* was furious that the Spartans could not be got off Sphacteria and regretted that a peace deal had not been signed. At an Assembly reported in detail by Thucydides, Cleon, aware that he was becoming unpopular because of his role in rejecting the peace deal, said that it was time to stop messing about and start military action to get the Spartans off the island – *now*; if he were *stratêgos* (military commander), that is what he would do. One of the elected *stratêgoi*, Nicias, immediately suggested that he should do just that. Cleon, thinking it was simply a debating point, agreed:

> but finding that it was seriously meant, he retracted, saying
> that Nicias, not he, was *stratêgos*... Nicias, however,

repeated his offer and resigned his command, calling the Athenians to witness that he did so. And as usual with a crowd, the more Cleon tried to back out of what he had said, the more they encouraged Nicias to hand over his command, and shouted at Cleon to go.

Realizing he was trapped, Cleon agreed, saying that:

within twenty days he would either bring back the Spartans alive, or kill them on the spot. The Athenians could not help laughing at this absurd boast; but the sensible men among them comforted themselves with the reflection that this was a win-win; either they would be rid of Cleon, which they thought the more likely, or if not, the Spartans would be theirs.

Now this is real *dêmokratia* – people power – in action: one can hardly imagine a prime minister or president today, shouted down in a public meeting, resigning his post and handing it over to the man demanding his resignation. It was Cleon's first public office of any sort.

And the result? Within twenty days Cleon got 292 of the 420 Spartans off, including the 120 Spartiates. But peace did not ensue. The emboldened Athenians redoubled their assaults, telling the Spartans that if they attacked Attica, the Spartans would all be executed. So the war ground on till 421 BC, when Nicias engineered a fifty-year peace treaty. Cleon was killed in battle in 422 BC.

'DISAPPEARED'

At this time, the Spartans became very worried about the possibility of a helot (slave) revolt. So they offered freedom to the 2,000 men whom the helots thought most worthy of it. The helots, delighted, chose the 2,000 they most wanted freed, put on garlands and went around celebrating. The Spartans, now knowing the helots most likely to cause trouble, anticipated the IRA by 2,400 years and proceeded to 'disappear' them (this is the literal meaning of *aphanizô*, the Greek word used here).

HEAD IN THE CLOUDS – OR VICE VERSA

In 423 BC Aristophanes produced his *Clouds*, a comedy about Socrates. It was a flop. Aristophanes partially revised it (this is the version we have), but it was never staged.

The plot centres around an old farmer, Strepsiades, who has a wastrel for a son, the horse-mad Pheidippides. Debts are mounting, and Strepsiades decides his son should go to Socrates' 'Reflectory'. There he would learn the new tricky ways of arguing that turned right into wrong (and vice versa) and would help him get off any lawsuits. Pheidippides refuses, so Strepsiades reluctantly decides to try it himself. He is baffled by all the scientific experiments going on, and even more by Socrates, who floats on-stage suspended in the air and initiates him into the Socratic mysteries, asking him to swear by 'Void, Cloud and Tongue' (see pp. 196–7). It is all too much for poor, dim Strepsiades, who is expelled for stupidity.

Pheidippides is now persuaded to give it a go, and after a specially staged public debate, he is duly handed over to Wrong, who in the debate is seen easily to defeat Right. Pheidippides is duly re-educated, and creditors are driven off when they come demanding their money; but father and son then fall out over modern poetry, which Strepsiades hates (especially Euripides), and traditional ways of doing things, which

Pheidippides despises. Strepsiades repents of his actions and with his slaves sets fire to the Reflectory, driving Socrates and his students away.

Incidentally, 'Reflectory' is the translation of an Aristophanic invented word *phrontistêrion*, literally 'think-shop'. In modern Greek, *phrontistêrio* means 'private school'.

ANYTHING FOR A LAUGH

It is clear that Aristophanes' Socrates bears no relation to the real Socrates, who was not interested in 'scientific' theories or sophistic argument, let alone ran a school charging fees. But at least three other comedians we know of made a fool of Socrates in the same sort of terms. In other words, Socrates was well known to the populace as a philosopher or intellectual, and could be made to stand for the whole tribe of them and their mad ideas (as the general populace saw them), whatever his actual ideas were. So today, one would take some well-known figure, the odder the better (Greeks, having no sensitivities about the disabled, would probably have gone for Stephen Hawking), and heap on him all the fashionable nonsense currently going the rounds.

VIII

421–399 BC

TIMELINE

421–418 BC	Athenian Alcibiades in the Peloponnese
416 BC	Athens captures Melos
415–413 BC	Athens' Sicilian disaster; defection of Alcibiades
411–410 BC	Brief oligarchic coup in Athens; Alcibiades returns
407 BC	Enter Persia – on Sparta's side
406 BC	Athens' success at Arginusae; the political aftermath
405 BC	Spartan Lysander captures Athenian fleet at Aegispotami
404 BC	Athens capitulates to Sparta; violent rule of the Thirty
403 BC	Democracy restored
401 BC	Xenophon and the 10,000
399 BC	Execution of Socrates

ATHENS CAPITULATES:

THE EXECUTION OF SOCRATES

M any of Sparta's allies were now quite disillusioned with Sparta, and much juggling of alliances took place. The fifty-year truce soon fell apart. Enter onto the political scene the young, rich, charismatic and daredevil Athenian Alcibiades to try to exploit the situation in Athens' interest, with a land-grab among Sparta's allies. But his efforts failed, so Athens turned its attention to its maritime empire. In 416 BC Athens forced neutral Melos into alliance, and then sent an embassy to answer an appeal for help from their ally Egesta in Sicily. Alcibiades urged a full-scale expedition there, against the advice of Nicias. The Assembly voted for it, but on the night of departure Alcibiades was involved in a scandal and was called back to face charges in Athens. He immediately defected to Sparta. The expedition ended in disaster in 413 BC, with the loss of the Athenian fleet in a battle in the harbour at Syracuse.

Sparta at once established a permanent garrison at Decelea, near Athens, so restricting Athens' movements. They encouraged Athens' allies to defect and started to build a fleet. Persia now enquired if they might be of help to Sparta, and Sparta sent Alcibiades to negotiate with them. However, Alcibiades' tactics aroused Spartan suspicions, and he promptly schemed to defect back to Athens! A coup in Athens in 411 BC led to the installing of an oligarchic government of 400, but the new Athenian fleet based in Samos would have none of it. The sailors welcomed Alcibiades to join them, in the belief that he could bring the Persians over to the Athenian side (he couldn't). Meanwhile in Athens, in 410 BC, the radical democracy was restored. But Alcibiades won victories against Sparta with the fleet in the Aegean, and in 407 BC was welcomed back to Athens.

At the same time, however, the Persians finally sided with the Spartan fleet under Lysander – the Spartans had agreed to abandon Greek cities in Asia Minor to the Persians – and tipped the balance of the war. After some mixed fortunes, in 405 BC Lysander trapped and captured almost the whole Athenian fleet at Aegispotami, and in 404 BC Athens surrendered. Sparta imposed an oligarchy of Thirty, backed up by a Spartan garrison of 700. A reign of terror ensued, but in 403 BC the democracy was restored. These were edgy times, however, and in 399 BC Socrates was executed. Athenian self-confidence had been drained. Intellectuals who might threaten traditional values could not be endured in the current climate.

Meanwhile, Sparta replaced Athenian rule with its own all over the Aegean, so coalitions of those fearing Sparta's growing power began to form. Sparta also secretly backed the attempt by the pro-Sparta Persian Cyrus to replace his brother Artaxerxes as king of Persia. The Athenian Xenophon joined the expedition. It failed.

MIGHT IS RIGHT: THE MELOS DEBATE

In 416 BC, in an act of pure, unprovoked imperial aggression, Athens decided to attack the island of Melos. It was populated by colonists from Sparta but had remained strictly neutral in the war. Before Athens did so, however, it sent a deputation. Thucydides records the ensuing debate in the form of a dialogue (here extracted and somewhat paraphrased):

Melians: Such is your state of mind, it is clear that the result of the discussions will be either war or our enslavement.

Athenians: There will be no point in continuing with these talks if you are simply going to speculate about the future and not face up to the real issue, i.e. how you can save your city from destruction.

Melians: We get the point.

Athenians: We are not going to say we have any right to control this part of the world; nor will it do you any good to say that you have remained neutral. The point is, as you well know, that when these matters are discussed by practical people, right is in question only between those who are equal in power, and that in fact the strong do what they have the power to do, and the weak accept whatever they have to accept.

Melians: But there is a principle at stake of common interest to all, that of fair play and just dealing. This affects you as much as anyone, since your fall would be accompanied by the most terrible vengeance, an example to the world.

Athenians: It is a risk we are prepared to take. Now: for or against?

Melians: We could not, we suppose, remain neutral.

Athenians: Certainly not. That would be a sign of weakness in us.

Melians: But will that not make enemies of all the states that are presently neutral, who will immediately assume you will attack them too? Thus you will strengthen the enemies you have already and force others, against their inclinations, to turn against you.

Athenians: We are not worried about them. Gods, we believe, and men, we know, by a necessary law of nature rule wherever they can. We did not make this law. It existed before us, and will exist when we are gone. We merely act in accordance with it, knowing that anyone else in our position would do exactly the same. Think about it.

The Melians' pleas fell on deaf ears. The island was blockaded, and surrendered. Adult males were put to death, women and children sold into slavery. Not that Athens was unique in approving such cold-blooded slaughter. Immediately before the Melos episode, Thucydides reports – in a single sentence, without comment – that the Spartans captured Hysiae and killed all the free men they could lay their hands on.

THE WEALTH OF SICILY

Athens had long had interests in Sicily, the most fertile and productive of all the Mediterranean islands in timber (for shipbuilding), wheat, wool, vines, olives and honey in particular. It was a huntsman's paradise, rich in horses (and therefore cavalry). It was also a gateway to trade in the western Mediterranean, a trade dominated by the Etruscans in Italy and the powerful city of Carthage on the north coast of Africa. Carthage already had interests in Sicily: since the sixth century BC Greeks and Carthaginians had fought over it (what if Carthage had allied itself to Persia or Sparta...?). So when in 416 BC Athens' allies from Egesta in Sicily asked for help in the war against the city of Selinus, the Assembly ordered an expedition of sixty ships with Alcibiades, Nicias and Lamachus as *stratêgoi*. But Nicias wanted nothing to do with it, suspecting that the Athenians had far larger, unachievable ambitions – mastering all Sicily. Thucydides provides a stunning account of the debate at an ensuing Assembly.

SICILY: AN OLD MAN SPEAKS

When the Assembly met to discuss further measures for its proposed expedition to Sicily, Nicias urged caution. In particular he cast aspersions on 'someone here' who had packed the Assembly with his youthful supporters:

> And there is someone here who is overjoyed at being chosen
> to command, and urges you to make the expedition, merely
> for ends of his own – not least because he is still too young
> for office. He wants to be admired for his stud of horses, but

hopes merely that this expedition will help him offset the expense it involves. Do not allow such a one to maintain his private splendour at his country's expense. Remember that such persons injure the public fortune while they squander their own. This is a matter of great importance, and not for a young man to decide or hastily take in hand.

Everyone knew whom he meant.

SICILY: A YOUNG MAN REPLIES

Alcibiades stood up:

Athenians, I have a better right to command than others – I must begin with this as Nicias has attacked me – and at the same time I believe myself to be worthy of it. The things for which I am abused brought fame to my ancestors and to myself, and benefit to the country as well. Because of the magnificence with which I represented Athens at the Olympic Games, the Greeks, who had expected to see Athens exhausted by the war, concluded it was even greater than it really is. I entered seven chariots, a number never before entered by any private person, and won the first prize, and was also second and fourth, and took care to have everything else in a style worthy of my victory...

Again, any splendour that I may have exhibited at home in producing plays or otherwise is naturally envied by my fellow citizens, but in the eyes of foreigners has an air of strength... And this is no vain *folie de grandeur*, when a man

at his own private cost benefits not himself only, but his city:
nor is it unfair that he who prides himself on his position
should refuse to be treated equally with everyone else.

If ever one wanted a statement of Homeric values and the implied right of the wealthiest and most honoured to rule, this was it (see pp. 49–50, 62–3, and contrast liturgical values at p. 217). Desperately, Nicias tried to dampen enthusiasm by pointing out what vast resources would be entailed. The Athenians enthusiastically agreed, and gave the *stratêgoi* permission to take whatever was needed. 'All alike had fallen in love with the enterprise' was Thucydides' sombre comment. He knew what the result of falling in love usually was.

A BAD OMEN?

Shortly before the Sicilian expedition was due to sail, two events rocked Athens. First, the statues of Hermes the protector (and also, significantly for the expedition, god of travel), which stood in front of many houses and temples, were defaced; and then it was reported that the Eleusinian mysteries were being parodied in private houses – and that Alcibiades was behind it all. Alcibiades demanded to be charged at once in order to prove his innocence, but his enemies wanted time to collect the evidence. They persuaded the Assembly that the expedition should leave, and Alcibiades be called back if it came to a trial. The fleet sailed and had arrived in Sicily when the trireme to take Alcibiades back to face trial arrived. En route back to Athens, he defected to Sparta.

Alcibiades was among a number of suspect characters associated with Socrates. This was to do Socrates' reputation no good at all (see p. 251).

THE ELEUSINIAN MYSTERIES

Some myths 'explain' religious rituals: the myth of Demeter and her daughter Persephone (also known simply as Korê, 'young girl') is one. The following account is highly simplified.

Persephone was taken down to the underworld by the god Hades. Her mother Demeter, goddess of fertility (*Dêmêtêr* means 'earth mother'), fasting, miserably wandered the earth looking for her, while the crops refused to grow. This was a disaster for mankind and also for the gods: who would worship them? At Eleusis a woman, Iambê, made some obscene jokes, bringing a smile to Demeter's face, and offered her a barley drink. The gods were unable to persuade Demeter to return to Olympus, so they ordered Hades to give back Persephone, which he did annually for half a year. Her daughter returned, and Demeter restored the cycle of fertility and the annual blessings of the fruits of the earth.

This myth became a rite of such great importance and complexity in Athens that a fifty-five-day truce was declared to allow anyone to travel to partake in it, and anyone, slave or free, as long as they were Greek, could be initiated. Among much other ceremonial, initiates enacting Demeter's journey walked, fasting, from Athens to Eleusis; obscenities were shouted at them; they broke their fast by consuming the barley drink; and in the darkened Hall of the Mysteries, they met a sudden blaze of light to represent Demeter's conversion from misery to joy. What else happened there is not known, but Sophocles said, 'Thrice-blessed are those who, after witnessing these rites, go down to Hades. Only for them is there life.'

No wonder the (apparent) desecration of this most sacred of mysteries created such uproar. It was punishable under the treason law (see p. 108).

DISASTER IN SICILY

In 414 BC the Athenian *stratêgos* Lamachus was killed, leaving a reluctant and ill Nicias in charge of the Sicilian escapade. In 413 BC he begged to be allowed to return home, but was instead reinforced with men and ships. Meanwhile, advised by Alcibiades, the Spartans sent Gylippus to stiffen Syracusan resistance. Matters in Sicily came to a head when the Athenian fleet was trapped in Syracuse harbour and a great battle ensued. Thucydides gives a masterful account of how the army viewed the battle as it unfolded in the harbour:

> Close to the scene of action and not all looking at the same point at once, some saw their friends victorious, took heart and fell to calling upon the gods not to deprive them of victory, while others, who had their eyes turned upon the losers, wailed and cried aloud, and, although spectators, were more overcome than the actual combatants. Others, again, were gazing at some spot where the battle was evenly balanced; as the contest went on without a clear result, their swaying bodies reflected the agitation of their minds, and they suffered the worst agony of all, always just within reach of safety, or just on the point of destruction.
>
> In short, in that one Athenian army, as long as the sea-fight remained doubtful, there was every sound to be heard at once – shrieks, cheers, 'We're winning', 'We're losing' and all the other various exclamations that a great army would necessarily utter in great peril; and with the men in the fleet it was nearly the same; until at last the Syracusans and

their allies, after the battle had lasted a long while, put the
Athenians to flight, and with much shouting and cheering
chased them in open rout to the shore.

The retreating army finally surrendered and that seemed to be that.
Amazingly, Athens did not surrender, despite their allies planning to
walk away. They melted down gold statues and drew on reserves to
build another fleet in Samos (close to where there were ample supplies
of timber) to continue the war.

NO SEX, PLEASE, WE WANT PEACE

In 411 BC Aristophanes' famous comedy *Lysistrata* was staged. In the play
the women of Greece are persuaded to refuse to sleep with their husbands
in an attempt to end the war; as a result, the sex-starved men, sporting
huge erections throughout, give in and the war ends. In fact the sex strike
is only the half of it. The women of Athens also seize the Acropolis, where
the financial reserves are kept, and 'manfully' protect it against counter-
attack from the elderly chorus (the only men left in Athens); and the
women of Sparta repeat the trick there. Thus deprived of cash, the two
sides are unable to prosecute the war anyway, sex strike or no.

The play is not about 'the liberation of women', but the destruction
of family life. The wives hate the disruptive effect of war on domestic
life. The frustrated males do not immediately resort to prostitutes, nor
the equally frustrated women to any passing lover. It is their spouses
they all long for, and the comedy ends with a celebration of restored
family life and conjugal love. Further, it is hard to see how the comedy
would work if Athenian wives lived a life of abject subservience to their
husbands.

Nor is *Lysistrata* an 'anti-war' play, let alone a comment on 'the futility of war', about which there is not one word. The aim of Lysistrata, the heroine of the play, is to force an end to *this* war, on equal terms for both sides, and a sex strike was a good comic device for achieving this. It was, however, an impossible dream. Athens in 411 BC was in deep trouble, and Sparta would never have agreed to any peace except on terms that would have been wholly unacceptable to the Athenians, let alone Lysistrata. She was not a loser.

DILLY-DALLYING

Aristophanes often depicts women as drink- and sex-mad. It makes for good comedy. Dildoes, made of leather, were regularly associated in comedy with wives and prostitutes. Giant versions feature on vase paintings, where they are used in a number of imaginative ways. Dildoes were a major export of Miletus, and in *Lysistrata* – as Miletus has just defected from Athens – their scarcity is lamented. Even the pretty useless five-inch ones (literally 'eight-finger-width') are no longer available!

MARRIAGE AND THE PERILS OF CHILD-BEARING

For legal purposes, the woman was the property of a male – father, guardian or husband. At marriage she was passed, with a dowry, into another family. The formula was: 'I give you this woman for the ploughing of legitimate children.' No question, then, what marriage was for. Given the uncertainties of childbirth for both mother and child, she would be married as soon as she could bear children. Males seem to have been married later in life. Aristotle recommended eighteen as the best age for a woman to start having children, and thirty-seven for a man, for the rather charming reason that they would both thus reach the end of their reproductive lives at about the same time. Average longevity for women seems to have been thirty-six; for men, forty-five. Child-bearing played a large part in this disparity.

CHILDREN: A FAMILY AND CIVIC DUTY

For ancients, producing children was a duty, with a specific, long-term, public and religious purpose.

First, children maintained the family line. Indeed, this was the only purpose of marriage. Without children, the family, its fortune, its traditions, its achievements and its worship of ancestors and gods died out. This was a social and religious disaster – the end of a line.

Second, as Thucydides puts it, 'Men are the state, not ships and walls empty of men.' In other words, children served the state too, by maintaining the level of manpower necessary to ensure it could fight a successful defensive war, the main condition of survival in the ancient world.

WOOING THE WANDERING WOMB

Since neither conception nor childbirth was guaranteed, ancient authorities offer much advice on the subject of checking fertility. To check if a woman's tubes are clear, place a strong-smelling substance like garlic at the bottom end and sniff the woman's breath. If you smell garlic, she can conceive. If not, her womb (*hustera*) has probably wandered out of its proper place. Bring it back by concocting a dish of sweet-smelling herbs and wave it around the bottom end. Attracted by the delicious aroma, the womb will immediately return to position A. Ancient doctors put many female problems down to a wandering womb; hence our 'hysteria'. Intercourse and having children solved the problem.

BEWARE OF LONG PENISES

According to the 'four humour' theory of medicine (see p. 174), women who wanted male children should stick to 'dry' foods, or fast, while men should eat 'strong' food, drink a little white wine, lie on their right side during intercourse, and tie up the left testicle. Since the semen must be hot, avoid men with long penises: the semen will be too cool by the time it reaches the womb. To ensure the seed stays in the womb, women should cross their legs after intercourse, and for a few days they should avoid violent exercise, baths, solid food, or getting their hair wet.

BIRTH 'CONTROL'

To avoid producing children, men should drink honeysuckle for thirty-seven days, or enjoy the burned testicles of mules, with willow (chaps, as usual, have all the luck). Herbal-based vaginal suppositories are recommended, though Egyptian and Arabian women favoured inserting crocodile or elephant dung. Hippocrates suggests olive oil. Children could also be exposed at birth. *Coitus interruptus*, however, is never mentioned, while condoms are a sixteenth-century invention. The vulcanization of rubber, invented in 1844, made them more widely available.

KEEPING IT IN THE FAMILY

If a woman actually inherited property because there were no males around to do so, she did so only to pass it on to her *son*. If she was not married, every effort would be made to keep the property in the family by marrying her to a relative by birth; if she was married, she might even be obliged to divorce her husband to remarry the relative in question. Maintaining the family was the priority. At the same time, one did not want the property split up among too many family members. Infanticide, of girls rather than boys, was practised, but how widely we do not know.

COULD THE ASSEMBLY DO WRONG?

In 406 BC the Athenian fleet defeated the Spartans at Arginusae, but owing to a storm was unable to pick up the survivors after the sea battle. Several thousand drowned. To start with, there was some sympathy in the Assembly for the *stratêgoi* involved, but the mood changed, and there was a demand that the *stratêgoi* be tried *en bloc*. It was pointed out that this was illegal, but the shout went up that 'it was outrageous that the *dêmos* should not be allowed to do whatever it wanted'.

Socrates was then a member of the *boulê* – the steering committee of 500 (see p. 190) – and on that day happened to be chairman presiding at the Assembly. He refused to accept the Assembly demand, because it was illegal. And he was right. But the next day's chairman, cowed by the Assembly, overturned this ruling, and the decision to try them all together was accepted. The six of the eight *stratêgoi* at Arginusae who had returned to Athens were found guilty and executed.

Some months later, the Assembly admitted that it had been wrong to change the law on the spot, and lodged proceedings against those who had proposed this illegal trial. It was no defence for them to argue that the Assembly had accepted it at the time. If the Assembly decided someone – any citizen – had persuaded them to take bad advice, that person could be put on trial for deceiving the people. As a critic of Athenian democracy said:

> If anything bad results from the people's plans, they allege that a few men working against them ruined things; but if something good results, they take the credit for themselves.

Radical democracy was no easy master.

THE FINAL BLOW

In 405 BC the Spartan general Lysander was besieging Lampsacus near the Hellespont. For five days he refused to engage with the Athenian fleet, which was moored opposite by an open shore at Aegispotami; he merely observed their tactics when they sailed out to offer battle and sailed back again in the evening. Alcibiades suggested the Greeks shift anchorage to a safer, less open spot, but was ignored. On the fifth day, when the Athenians, now contemptuous of Lysander's refusal to fight, had sailed back for the night, Lysander pounced, capturing the Athenian fleet without resistance and putting to death all the Athenians for their crimes against the Greeks.

ATHENS SURRENDERS

The Athenian general Conon escaped and sent the state trireme *Paralus* back to Athens with the news. Xenophon, picking up the story of the

Peloponnesian War where Thucydides had left it in 411 BC, wrote:

> It was night when the *Paralus* arrived in Athens. As news
> of the disaster spread, a howl of grief rose up first from the
> Piraeus, then along the Long Walls and into the city, as one
> man passed the news to another. That night no one slept.

Athens was at first defiant and determined to continue the fight.
But now that Sparta controlled the seas, they controlled Athens'
food supplies – a deadly foot on their throat. In 404 BC the starving
Athenians surrendered. Athens was not destroyed – though Thebes and
Corinth had urged it – but lost her empire and all of her fleet bar twelve
ships; the defences of the Piraeus and the Long Walls were demolished;
and a board of Thirty replaced the radical democracy, backed up with a
Spartan garrison of 700. One punishment they introduced was death by
drinking hemlock. A reign of terror ensued.

ALCIBIADES' LAST STAND

After the battle at Aegispotami, Alcibiades holed up in Phrygia, evidently
planning to bring in the Persian king Artaxerxes against Sparta. But the
Spartan leader Lysander got word of it and sent in his hit-men. Plutarch
reports what happened next:

> Those who were sent to assassinate him did not dare enter
> the house, but first surrounded it and then set it on fire. As
> soon as he saw this, Alcibiades got together great quantities
> of clothes and furniture and threw them on the fire to dowse
> it. Then he wrapped his cloak about his left arm, and holding

his drawn sword in his right, charged through the fire and got safely out before his clothes were burnt. As soon as the barbarians saw him, they retreated. Not one dared stand up to or engage with him. So they stood off him and finished him off at a distance with spears and arrows. His mistress Timandra took up the body and, covering and wrapping it up in her own robes, buried it as decently and as honourably as circumstances allowed.

THE FIRST AMNESTY

The reign of terror, led by one Critias, a friend of Socrates, and instituted by the Thirty, did not last long. An army consisting of democrats and some allies of Sparta – worried that Sparta would become too powerful – captured the Piraeus and killed some of the Thirty. Sparta sent one of their kings, Pausanias, with an army to sort it out, but he realized the democrats were too powerful. But what now? The wounds of the previous year's bloodletting were still raw, and the city was split down the middle. The result was the first-ever amnesty (Greek: *a-mnêstia*, 'not-remembering'), which stipulated that, with the exception of the Thirty and some officials, 'no one was to remember the past misdeeds of anyone'. The democracy was restored, and the slate wiped clean. Xenophon comments:

> To this day both parties live together as fellow-citizens, and the people abide by the oaths which they have sworn.

At this time, pay for those attending the Assembly was introduced, at the rate of two obols a day (roughly half a living wage).

XENOPHON: HISTORIAN, MERCENARY, ESSAYIST

Born around 430 BC into a wealthy but not politically well-known family, the Athenian Xenophon became an enthusiastic supporter of Socrates (leaving some memoirs of him and an *Apology*: see p. 251). But he was not especially sympathetic to the democracy, so he trod something of a tightrope in Athens. In 401 BC he hired himself out as one of the Greek mercenaries known as 'The Ten Thousand' to the Persian Cyrus (II), a Spartan sympathizer, who wanted to depose his brother Artaxerxes as king. Though the battle at Cunaxa was technically won, Cyrus himself was killed, so the purpose of the Greek mission was over. It fell to Xenophon to lead 'The Ten Thousand' back to Greece, which he did (for his account of the terrible march, see below). He became a mercenary of the Spartans, but after their defeat at the battle of Leuctra in 371 BC (see p. 269), he lived the rest of his life in Corinth, eventually becoming reconciled with the Athenians. His *Hellênika*, a generally pro-Spartan account of Greek history, is an important source for the period from 411 to 362 BC.

SOLDIERS FOR HIRE

Ancient mercenary soldiers served anyone, anywhere. Markets where they could be hired emerged all over the Mediterranean, the most famous being at the southernmost point of mainland Greece, the place now known as Cape Matapan. In 322 BC the Spartan Thibron was in trouble in Cyrene (Libya) and decided he needed a bit of rapid reaction. His envoys found 2,500 mercenaries waiting for employment at Cape Matapan and hired the lot. In the course of conquering the known world from 334 BC, Alexander the Great enhanced his international reputation with some 50,000 mercenaries.

It was the mercenary's expertise that was so much admired. Xenophon observes that the Spartan cavalry had been pretty much of a muchness until 388 BC, when Dionysius I of Syracuse sent them a troop of his own fully trained mercenary cavalrymen. Aristotle backs up Xenophon's analysis:

> War seems filled with empty alarms, but mercenaries know all
> about them. In these situations, they bring their experience
> to bear and avoid unnecessary suffering. They know how to
> use their equipment and how best of all to use it to attack and
> defend themselves.

Indeed, so organized did the system of employing such forces become that many states concluded agreements among themselves, giving them exclusive rights or first choice. The Greek words for 'mercenary', 'foreigner' and 'soldier' became virtually interchangeable.

THE SEA! THE SEA!

For Xenophon and the Ten Thousand, the march of 800 miles (1,290 km) overland from Cunaxa (see above) to the Black Sea, where they would be among friendly Greek cities, turned into a nightmare. In his *Anabasis* ('March Up-Country'), Xenophon tells how, from September 401 to May 400 BC, they were attacked without let-up as they travelled through tortuous terrain and unforgiving winter conditions. The following passage became a model for many later writers to express feelings of overwhelming relief that the door had finally closed on a long period of emotional anguish and physical suffering:

> Now as soon as the army got to the top of Mount Theches, a
> great shout went up. And when Xenophon and the rearguard
> heard it, they imagined that other enemies were attacking...
> But the shout kept getting louder and nearer, as the
> successive ranks that came up all began to run at full speed
> toward the ranks ahead that were one after another joining
> in the shout; and as the shout kept growing far louder as the
> number of men grew steadily greater, it became quite clear to
> Xenophon that here was something of unusual importance.
> So he mounted a horse, took with him Lycius and the cavalry,
> and pushed ahead to bring help; and at once they heard the
> soldiers shouting 'The sea! The sea!' and passing the word
> along. Then all the troops of the rearguard likewise broke into
> a run, and the pack animals and horses began racing ahead.
> And when they had all reached the summit, they fell to
> embracing one another, generals and captains too, with tears
> in their eyes. And suddenly, someone gave the word and the
> soldiers began to bring stones and build a great cairn.

In fact, after travelling by land and sea to Byzantium, Xenophon's
men then enlisted to fight in Thrace, and the *Anabasis* ends with them
signing up in the Spartan army. That's mercenaries for you.

SOCRATES' APOLOGY – AND NO APOLOGY

In 399 BC Socrates was put on trial for 'refusing to recognize the gods of
the state and introducing other new gods. He is also guilty of corrupting

the young.' At the time there were a number of trials in progress associated with the Thirty (see p. 247), and fifty years later the orator Aeschines declared:

> Athenians, you executed the sophist Socrates because he had quite obviously been the teacher of Critias, who was one of the Thirty who put an end to democracy.

Nor can it have helped Socrates' case that one of his friends had been Alcibiades, while in his trial Socrates himself mentioned the prejudice that Aristophanes' *Clouds* had created against him (see p. 226).

But whether politics or comedy were at the heart of it or not, the charge was serious enough as it stood, and these were fraught times in Athens. Socrates was found guilty by a vote of 280 to 221. Since there was no set punishment on this charge, both sides were asked to propose one, on which the dikasts (jurors) would then vote. The prosecution proposed death. Socrates, typically, argued that he had done nothing but good, and should therefore be rewarded with free meals for life at state expense. His friends immediately intervened and suggested a fine of 3,000 drachmas, which *they* (of course) would pay. None of this went down well with the jury, who voted for death 360 to 141.

The Greek for 'defence speech' is *apologia*. That is why Socrates' defence of himself is known as his 'Apology'. It has nothing to do with apologizing. Many 'Apologies' were written after his death, the best known (inevitably) by Plato. It is an extraordinarily powerful document, all the more so for being so simple and straightforward.

THE DEATH OF SOCRATES

Plato describes the death of Socrates in prison in Athens, following a long discussion on the immortality of the soul. After he has bathed so that he is purified for death, and the jailer has delivered the hemlock, Socrates says:

> 'But come, Crito, let someone bring the poison, if it is ready; and if not, let the man prepare it.' And Crito said: 'But I think, Socrates, the sun is still on the mountains and has not yet set; and I know that others have taken the poison very late, after the order has come to them, and have eaten and drunk; some of them have made love. Do not hurry; for there is still time.'
>
> And Socrates said: 'Crito, those whom you mention are right in doing as they do, because they think they gain by it; and I shall be right in not doing as they do; because I think I should gain nothing by taking the poison a little later. I should only make myself ridiculous in my own eyes if I clung to life and spared it, when there is no more profit in it. Come,' he said, 'do as I ask and do not refuse.'

Socrates takes the cup and drains it. At this they all burst into tears, bar Socrates, who rebukes them.

> He walked about and, when he said his legs were heavy, lay down on his back, for such was the advice of the attendant. The man who had administered the poison laid his hands on him and after a while examined his feet and legs, then

pinched his foot hard and asked if he felt it. He said 'No'; then after that, his thighs; and passing upwards in this way he showed us that he was growing cold and rigid. And again he touched him and said that when it reached his heart, he would be gone.

The chill had now reached the region about the groin, and uncovering his face, which had been covered, he said – and these were his last words – 'Crito, we owe a cock to Asclepius [god of healing! A joke?]. Pay it and do not neglect it.' 'That,' said Crito, 'shall be done; but see if you have anything else to say.' To this question he made no reply, but after a little while he moved; the attendant uncovered him; his eyes were fixed. And Crito, when he saw it, closed his mouth and eyes.

Such was the end of our friend, who was, as we may say, of all those of his time whom we have known, the best and wisest and most righteous man.

A PASSION FOR BOYS

There was in fact no Greek word for homosexuality in our sense: gays pursuing a gay lifestyle with similar-thinking gays for the whole of their existence did not exist in ancient Athens. What did exist was pederasty: the passion of an older male lover (*erastês*) for a beloved (*erômenos*) prepubescent youth, until the boy reached puberty and grew a beard, when he was replaced. Greek literature is full of passionate poetry about this kind of love.

But this practice is widely attested only because it was an educated, upper-class habit, and all the ancient literature that we possess today was written by the educated upper class. It was the great upper-class fantasy. Even so, it must be stressed that these aristocratic males were not homosexual. They were bisexual: they lived in a world where family life and private life were two quite separate existences.

If one asks what advantages were in it for the young male, Greeks argued in educational terms. The relationship was idealized as greater than that of family and friends put together. The younger male had masculine strength of a type admired in any military community. The older male was expected to attract the younger by his wisdom, experience and value as a role model, maintaining high standards of probity and conduct. That meant, in theory at least, no penetration of the young male by the older: that would be to turn him into a woman. In 581 BC Periander, tyrant of Ambracia, was thrown out by the people because, when he was drinking with his *erômenos*, he asked, 'Are you pregnant yet?' In copious depictions on Greek pottery, intercrural intercourse between males was the accepted norm, with the younger showing no signs of arousal.

IX

399–362 BC

TIMELINE

396–395 BC	Spartan king Agesilaus attacks Persia
387 BC	The Persian 'common peace'
371 BC	Sparta defeated by Thebes at battle of Leuctra
362 BC	Thebes held to a draw by Greek states at battle of Mantinea

CITY-STATES AT WAR IN GREECE

As a result of so many Greeks going (in vain) to help Cyrus against his brother Artaxerxes, king of Persia (see p. 248), Greeks in Asia Minor appealed to Sparta for protection from Persian retribution. Forgetting their previous alliance with Persia, the Spartan king Agesilaus set off, but was called back the next year to protect Sparta against its Greek enemies. For the next forty years, the story was that, as one or other Greek city-state (*polis*) gained power (mainly Sparta, Thebes and later Athens), everyone else ganged up on them, with Persia occasionally intervening with slush money. Unsurprisingly, the Peloponnesian War had solved nothing: it was business as usual among the virulently competitive Greek *poleis*.

By 393 BC Athens had rebuilt her fleet and her Long Walls, thanks to Persian gold, but there were no more decorative buildings: no empire, no money. Meanwhile, Athens was forming alliances in the Aegean, as was Thebes in Boeotia. Sparta and Persia did not like this, and in 387 BC the king of Persia imposed a 'common peace' on them all, backed by Sparta, which required that each city be autonomous. The result was that the Greek mainland became the centre of the action, while the Greeks in Asia Minor were formally returned to Persian control (a hold broken only by Alexander the Great some fifty years later). This 'common peace' did not last. For example, in 382 BC Sparta took over Thebes, imposing a garrison there; in 379 BC, it was dramatically kicked out. In 378 BC Athens, its power at sea restored, formed an allied 'confederacy' against Spartan ambitions.

At Leuctra in 371 BC the brilliant Theban general Epaminondas defeated Sparta and freed the Messenians from helotry (see p. 79) – the end of Spartan domination. But Theban ascendancy was no more able to maintain order than anyone else's, and in 362 BC Thebes fought a draw against an alliance of Athens, Sparta and others at Mantinea. Nothing was resolved.

PEACE TREATIES

Given the regularity with which city-states (*poleis*) changed alliances in the Greek world, one wonders why they bothered with peace treaties at all. Such treaties involved various technical details: the length of time during which the treaty was to be in force, the handover of prisoners, exchange of hostages, publication of the terms, and the precise form of the oath. This was taken in the name of the gods who would feel insulted were it broken. But at the heart of any treaty was one simple condition: *summakhia*, literally 'fighting together', often expressed as 'having the same friends and enemies'. In reality, it must have been difficult to be certain who were friends and who enemies from one week to the next.

CLOAKS AND OXEN: MAKING FRIENDS OF ENEMIES

Traditionally, Greeks were committed to helping their friends and harming their enemies (see p. 74). Agesilaus, one of the most influential kings Sparta had ever had, went out of his way to ensure that he had no enemies. As a king, he was held in check by the *gerousia* (a council of thirty distinguished senior citizens, see p. 83), but while that had usually led to friction, Agesilaus courted the *gerousia*'s favour, sought its advice and always greeted its members warmly. When a new member was elected, he sent him a cloak and an ox in recognition of his appointment. As for enemies, he never acted against them without just cause, and even when he did, he would often use his influence on their behalf to get them off, thus making friends of them. Further, he was always lenient with friends, even if they had done wrong. Even so, being king, he still had a position to uphold. One of his friends once saw him sitting astride a stick and galloping round the house with some small children (of whom he was fond). Agesilaus told him to keep quiet about it until he himself was a father.

COUNTING THE TROOPS

Some of Sparta's allies began complaining that their men made up most of the allied forces. King Agesilaus summoned them all to sit down in a meeting, the allies in one place, the Spartiates (Spartan elite warriors) in another. Then he ordered the herald to invite all the potters to stand up, then the smiths, then the carpenters, then the masons and so on. Most of the allies stood up, but not one Spartiate, as they were forbidden to practise anything but the art of war. Agesilaus laughed and said, 'You can see how many more soldiers we send out than you do.'

TRICKING SPARTANS OUT OF THEBES

In 382 BC a Spartan *junta* took over Thebes. In 379 BC the Theban general Pelopidas, who had fled into exile in Athens, secretly led a dozen Theban exiles back into Thebes and joined thirty-six more resistance fighters in a safe house owned by a friendly Theban. Meanwhile another sympathizer, Phillidas, had already made himself secretary to the two Spartan generals. Phillidas, as agreed, laid on a party for them, with lots of drink and a promise of women. There was a scare for the conspirators when the generals received two notes warning of a possible attack. 'Serious matters for tomorrow,' said the Spartans, and got back to the bottle. Pelopidas and his men disguised themselves as women, minced into the room and killed them all. Thus ended Spartan control over Thebes.

Later, we are told that, when Pelopidas was leaving for battle, his wife begged him to take care of his life. 'Good advice for soldiers,' Pelopidas replied, 'but generals need to be told to take care of the lives of others.'

PRIVATE BANKING

'There is no more pestilential tribe than bankers,' exclaimed one comic poet. But no failed bank could bring down Athens either, because in fourth-century Athens banks were private, personal, one-man businesses, kept within the family, reliant on the ability and connections of their owner, who had learned banking as a trade.

Legal cases taken by the orator Demosthenes indicate that relationships between bankers and depositors were extremely close. When financial problems arose, an Athenian went straight to his personal banker, and that probably meant going to his house, where documents and money would be safely stored. The banker did not hire outsiders to help him, but trained up his slaves in the appropriate financial and documentary skills, keeping it all within the family. We hear of slaves evaluating security for loans, paying out large sums of money and regularly acting on their own initiative. Wives too were fully *au fait* with, and influential in, their husbands' affairs, as many legal cases reveal. We know of one freed, ex-slave banker, Pasion, who at his death married his wife off to Phormio, his own ex-slave, now freed, co-banker, thus keeping the business in the family.

So the family could be trusted: a man who either needed a big loan – banks were instrumental in providing maritime loans for vital operations like grain-trading – or for one reason or another wanted to conceal his wealth (for instance, to avoid property taxes) knew where he could safely do so. Unscrupulous bankers, naturally, might not distinguish between their own personal fortune and the money deposited with them; we do hear of a case in which some bankers lost their personal fortunes when they could not repay depositors.

PLATO (429–347 B<)

We are told that Plato's birth-name was Aristocles (and he wore an earring when he was young, too). *Platôn*, 'broad', perhaps referring to his physique or interests, was his nickname. He was an ardent admirer of Socrates (who never wrote a word) and couched nearly all of his writings in dialogue form, with Socrates taking centre stage (Plato invented the dialogue form because he thought that argued dialogue – dialectic – was the only way to the truth; see p. 211). So what Socrates thought and what Plato thought are subjects of much debate. Aristotle put it roughly like this: Socrates drew his conclusions from talking to people around him, while Plato elevated Socrates' beliefs into a metaphysical theory about a divinely constructed universe, in which man's purpose was to search for knowledge of, and commitment to, ultimate 'Goodness'.

IN SEARCH OF FORMS

One of Plato's most famous theories was that of 'Forms'. He believed that above and beyond our perceptions of reality were real entities, 'Forms' or 'Ideas', as he called them, that existed, unchanging, absolute and eternal. He thought that, while we can see particular people or things that look to us (say) good or beautiful, what makes them good or beautiful is that they share dimly in the Form or Idea of Absolute Goodness or Beauty; and that humans live best if they work to train their soul to get certain knowledge of these Forms. His job as a philosopher was to worry away at how this could be done. One consequence of his belief in these absolutes was that he had no time for sophists like Protagoras, who were all relativists (see p. 194). Such has been Plato's influence that the term 'sophist' has ever since been accompanied by a sneer, with undertones of 'charlatan' or 'fraud'.

UNREALITY SHOW

Plato likened man's normal condition to people living in an underground cave. Chained into position from birth, they can see only what is directly in front of them. Behind them is a puppet show of men and animals, and behind that is the light of a fire (no electric light in the ancient world!). The flickering firelight casts shadows of the puppets onto the wall in front of chained mankind. Such is reality for man – the shadows of puppets.

Now suppose, Plato says, that one of these prisoners should be released and led out of the cave into the real world above. He would be almost blinded, but eventually he would get used to it. Let him then to return to the cave. What a valueless place it would seem! But how would those down there respond when he told them how valueless it was?

> They would laugh at him, and say he had gone up only to come back with his sight ruined: if only they could lay hands on the person trying to free them and take them up there, they would kill him.

Welcome to today's image-dominated digitized world.

THE MYSTERY OF ATLANTIS

The story about the earliest event in Greek history is told by Plato. He recounts the rise of an early, highly aggressive superpower called Atlantis, an island in front of the mouth of the straits of Gibraltar in the tenth millennium BC. From its Atlantic base and with its fleet of triremes, it had ruled Africa as far as Egypt and Europe as far as Italy. But then it came into conflict with Athens, was defeated, and in a single day and night was engulfed in a flood of waves and mud, collapsed and sank into the ocean.

Some scholars think a long-distant memory of the Thera explosion was the source of Plato's idea (see p. 9). That seems most unlikely. Plato was doing what all philosophers have done ever since: making up a story as an allegory, to start off (in his case) a discussion of the divine structure of the universe and how states needed to be divinely constructed (which Atlantis was not) if they were to be successful. As Aristotle, Plato's pupil who knew very well what Plato was doing, put it: Plato created Atlantis only to destroy it.

WORDS AND MEANING

Etymology was of considerable interest to Greek thinkers. Plato's dialogue *Cratylus* is entirely devoted to the subject and takes the form of a discussion about the relationship between language and reality. Cratylus argues that words and names are 'natural', applied to things because that is what the things really *are*; etymology (Greek *etumos*, 'true, real'), in other words, really gets to the heart of the thing to which it is applied. Hermogenes, on the other hand, argues that words are just arbitrary sounds, applied to things by convention or agreement.

Socrates now takes over. He partly agrees with Cratylus, but also agrees with Hermogenes to the extent that words are not *perfect* representations of reality (otherwise one could not distinguish between the word and the thing). So, Socrates concludes, words, though helpful, can be ambiguous guides to understanding the real world. Greeks, in other words, got there long before all those excitingly vibrant twentieth-century French literary theorists.

THE FIRST UTOPIA

The word 'Utopia' was invented in 1516 by Sir Thomas More for his book of that name. It is constructed from two Greek words: *ou*, 'not', and *topos*, 'place' – in other words, there is no such place. Plato invented the first Utopia in the dialogue *Republic* (*c.* 375 BC). This is not a practical construct, but a vision of an imaginary, ideal community whose purpose is to act as a model for how things might be in a perfect world. He produces it by sketching a picture of the educational and moral underpinning that would go into making a good human, and from that constructs an institutional programme that would create the best state that humans on earth could ever achieve. But Plato knew that this could never be achieved voluntarily; the moral purity it required would have to be imposed by Plato's indoctrinated leaders, called 'Guardians'. It would be a tyranny.

SUN-TAN EDUCATION

At one stage in his life (according to a letter he apparently wrote), Plato was asked to turn Dionysius II, tyrant of Syracuse, into a philosopher-king of the sort that he (Plato) was convinced could alone cure the troubles of mankind. It did not turn out well. Plato became involved in court politics, and Dionysius, who was 'full of second-hand ideas', turned out to be uneducable. In a brilliant image, Plato likens people such as Dionysius to those who, once they have seen 'how much there is to learn and the labour involved and the disciplined way of life the subject requires', prefer an education resembling 'a superficial veneer, like men developing a sun-tan', turning over occasionally till lightly educated on both sides.

UTOPIA REALIZED?

Plato's last work, *Laws*, which does not feature Socrates, attempts to imagine the legal framework that a Utopia would require in real life. It is a fascinating document that covers everything from size of state, population, occupations and education, to religion, laws and government. It tries to balance the demands of freedom/rational politics on the one hand, against coercion/political trickery on the other.

THE BLESSINGS OF PUNISHMENT

In his discussion of the justice system in *Laws*, Plato lays down the principles that lie behind almost every humane theory and practice of punishment. He argues that treatment of a criminal should be seen as the same sort of activity as curing a disease. No one willingly contracts a disease; such a person deserves sympathy and help. So with a criminal. The purpose of his punishment, Plato argues, is to cure him of his belief that evil can ever be advantageous. Retribution, in other words, does not come into it: punishment of the proper sort is *good* for you (see p. 212). There should also be payment of compensation for the damage inflicted, reconciliation between criminal and victim, and public protection too, until the criminal is cured – all good modern practice. But – and it is a big but – what if the man turns out to be beyond cure? 'The lawgiver will recognize that the best thing for such people is to cease to live – best even for themselves.' So, he concludes, another purpose of punishment is deterrence.

DEMOCKERY

Plato, having little respect for the common man, had no time for Athens' radical democracy. In his *Republic*, he presents a marvellous picture of democratic man and his world which cannot be said to differ greatly from aspects of ours. He sees the young person's mind as a citadel which can, in the wrong circumstances, be stormed by any fleeting desire that takes its fancy. If the mind is drugged on the concept of 'liberation' and consequently sceptical of the value of inhibition, self-control and moderation, it loses the capacity to differentiate between right and wrong desires and develops no natural defences against what is evil. As a result, it is easily stormed and taken by whatever passing pleasure attracts the attention. Such a liberated person

> one day gets drunk at a party; the next is sipping water and trying to lose weight; sometimes takes exercise, sometimes slobs out without a care in the world, and then takes up philosophy... Then he gets involved in community affairs and public speaking, then joins the army, then goes into business. His lifestyle has no rhyme or reason, but he thinks it enjoyable, free and enviable and he never dispenses with it... he becomes multi-hued and multi-faceted, a gorgeous and varied patchwork... his way of life can be admired by many men and women because it contains so much variety in it.

Taken to extremes, the demand for freedom means that

> fathers are afraid of their sons and sons neither respect nor stand in awe of their parents; the teacher fears and panders to his pupils and the pupils despise their teachers... the old then adapt themselves to the young, aping them and mixing frivolously with them, because they do not wish to be thought strict and disagreeable.

JUST GET THE EDUCATION RIGHT...

In his *Republic*, Plato argues that the key to a healthy society is a proper education – 'the one big thing', as Plato calls it, from which everything else follows. Get that right and

> the process of growth will be cumulative. A good education system produces people of good character; and they in turn produce children better than themselves, and so it goes on. Animals provide a good analogy.

Then, he goes on, proper behaviour like 'being silent in the presence of elders, giving up your seat to them, standing when they enter the room, and looking after your parents' is automatic, and issues of 'hairstyle, clothing, footwear and the general way one presents oneself' solve themselves. Significantly, he goes on: 'In my opinion only an idiot would legislate on such matters. These rules do not come into being, nor would they remain in force, through being formulated and written down.'

The same, argues Plato, goes for the world of business: 'Contracts with labourers, lawsuits, empanelling juries, rent collection, regulations affecting markets or police or ports – shall we take on legislation and rules in these matters?' Of course not. Properly educated people will work all this out for themselves as long as the principles of their education are sound. If, however, their education is valueless,

> they'll spend their whole lives making rule after rule, and then trying to improve them, in the hope that they'll hit upon a successful formula. They'll live like the ill, who lack the

discipline to give up a way of life that is bad for them. All their treatments get them nowhere, yet they live in hope that their next recommended medicine will restore them to health, and detest those who suggest that, until they put an end to their lifestyle, no amount of medicine or cautery or surgery will do them any good at all.

He concludes that it is the mark of a badly governed society to need rafts of legislation about everything. Such lawmakers, he goes on in a brilliant image, 'are unaware of the fact that they are slashing away at a kind of Hydra' – the many-headed monster which grew two heads for every one chopped off.

DRUNK INTO BATTLE

Both Sparta and Thebes were keen to decide who was to be the leader of Greece. At Leuctra in 371 BC Sparta went into the fight with around 11,000 men, Thebes under their superb general Epaminondas with about 7,000. But Spartan morale was low: they had not fought a major pitched battle for twenty-three years, had only 700 Spartiates on their side, and their general Cleombrotus was not up for the fight. As a result, his men took to the bottle and were not at their best. But Epaminondas had his battle plan: hit the Spartan element of the army hard, and (with an eye to the future) lay off their allies as far as possible. His cavalry forced Sparta's inferior cavalry back into the Spartan line, causing confusion; his line – fifty deep! – then launched themselves into the Spartans. It was all over. All Sparta's allies at once set about revolting, drawing up new concords with other *poleis*, and so on – as usual.

SPARTA'S COLLAPSING POPULATION

By the fourth century BC Sparta had suffered a dramatic drop in population: Spartan male citizens were down from around 9,000 to maybe 1,200; and of these some 400 of the 700 fighting at Leuctra were killed. Why? Sparta placed a high importance on the birth of male children. Pederasty was a feature of the relationship between the young soldier and his superiors; there was restricted access to marriage; and it may be that more females than usual were abandoned at birth. On top of that, Spartan inheritance laws split everything equally between all children, thus (over time) reducing their estates to virtually nothing – something that in itself encouraged small families. So desperate measures in the other direction were now taken. Wives of child-bearing age with old husbands were encouraged to take virile young lovers, and incentives were offered to have large families.

LAUGHED OUT OF COURT

In 369 BC the Theban general Epaminondas illegally extended his and his fellow generals' term of office by four months in order to complete a successful attack on, among others, Sparta. So when he returned home, it was to find himself on a capital charge, brought by political enemies. He demanded that, if executed, the following notice should be posted:

> Epaminondas was executed by the Thebans because he forced them to defeat the Spartans whom they had never even dared to look in the face before, rescued Thebes and liberated all Greece...

The jury fell about laughing, and all charges were dropped.

NUDE SPARTAN HERO FINED SHOCK

Now that Thebes was top dog, it was inevitable that everyone would gang up against it. The issue was to be settled at Mantinea in 362 BC. Epaminondas decided on a diversionary tactic: an attack against the city of Sparta itself. In this way he would pin down a section of the Spartan troops in defence of their town, away from the main conflict. So it happened: when King Agesilaus heard that Thebans were marching on Sparta, he rushed back to save it (he was over eighty at the time!) and did so with great audacity, helped by the narrow, winding streets of the city (see Plataea, p. 198). But it was the Spartan Isidas who caught the eye, as Plutarch recounts:

> He was conspicuously tall and handsome, and at an age when the human form reaches the flower of its beauty, the boy merging into the man. Naked as he was, without either armour or clothes – he had just anointed his body with oil – he took a spear in one hand, a sword in the other, leaped out from his house, and after pushing his way through the combatants, charged up and down among the enemy, laying low everyone who encountered him, and without a wound... For this exploit it is said that he was garlanded – and then fined a thousand drachmas, because he had been so foolish as to risk his life in battle without armour.

In the battle at Mantinea a few days later, Epaminondas was killed, and another 'common peace' concluded.

GRAPE EXPECTATIONS

In the fourth century BC, artists and sculptors began to develop a new range of naturalistic, emotional and individualized expression, involving children, animals, drunks, cripples, and so on – even jokes. Exquisite realism was the name of the game. When Zeuxis painted his *Child with Grapes*, birds came to peck at the fruit. Zeuxis was incensed: 'I've painted the grapes better than the child, since the birds ought to have been afraid of the child, if I had got him right.' Zeuxis and Parrhasius apparently staged a painting competition to decide the better man. Zeuxis painted grapes, with the same avian response. He then told Parrhasius to pull back the curtain from his painting. But the curtain was the painting! Zeuxis conceded victory with the words: 'I deceived the birds, but Parrhasius deceived me.'

BLOWING YOUR OWN TRUMPET, GREEK STYLE

Olympia was occupied for 1,200 years. Today's visitors will see all sorts of things – ruins of temples, training grounds, officials' residences, shrines, treasuries, workshops (including that of the great Athenian artist Pheidias), a house of the Roman emperor Nero (he loved the games and competed in them regularly, often coming last but still being given the winner's prize, of course) – but most of all statue bases. The point is that it was a tremendous honour to be associated with and displayed in this greatest and most important of all Greek sanctuaries – even more so if you won. Put up a statue of yourself, and you would be honouring and paying respects to the gods who helped you win, and every four years crowds would gawp in wonder at it; a city building a treasure-house there marked its importance and prestige, while at the same time honouring the gods and hoping to win their favour. Think of the great cathedrals of Britain, loaded with statues and memorials to the great and good – commemorating, honouring and thanking God.

GARRULOUS GUIDES

Tourism flourished in Greece as much then as now. Temples were a major attraction, and while one could view the statuary outside just by turning up, one had to know the opening hours or find the key-holder to view the precious objects kept inside (temples were pillaged as ruthlessly as churches now). Guide books not being readily available, local guides lay in wait. In a satirical sketch, Lucian, writing in the second century AD, describes examining some paintings in a sanctuary 'and right away two or three people ran up to tell me all about them – for a small fee'. Nor would the guides shut up once they had got going. Plutarch, also of the second century AD, tells of a party going round Delphi complaining that the guides 'paid no attention to our entreaties to cut the talk short'. Another contemporary, the travel writer Pausanias, moans that the guides in Argos know very well they are talking rubbish, but say it anyway because people don't easily change their minds (see pp. 318, 354–5).

COUBERTIN AND THE OLYMPIC IDEAL

The official view of the modern Olympic Games is all wrapped up in the concept of the Olympic ideal, propagated by the founding father of the modern Olympics, the Frenchman Baron Pierre de Coubertin (1863–1937), who was inspired both by the site of Olympia (which had only recently been excavated at the time) and by what he took to be the Olympic spirit. His vision was world peace through healthy sporting competition. He thought the French were over-intellectual, and he hugely admired the English balance of work and play, and the English concept of team games and the formative effect they apparently had on character (he even approved of cricket). Coubertin was fascinated by the annual Wenlock Olympic Games in Shropshire, founded by William Penny Brookes in 1850 (they continue to this day), and the even earlier Cotswold Olympics, devised by Robert Dover in the early seventeenth century at Chipping Camden, where one of the events was shin-kicking. He was also touched by the enthusiasm for intercollegiate sports that he found in North America. Coubertin's vision was not shared by the French, however, and he died a bankrupt in 1937 – 'one of the few Frenchmen left undecorated,' as a biographer points out.

THE FIRST MODERN OLYMPICS

The first modern Olympic Games were held in Athens in 1896. They were a success, despite the freezing weather. There were 311 competitors, all thoroughly amateur: 230 of them were Greek, fewer than ten came from the UK, and fourteen were from the USA (mostly Princeton and Harvard), all happy to compete in whatever events took their fancy. The Americans, as usual, won more silvers (today's golds) than anyone else, including the discus, which their man, Robert Garrett, had never thrown before. Their swimmer, though, Gardner Williams, plunged keenly into the sea (no pools) for a swimming event, and exclaiming 'Jesu Christo, it's freezing', immediately leapt out. Not quite the Olympic spirit. The Greek hero of the day was Spyridon Louis, who won the Marathon amidst ecstatic scenes and was said to have been offered (among much else) free shaves and free rail travel for life, with space for his bicycle in the goods van.

THE OLYMPIC FLAME: TO BURN FOR A THOUSAND YEARS...

These days, the Olympic torch is lit in Olympia and carried to the city where the games are going to be held. But since the games in ancient Greece were always held in Olympia, there would have been nowhere to carry the flame to. In other words, the torch ceremony is a modern invention, and a Nazi one at that.

The idea was dreamed up by the German sports administrator Carl Diem. On 20 July 1936 the 'sacred' Olympic flame was duly created from steel reflectors (by Zeiss) – the same technique is still used today – in a ceremony featuring virginal priestesses in short skirts, a high priestess, and a choir singing a Pindaric ode (see p. 102), and duly transmitted to a magnesium-fuelled torch (by Krupp) held by a Greek athlete. Thence it was relayed over the 1,400 miles to Berlin, mainly via countries that within a few years would find themselves under the peace-loving Nazi jackboot. On 1 August, in an arena hung with huge banners sporting the swastika, Hitler assured the crowds that sport helped create peace between nations and expressed the wish that the Olympic flame should never die. The 3,075th runner lit the 'eternal' flame, and Hitler was presented with an olive branch from Olympia. The games? Political? Don't be ridiculous!

BAD BREATH

At the court in Macedon, a certain Decamnichus was a member of the team that assassinated King Archelaus during a hunt in 399 BC. The reason was that Decamnichus claimed Euripides had foul-smelling breath, and Archelaus handed him over to Euripides to be whipped.

X

360–336 BC

TIMELINE

357 BC	Philip II of Macedon takes Amphipolis and Pydna
357 BC	Birth of Alexander the Great
348 BC	Philip razes Olynthus
347 BC	Death of Plato
346 BC	Philip makes peace with Athens
338 BC	Final Greek defeat at Chaeronea
337 BC	Philip prepares an attack on Persia
336 BC	Assassination of Philip

THE RISE OF MACEDON:

PHILIP II TAKES OVER GREECE

From 360 to 336 BC, the new threat came from Macedon to the north, where Philip II (father of Alexander the Great) spotted the inherent weakness of the squabbling Greek cities. Through diplomacy and military action, he was to make himself the effective leader of the Greek world, despite the efforts of the Athenian statesman Demosthenes to rally Greeks against him.

The point about Philip was that Greeks saw him as they saw their rival Greek *poleis* (city-states): either as a threat to their freedom or as an ally against other *poleis* – or, on the international scale, as a champion against the Persians. In other words, there was no common Greek point of view. Was there ever? So Philip knew that the Greek *poleis* would, as usual, jockey among themselves in relation to him, changing sides at will in accordance with their own perceived interests, but would never unite significantly against him. The battle at Chaeronea in 338 BC finally ended Greek resistance to him, and Philip created a federation of all Greek states (except Sparta) – the so-called 'League of Corinth' – to support his proposed attack on Persia. It was the first time Greece became something approaching a single political entity.

PHILIP II OF MACEDON: TAMING THE WARLORDS

Greeks regarded Macedonians to the north of Greece as a collection of thuggish oiks – short, hairy, illiterate and definitely not 'one of us'. In fact under the Macedonian king Archelaus (I), Euripides wrote his tragedy *Bacchae* and died there; Zeuxis the painter worked there; Macedon held its own 'Olympia' games; and tombs of the Macedonian elite show some similarities with the artistry of Athens. It was Philip II (king from 359 to 336 BC) who, as an ancient writer put it, turned a volatile Macedon into 'a united kingdom from many tribes and nations', covering a huge area from northern Greece to the Black Sea. He did this by converting an independent-minded assortment of fractious Macedonian warlords into a court nobility at the service of the Macedonian state. The key to success was inviting their *sons* to join his royal entourage. They waited on him at table, joined royal hunts, and were generally inducted into the life of a king and his courtiers.

UNDER THE TABLE WITH PHILIP

Philip knew all about male bonding. He himself kept his foot hard down on the alcohol, and his court was a riotous place. Drink and violence were its staple diet. By god, said an Athenian ambassador about Philip (and Greeks knew all about symposia), he is the greatest man to drink with. With reason: these 'barbarian' Macedonians did not dilute their wine with water as Greeks did. Winston Churchill would have approved: at dinner parties he liked to calculate to what depth he would flood the room were he to fill it with all the alcohol he had consumed during his life.

AN IRRESISTIBLE FIGHTING MACHINE

Philip put together the basis of what his son Alexander would turn into a superb, virtually unbeatable army. The key to its success lay in the different types of unit of which it was composed – light-armed, heavy-armed, infantry, cavalry, commandos – all integrated and interacting with highly professional discipline and skill. The massed infantry phalanx, with its 18-foot-long pikes (*sarisa*), was almost unbreakable; cavalry charges from the flanks gave it momentum; and the commando-style units, with archers and spearmen attached, were deployed in rapidly moving columns. No enemy of the time could match their flexibility and speed of reaction, let alone Alexander's tactical skill in manipulating them. Philip likewise harnessed technology to create siege engines more effective than any others: the torsion catapult with a range up to 330 yards (300 metres), mechanical rock-throwers, and taller, stronger, more mobile siege towers. His sieges were over in days and weeks rather than months and years.

A LEADER OF MEN

An army is nothing without its generals, and here Philip taught Alexander what it was to be a leader of men. Philip led the army from the front (he was wounded seven times in all). He was a rigid disciplinarian. His army trained and drilled without cease. He taught his men self-sufficiency, making enormous savings in provisions and equipment by cutting their number of personal slaves from one each to one between ten. Moreover, at a time when (for agricultural reasons) wars were fought only during the fallow summer months before the main harvest, he fought all the year round. Philip knew that practice makes perfect. He was no less quick on his feet diplomatically, not above bribery and treachery, and had a keen eye for the useful marriage (he made seven in all with various neighbouring states). Greeks were no match for him on any front.

THE MOVE INTO GREECE

In 357 BC Philip had an army of 10,000 behind him. He took Amphipolis and the gold and silver mines of the north Aegean, generating vast wealth to pay his army and mercenaries. In 356 BC Alexander was born, and Philip's horses won at Olympia, despite grumbles that he was not really 'Greek'. In 352 BC he overran Thessaly and was made its archon (ruler). In the process he defeated the Phocians, crucifying their general and forcing 3,000 of their mercenaries to jump off a cliff to their deaths in the sea below. It was now clear that Philip's ambition was the submission of Greece. If Athens was to do anything about him, it had to be done at once. Despite the urgent warnings of their statesman and greatest orator Demosthenes, they did not heed the danger signs.

GREECE'S GREATEST SPEAKER

On one occasion, Demosthenes and his bitter political (pro-Philip) rival Aeschines were visiting Macedon on an embassy, and Aeschines complimented Philip on being the finest speaker, best-looking man and greatest drinker. Demosthenes commented that the first of these compliments was admirable for a sophist, the second for a woman and the third for a sponge – but none for a king.

Born a sickly youth, Demosthenes (384–322 BC) developed his voice by orating while running up hills or walking beside the loud-resounding sea, his mouth filled with pebbles. Certainly, his sixty or so surviving speeches, covering legal and political cases, earned him the general accolade of Greece's greatest orator, while those directed against Philip of Macedon turned him into Athens' finest patriot as he urged Athens to stand against the 'tyrant'. But note that Demosthenes did not himself deliver the legal speeches: he wrote them for the litigant to deliver.

Aeschines, his rival in the Assembly in Athens, was a man in the pay of Philip who urged the Athenians not to listen to Demosthenes but to do a deal with the king. There was nothing unusual about this. Many Greek *poleis* felt the same, as did many influential Athenians: Athens was not the force it once had been. But there is no doubt that Philip took Demosthenes very seriously. So did the Persians, who were keen that Demosthenes keep Philip involved in Greece: they did not want Philip casting his eyes in *their* direction!

THE GATHERING STORM

Philip out-thought Demosthenes, threatening to extend the war south, but offering peace at the same time. In 346 BC, as Athens dithered over a peace treaty, Philip swooped, marching south and installing himself on Delphi's governing council. He now began overtures to the Peloponnesian *poleis*. Athens prodded away at him where it could, even preventing him taking Byzantium, where he could have strangled Athens' major food supply line (see p. 246). All the time

Philip was offering the chance of peace, and finally his patience broke: he seized Elatea, two days' march from Athens. Demosthenes was sent to persuade Thebes to ally with Athens. Thebes agreed. The armies met at Chaeronea.

CHAERONEA: THE FINAL SHOWDOWN

The final showdown between Philip and the Greek alliance took place on 2 August 338 BC at Chaeronea in Boeotia. Philip commanded the Macedonian infantry, his eighteen-year-old son Alexander (the Great) the cavalry. Ten thousand Athenians and their allies died that day; 2,000 were captured. According to Plutarch, Demosthenes, with 'Good Luck' emblazoned on his shield, 'acting without honour, courage and in flagrant breach of his own exhortations, disgracefully ran for it, abandoning his position and jettisoning his weapons'.

But Philip nobly released those he had captured, and when they came back asking for their clothing and bedding to be returned, he refused, laughing, and said, 'Anyone would imagine these Athenians think they've been beaten at a board game!'

MILITARY LOVERS

The most famous example of institutionalized homosexuality was provided by the Theban 'Sacred Band', an elite troop of 150 pairs of lovers. This band was never beaten until the battle of Chaeronea against Philip. When Philip came across the place where they had 'fallen in their armour, all mixed up together, facing the enemy head on, he wept and said "Perish all those who claim that these men did, or allowed to be done to them, anything shameful."' Two hundred and fifty-four skeletons have been found in the vicinity, laid out in seven rows – could they be the very men?

Plato thought that Sparta and Crete were largely responsible for introducing a homosexual ethos into the military. The biographer Plutarch explained the rationale by arguing that a regiment bonded by sexual feelings was 'indissoluble and unbreakable' because they did not flinch in the face of danger out of their feelings for each other. But he had his doubts. Xenophon once formed a regiment of the handsome because of the example of one Episthenes: his youthful beloved was due to be executed, and Episthenes had offered himself to die in his place. Plutarch commented that desire for wasteful self-sacrifice was not much use in a soldier: 'such lovers often seek danger beyond the call of duty.'

CHAERONEA: THE SETTLEMENT

After Chaeronea, when Philip sent Alexander and his most trusted general Antipater to Athens to make a settlement, the Athenians feared the worst. But together with a second batch of Athenian prisoners and the ashes of their comrades, they brought not fines, nor retribution, but peace. The Athenians could hardly believe their luck. Philip repeated the offer for almost every other *polis* in Greece. It was an offer they could not refuse, and the League of Corinth was formed. The point is that Philip now had his eyes on much bigger fry: Persia. He would need the Athenian fleet and a settled Greece to achieve that. Besides, what ought to appeal more to Greeks than revenge against Persia for that invasion 150 years earlier? Athens voted Philip honours and put up a statue to him. Other Greek cities agreed to join in the attack on Persia under Alexander's leadership.

BE MORE DOG

Diogenes was an author (though nothing survives), preacher and iconoclast. He came from Sinope (in modern-day Turkey) but was living in Corinth when he was paid a visit by Alexander. Diogenes was basking in the sun, and Alexander enquired whether he could do anything for him. 'Just move to one side a little and get out of the light' came the reply. Alexander said to his chuckling friends, 'Say what you like, if I were not Alexander, I would be Diogenes.'

A contemporary of Plato and Aristotle, Diogenes lived in Athens in a large earthenware jar. He had no interest in logic, science or metaphysics (he thought Plato's lectures 'a waste of time'). Believing real human nature to be primitive and animal-like, he rejected all ties of family and nationality and flouted all conventions and standards of behaviour, happily masturbating in public. He lived (it seemed) as shamelessly as a dog. So he was first of the 'Cynic' philosophers (from Greek *kunikos*, 'dog-like'). Stories about him are legion. When Plato defined 'man' as a featherless biped, Diogenes came into his class with a plucked chicken, saying, 'Here is Plato's man.' When asked if there was a great crowd at the Olympic Games, he replied, 'Yes, a great crowd, but few that could be called men.' He declared the love of money to be the 'metropolis' of all evils. He wrote an *Oedipus* and an *Atreus*, highlighting points in favour of incest and cannibalism. Plato described him as 'Socrates gone mad'.

Diogenes did resemble Socrates to the extent that he believed happiness to be unconnected with worldly goods, but dependent rather on inner resources which could be nurtured only by severe physical and mental self-discipline. Self-sufficiency, freedom of speech, indifference to hardship and lack of shame were Cynic hallmarks; Diogenes declared himself a citizen of the world (*kosmopolitês*, whence 'cosmopolitan'). Such extremism was attractive (it is the nearest the ancient world got to mendicant friars), but even then it easily degenerated into shoddy exhibitionist beggary.

COCK OF THE WALK

Around 350 BC Demosthenes wrote a speech for one Ariston, who was bringing a case against Conon for assault and battery. Ariston said he had been the object of a number of unprovoked assaults while he was on garrison duty, and some time later back in Athens he was taking the night air in the agora when he was set upon and beaten to a pulp by Conon and his friends. Not only that: Conon 'started crowing in imitation of victorious fighting cocks, while his friends urged him to flap his elbows against his sides like wings'.

That, said Ariston, was a sign of his *hubris*. Hubris is used in English to mean 'excessive pride', usually going before a fall. But that is not quite its Greek meaning. It originally meant doing physical violence to someone; by extension, it came to mean humiliating someone in order to get the upper hand over them, to show them who was boss, physically or socially. The aim was to degrade or demean the other person, as Aristotle says, for the sheer pleasure of demonstrating your superiority. That was something no proud Greek would take from anyone; and no god would take from any mere mortal.

THE INVENTION OF WESTERN EDUCATION

Isocrates, an Athenian orator and professor of education (436–338 BC), had little time for Plato's Utopia (see p. 264). As a teacher of rhetoric, or 'communication skills', he saw himself as a practical man and contrasted himself with philosophers, the theorists of the day. These people, he argued, despised vocational skills like rhetoric and were interested only in *abstract* truth. In what looks like a brochure advertising his own teaching aims and objectives, he condemns philosophers as follows:

> They ought to abandon this claptrap, which pretends to prove things by verbal quibbles, and to pursue truth and instruct their pupils in the practical affairs of government: for probability in what is useful is far preferable to exactness in what is not.

The philosophers' answer was that communication skills were merely the means to ends and consequently could actually do harm if the ends were wicked. Consequently, they argued, only the philosopher, knowing the distinction between right and wrong, could be trusted with such potentially dangerous means. Philosophy, or theory, must therefore come first. But Isocrates won the day as far as the West is concerned.

LIKE FATHER, LIKE SON

In 336 BC Philip returned from preparations in the north Aegean for the invasion of Persia to celebrate his daughter's wedding. There he was assassinated by one Pausanias. The real motives remain obscure. Was Alexander part of the plot? Or Alexander's mother Olympias, since Philip's latest high-power Macedonian wife (number seven) had recently born a son? But the inevitable result was rebellion among many Greek states. They were free at last! The League of Corinth began to crumble. Demosthenes, who for all his cowardice was still a revered figure in Athens, was in his element again. Thebes began the revolt. But the Greeks had reckoned without a certain twenty-year-old.

First, Alexander wiped out all possible rivals in the Macedonian court. He then took out Thessaly – cutting steps into Mount Ossa, 6,500 feet (2,000 metres) high, to get to the troops at the top – and moved north to settle rebellion round the Danube. He then heard that Thebes had revolted. Within two weeks he had covered the 450 miles (700 km) back south. He offered an amnesty in return for the Theban leaders. He was rejected. A number of Greek *poleis* had remained in the League of Corinth, and when Alexander asked them what to do about Thebes, they sided with him. So Thebes was obliterated – 6,000 killed in battle, the rest (30,000) sold into slavery. Only the house of the poet Pindar, who 150 years earlier had written a poem praising an ancestor of Alexander, was left standing. Thebes was rebuilt on a smaller scale from 316 BC.

TARTS AND COURTESANS

The Greek for a prostitute was *pornê*, derived from a Greek word meaning 'sell' – she was bought, for cash. The transaction, then, was one that, by its very nature, was impersonal, done and dusted. We hear of one *pornê* called Clepsydra, 'water-clock': she stopped when the water ran out. In a comedy we learn of a scale of charges for a prostitute's favours: 'bent over' is cheapest (the man standing behind her); then 'bent back' (she leans back against the man's chest); and the most expensive, 'racehorse' (she sits on top of the man). One day Gnathaena, a famous whore well past her prime, was shopping for meat and asked the handsome young butcher, 'How much?' 'Three obols' came the reply – 'bent over.'

A courtesan was a *hetaira*, meaning 'female companion'. She dealt in gifts, suggesting something much more like a personal relationship. Ancient love epigrams, written by men, tended to focus on the servile devotion of the man and evasiveness of the *hetaira*: the men are always fighting off other lovers and singing mournful songs outside her locked door. But that is the point: the *hetaira* retained her grip on her lovers by making herself available only when she felt like it, and on her own terms: it was essential to be fickle in the granting of favours.

Some *hetairai* won fame and fortune. Phryne, the most famous of all, volunteered to rebuild the city wall of Thebes as long as the Thebans put up the witty inscription: 'Alexander collapsed it: Phryne the *hetaira* got it up again.'

SHOCK OF THE NUDE

Phryne, which means 'Toad', was a nickname: the famous *hetaira*'s real name was *Mnêsaretê* – meaning 'commemorating virtue'! She was said to have been the model for the first nude *female* statue ('heroic' male statues were usually nude), sculpted by one of her lovers, Praxiteles. This statue created a tremendous stir and was rejected by the town (Cos) that had commissioned it. The people of Cnidus (an important harbour town) snapped it up and used it as a representation of Aphrodite in a temple dedicated to her. The story went round that Aphrodite herself came to see it and asked, 'When did Praxiteles see me naked?' Another story was told that a man got himself locked in the temple overnight in order to make love to the statue, leaving a stain on its thigh in the process.

SEX AND REVENGE

A court case, dated about 343 BC, gives us an extraordinary glimpse of the life of a sex worker – though since the speaker's purpose is to blacken the prostitute Neaera, the details cannot be wholly trusted.

Born around 395 BC, Neaera was bought as a very young girl by a madam in Corinth, who trained her up for the sex business. In 378 BC she attended the Panathenaic Games in Athens with her lover Simus, a wealthy aristocrat. In 376 BC she was bought for 3,000 drachmas – at least five times the price of a skilled slave – by two men from Leucas. But they then wanted to get married, so with the help of a debauched lover Phrynion, she bought her freedom for 2,000 drachmas and lived with him for some time in Athens: 'He had sex with her quite openly whenever and wherever he wanted, making a display of his privilege in front of the onlookers.'

In 374 BC she attended a party for Chabrias, a victor in the Pythian Games, and wound up having sex with many people, 'even slaves'. Tired of this abuse, she fled to Megara, where her work brought her into contact with the Athenian Stephanus. Under his protection, she went to Athens, continuing to work as a prostitute. Phrynion and Stephanus reached an agreement to share her – she was now of freedman status, not a slave – but Phrynion disappeared from the picture. By this time she had three children, two boys and a girl, Phano, who (according to the speaker) also became involved in the sex trade.

The case centred on Neaera's status – on the fact that she, a non-Athenian, had married Stephanus and that they were claiming her children were true-born Athenians (see p. 147). But Stephanus was the target. The case had been brought by a political opponent of

Stephanus, one Apollodorus, who was determined to prove Stephanus had committed a crime by marrying an alien. Apollodorus' motive? As he freely admitted at the start of the case, revenge – for earlier attacks by Stephanus on him. In ancient Greece, that was a wholly praiseworthy motive for legal action, which is why Apollodorus could say it in open court before the dikasts (jurors). He clearly expected the sentiment to meet with their approval.

XI

336–322 BC

TIMELINE

334 BC   Alexander's victory at Granicus

332 BC   Alexander at Siwah

331 BC   Alexander's victory at Gaugamela

326 BC   Alexander's retreat from India

323 BC   Death of Alexander in Babylon

323 BC   Death of the Cynic Diogenes

323 BC   Lamian war: Greeks fail to defeat Macedon

322 BC   Death of Aristotle

ALEXANDER THE GREAT AND THE END OF DEMOCRACY

From Philip's assassination in 336 BC, we follow Alexander the Great's assault on Persia in revenge for the Persian wars.

He crossed into Asia Minor in 334 BC and subdued the Persian army under Darius III; pursued the leader of the Persian resistance, Bessus (who had killed Darius), into Afghanistan; and pushed on over the mountains of the Hindu Kush and into Tashkent and Kashmir, before turning south to near Karachi, and west back to Babylon, where he died in 323 BC. He left his men in charge of the cities he conquered.

As a result of this 'Hellenizing' of the eastern world, this is the start of the so-called 'Hellenistic age', which ends with the death of Cleopatra in 30 BC. The term is a nineteenth-century one (invented by the German historian J. G. Droysen). Ancients did not see it like that. Greek culture undoubtedly had its influence, but it was far from a complete fusion of western and eastern cultures.

ALEXANDER THE GRAECOPHILE

As we have seen (p. 280), Greeks were rather sniffy about Macedonians. Alexander was certainly determined to prove he was more Greek than any Greek. His literary hero was the poet Homer; his model was the mythical hero Achilles; and he loved the story of the Trojan War. So it is entirely consonant with the ambitions of a young man of his background to take up his father's torch and seek revenge against the might of the Persian empire for having dared to attack Greece 150 years earlier. There was clearly another motive to all this too: not just wealth (the way to riches in the ancient world was to conquer rich countries) but eternal glory – just like his hero Achilles.

A GUIDED TOUR OF ALEXANDER

334–331 BC

With about 50,000 seasoned campaigners at his back, Alexander sets off for Asia Minor, first visiting Troy, where he races naked around the tomb of his hero Achilles. He takes out Persians at the battle of Granicus, where he was saved by his officer Cleitus, who sliced the arm off a Persian about to kill him; and at Issus, where 100,000 Persians were killed and Darius III 'led the race for safety'. He circles back through Syria, Palestine, Judaea and Egypt to consult the oracle of Zeus Ammon at Siwah. The booty he gathered from this set of conquests alone was staggering.

331–330 BC

Alexander conquers Iraq and Iran (the Persian homeland), defeating the Persian king Darius III once and for all at Gaugamela. He advances to Babylon, Susa and Persepolis, and commandeers there the financial reserves of the Persian empire – 'huge almost beyond belief, including mounds of gold and silver, huge quantities of clothing, ostentatious furniture,' says the historian Quintus Curtius. This led 'to the men fighting among themselves, ripping royal robes apart, dismembering statues, axing precious vases to pieces'. At Persepolis, in the orgy of all orgies, a drunken Alexander, urged on by the even drunker whore Thais to do what all Greeks expected him to do, incinerates the mighty palace that had once ruled the East. It was an act of which the next day he was to feel deeply ashamed.

330–327 BC

Alexander now launches out into his famous 'pacification' of the East. From October 330 BC he wages tough guerrilla warfare through Iran, Afghanistan and the Hindu Kush to Bactria and Sogdia in pursuit of Darius' successor Bessus, who had proclaimed himself King of Kings. He marries the Sogdian princess Roxane.

327–325 BC

He moves south into Kashmir/Pakistan – where, when he is on the point of attacking the Ganges delta, his army eventually calls 'Enough'.

324–323 BC

Alexander returns to Babylon (Baghdad), preparing to attack Arabia and then to move back to the Mediterranean, where (with Egypt already in his pocket) he has his eyes (perhaps) on North Africa, Sicily and southern Italy, but in 323 BC (aged thirty-three) he dies. At his death, his empire falls apart like a badly tied parcel, and its parts are carved up among the Macedonian generals he had left in charge of the various areas. They turn themselves into kings, making their areas enclaves of Greek culture.

PRIORITIES

In September 333 BC Alexander arrived in Anchialus and had translated an inscription composed by Assurbanipal (also called Sardanapalus), the seventh-century Assyrian king, under a picture of the king clapping his hands above his head. It read:

> Sardanapalus built Anchialus and Tarsus in a single day.
> Stranger, eat, drink and fuck, because other human activities
> are not worth *this* [i.e. a hand-clap].

One rather imagines a man like Alexander would have agreed with the sentiment, but not with the reasoning.

ALEXANDER, SON OF ZEUS

Plato gave three oracles a five-star rating: Delphi and Dodona in Greece, and Siwah, an oasis in Egypt. It was this last one, the fabulously rich oracle of Zeus Ammon, that Alexander consulted. The god, a shapeless idol, was covered in emeralds and other jewels and carried along on a golden barge supported on the shoulders of twenty-four priests. They appeared to move automatically, as if urged on by the god's will. They were followed by a procession of girls and women, singing paeans to Apollo and other hymns. The question for the oracle, so phrased as to be answerable by 'yes' or 'no', was placed on the ground, and the extent to which the barge moved towards it ('yes') or away from it ('no') represented the god's answer. We have no idea what Alexander asked it; all we know is that *he* understood it to have said that he was a 'son of Zeus'. The artist Apelles responded by depicting Alexander wielding a thunderbolt; others gave him hair like the sun-god, leonine features, or a divinely inspired, numinous gaze.

HOW TO BURN DOWN A TEMPLE

One of the seven wonders of the world, the vast temple of Artemis – said to be the first constructed out of marble – was built around 550 BC, partly funded by the Lydian king Croesus. In 356 BC it was burned to the ground by Herostratus, who was determined to make a name for himself somehow (you burn down a marble temple by setting fire to the wooden roof timbers – that brings down the roof and pillars with it). Alexander volunteered to pay for its reconstruction – but the Ephesians were not keen on the idea. They came up with a brilliant excuse for rejecting him: 'it did not befit one god to honour another.'

EMPIRE OF THE MIND

Alexander was doing more than mastering territory: he was also mastering knowledge, making an intellectual as much as a physical conquest (one is reminded of Napoleon in Egypt). He took not only geographers, navigators, surveyors and pilots with him on his long adventure – how else was he to march into the unknown? – but also historians and philosophers. The Roman natural historian Pliny wrote of him:

> Alexander was fired with a desire to know the natures of
> animals and delegated the pursuit of this study to Aristotle,

as a man of supreme eminence in every branch of knowledge. So orders were given to some thousands of persons throughout the whole of Asia and Greece, all those who made their living by hunting, fowling and fishing and those who were in charge of warrens, herds, apiaries, fishponds and aviaries, to be at pains to make sure that Aristotle should not remain ignorant of any animal born anywhere.

TRUE PUPIL OF ARISTOTLE?

Rather in the fashion of a keen father looking out for a maths tutor for his son and ending up with Stephen Hawking, Philip hired Aristotle (whose father had been doctor to an earlier Macedonian king) as tutor to Alexander. So it may well be the case that Alexander was given instructions by Aristotle about how to record data for his research.

For example, when Aristotle talks about elephants, they are Indian, not African, elephants. He discusses how the Indians separate males from females to maintain peace among the herds; how domestic elephants help to tame wild ones; and how a full diet keeps them happy. This is followed by a discussion of elephantine flatulence – surely the result of direct and perhaps painful experience – and its cure: you feed them olive oil, salt, honey and roast pork. And when he discusses how much an elephant eats, he does so in Macedonian measures. Further, he is able to describe precisely those features which he always talks about whenever he is a talking about animals: digestive organs, teeth, sex organs, method of movement, age of maturity, and length of pregnancy. So it looks as if Aristotle sent out with Alexander's army something like a questionnaire to be filled in and returned as and when they came across new species.

WHAT WAS IT ALL FOR?

What was the point of all Alexander's exertions? The easy answer is: for the personal glory of Alexander. Doubtless true, but that solves nothing; it merely raises the question: 'In what did he think his glory would consist?' As his army advanced across the East, Alexander planted cities, leaving members of his own perhaps reluctant elites in regional charge, supported off the land by equally reluctant locals – cities that were beacons of civilized Greek language and culture to some, oppressive imperial outposts to others. We are told that he named about seventy cities after himself. It was probably nearer a more modest twelve (note that 'Iskander' and 'Iksander' are both Arabic forms of 'Alexander').

The result was an extensive, if rickety, eastern empire. But Alexander knew the imperial project was doomed unless he gained the willing co-operation of *local* elites – Persians, Bactrians, Indians, and all the rest. So, like his father Philip, he welcomed local warlords into his court, often giving them pride of place. Like his father, he used marriage alliances to achieve this end (he himself married Roxane, daughter of a local Sogdian baron, and encouraged such marriages among his men). Like his father, he welcomed foreign troops into his army. Further, in order to win the respect of his eastern subjects, Alexander started partly dressing and behaving like an oriental too (even demanding worship like one). All this caused enormous resentment among his Macedonian loyalists, who felt themselves being kicked in the teeth. Hence the increasing strife at his court.

DIVINE ALEXANDER

So convinced was Alexander of his divinity that in 327 BC he tried to persuade his men to worship him with *proskunêsis*, which to Persians meant simply bowing before the monarch, but to Greeks was a cultic act, performed for the gods (*proskunêsis* meant 'obeisance, often involving blowing a kiss to'). This request was strongly resisted by his army. It is a sign of how far Alexander believed his own propaganda about his divinity that he tried to institute such an act. For all that, when he died, he was worshipped as a divinity, the first monarch to receive full ruler cult on his death. It established a pattern that was to become commonplace among the kings of Alexander's 'empire', all part of the propaganda that legitimized their rule over their subjects. Roman emperors took keenly to the concept and were immediately deified on death and worshipped.

DRUNKEN SON OF HIS FATHER

Alexander inherited something of a yobbish tendency from his father, and his court was just as riotous. The historian Arrian talks of him beginning to drink to 'barbaric excess' as the army marched on, and of almost daily symposia regularly leaving him in a state of perfect equilibrium – half man, half alcohol. On one miserable occasion his close friend Cleitus began to berate him for his drunkenness and the sycophancy of his courtiers. This is what happened (see pp. 296–7):

> Cleitus began to magnify Philip's achievements and belittle
> Alexander's; his words came pouring out; he was, by
> now, very drunk indeed and, among much else, he taunted
> Alexander with the reminder that he had saved his life, when

they fought the Persian cavalry on the Granicus. 'This is
the hand,' he cried, holding it out with a flourish, 'that saved
you, Alexander, on that day.' Alexander could stand no more
drunken abuse from his friend. Angrily he leapt from his
seat as if to strike him, but the others held him back. Cleitus
continued to pour out his insulting remarks, and Alexander
called for the Guard. No one answered. 'What?' he cried,
'Have I nothing left of royalty but the name? Am I to be like
Darius, dragged in chains by Bessus and his cronies?' Now
nobody could hold him; springing to his feet, he snatched a
spear from one of the attendants and struck Cleitus dead.

Our sources report plenty of drink being consumed right up to the
moment when Alexander died. It would not be at all surprising if his
drinking was a factor in his early demise, if not the final cause.

ALEXANDER'S DEATH

The historian Arrian tells us Alexander fell ill with a fever, which
progressively worsened. He ate little and slept a lot, emerging only
to issue orders and offer sacrifice. After a few days he was constantly
feverish, and becoming weaker by the hour. Arrian records the end:

Now very seriously ill, he still refused to neglect his religious
duties; he gave orders, however, that his senior officers
should wait in the court, and the battalion and company
commanders outside his door. He recognized his officers when
they entered his room, but could no longer speak to them.
From that moment until the end he uttered no word.

Malaria, perhaps? But Arrian goes on to say that there were stories that he had been poisoned during a drinking party. Arrian dismisses them, but many others did not.

PROJE<T UNITY

Though its authenticity has been questioned, Alexander apparently left a will in which he proposed nothing less than a complete fusion of power between East and West under one monarch. He seems to have been dreaming of a new world order in which

> cities should be merged and slaves and manpower exchanged between Asia and Europe, Europe and Asia, in order to bring the two greatest continents to common concord and family friendship by mixed marriages and ties of kith and kin.

Simple megalomania it might be, but its vision has powerful resonances for today's world.

THE FI<HT FOR THE BODY

Alexander had wanted to be buried at Siwah. Macedonians wanted him back in Macedonia. This was agreed, and a fabulous gold coffin was constructed – intricately and heavily decorated, with a canopy that was 36 feet (11 metres) high. Sixty-four hand-picked mules under four yokes were selected to draw it. Engineers and road-menders were to accompany it to ensure a hassle-free journey. However, Ptolemy I, Alexander's general left in charge of Egypt, would have none of that. Nothing, Ptolemy felt, would enhance his authority more, or better legitimize his breakaway state, than to be able to say that the embalmed corpse of Alexander the Great had come to rest on his soil. So he chatted up the cortege's officer-in-command, and the whole cortege left in secret for Egypt. Ptolemy was right. For the next 600 years the body, encased in a magnificent gold coffin, was visited by power-brokers from all over the Mediterranean. Some say that, when men were sent to retrieve St Mark's bones from Egypt in the ninth century AD, they in fact took Alexander's and his bones now lie in St Mark's in Venice!

AN AGENT TO DIE FOR

Whoever was Alexander's public relations officer would have earned his bonuses. Alexander's name has become revered across cultures all over the world to this very day – in India, Arabia, Russia, Malaya, Spain, Armenia, Syria, Ethiopia, Israel, the Balkans… Even in Iceland and Ireland tales in the local language of Alexander were told and retold down the millennia. In other words, he became a universal brand, an everyman: he captured the imagination not just of peoples with whom he came into contact but also of those who had heard of and wondered at his story.

Hebrew legend makes him a preacher and prophet, Christian Greek legend an obedient servant of God. In the European Middle Ages he became a chivalrous knight; for Persians, on the other hand, he was an arch-devil, Satan himself, because he destroyed the fire altars of the Zoroastrian religion. Because of his adventures in the East, ancient Greeks practised as Buddhists; Homer would be translated into Indian languages and read in Sri Lanka; the myth of Cupid and Psyche would be found carved on ivory and left with the elephant goads belonging to a local Indian mahout. There are still Afghan warlords who claim descent from his blood.

ALEXANDER SUPERMAN

Extraordinary stories sprang up about Alexander. He became a miracle-working hero, a superman, his name linked with submarines and flying machines. One of the wise men who attended the birth of Jesus was said to have brought gold from Alexander's treasury. We hear of Alexander coming across 25 lb mushrooms, three-eyed lions and killer crabs with claws 6 feet long. He is let down to the bottom of the ocean in an early bathyscaphe, an iron cage with a glass jar inside, with a hole in it for Alexander to stick his hand out to trawl for whatever he can find along the ocean bed. He meets the Egyptian queen Candace, who has a house with see-through walls and another one built on wheeled stilts pulled around by twenty elephants. He has an exchange of letters with the Queen of the Amazons, whose land is populated by 270,000 armed virgins. In order not to be attacked, they agree to send Alexander 500 a year, with replacements for any that are deflowered. He meets men with no heads but eyes and mouths in their chests, and donkeys 30 feet long with six eyes but using only two to see with. All this, and more, appears in the *Alexander Romance*, a collection of stories about him gathered from the second century BC.

THE DEATH OF DEMOCRACY

It will come as no surprise to learn that, when the Greek cities heard about Alexander's death, they rose in revolt. Athens and other cities defeated the Macedonian general Antipater, who had been ordered by Alexander to keep the Greek cities quiet when he left for Persia, and laid siege to him at Lamia for a year. In 322 BC reinforcements from Macedon arrived, and at the battle of Crannon Athens was defeated.

The Macedonians installed a garrison and cut back the democracy, allowing only 9,000 of the wealthiest citizens (out of 21,000) to retain full citizen rights. The Athenian experiment in radical democracy was over, 180 years after Cleisthenes had invented it.

THE ⟨LEVEREST/BUSIEST MAN IN THE WORLD⟩?

Plato called him 'the Brain' and said that while others needed spurring on, he needed reining back. One of the cleverest men who have ever lived, Aristotle (384–322 BC) was born in Stagira, became a pupil of Plato in Athens, moved to Assos, then Lesbos, where he studied marine life, became tutor to the thirteen-year-old Alexander the Great in 343, and returned to Athens to set up a research centre, the Lyceum, about 335 BC. His output is unmatched, even though only one-fifth of it survives. As the philosopher Jonathan Barnes says (1982):

> The catalogue of his titles includes On Justice, On the Poets, On Wealth, On the Soul, On Pleasure, On the Sciences, On Species and Genus, Deductions, Definitions, Lectures on Political Theory (in eight books), The Art of Rhetoric, On the Pythagoreans, On Animals (in nine books), Dissections (in seven books), On Plants, On Motion, On Astronomy, Homeric Problems (in six books), On Magnets, Olympic Victors, Proverbs, On the River Nile. There are works on logic and on language; on the arts; on ethics and politics and law; on constitutional history and on intellectual history; on psychology and physiology; on natural history – zoology,

biology, botany; on chemistry, astronomy, mechanics, mathematics; on the philosophy of science and the nature of motion, space and time; on metaphysics and the theory of knowledge.

But he did have his off days. He is said to have advised the youthful Alexander:

deal with Greeks as a leader and with foreigners as a master, caring for the former as friends and relatives, and treating the latter as animals and plants.

THE MIDDLE WAY

Aristotle's doctrine of the 'mean' had a number of applications, one of which was to deal with the tensions which any society generates within itself. It resulted in his favouring a large middle class, because it typified a moderation which avoided excess in conduct and aspiration. Such people, being neither excessively rich nor excessively poor, avoided the vices of the wealthy (contempt for others and refusal to be ruled) and of the impoverished (envy and a servile mentality). Again, since the middle class was not envied for their possessions by the rich, and the middle class was not itself covetous of others' goods (unlike the poor), it was a stable group.

NATURE DOES NOTHING IN VAIN

Aristotle not only identified 495 species of animal, he produced the first ever classification of them, and so invented biology. He dissected creatures, inspected them minutely, drew physiological conclusions, looked for recurring patterns and correlated all this against their life-styles. His purpose was to find out how and why they functioned as they did. He asked of them four questions ('the four causes'): (i) what is this creature's goal, and so how does it adapt, develop, reproduce and so on?; (ii) what is its formal cause, i.e. the information it received from its parents?; (iii) what is it made of?; and (iv) what causes it to change and move? These still form the broad basis of biological investigation. He was a teleologist, i.e. every part of the animal served an explicable function. For example, why does the elephant have a trunk? Because it lived in swamps, so might need to breathe underwater. Amazingly, he was right – we now know elephants evolved from an aquatic animal! But of course, he still got an enormous amount wrong.

RESPONSIBILITY: CHOOSING TO BE GOOD OR BAD

Aristotle takes a very black and white view of responsibility for action. We can wish for whatever we like, but goodness is about what we *do*, and we have the power to choose whether to do good or evil. If that is the case, he goes on:

> virtue and vice depend on ourselves, since where it is in our power to act, it is also in our power not to act, and where we can say 'yes', we can also say 'no'.

What, however, if we are careless or thoughtless? That surely renders us incapable of controlling our behaviour. No, says Aristotle. Our character is controlled by the actions we *choose* to engage in. Choose to act carelessly or thoughtlessly, and that is how we will turn out; it is unreasonable to maintain that a man who acts carelessly or thoughtlessly does not *wish* to be careless or thoughtless. After all, merely wishing will not make a man just or healthy: we must *do* justice and *promote* health.

Aristotle leaves the crunch argument until the end. If it is the case that we have control over the decision whether to be good or bad, it follows that both virtue and vice spring from the same source: ourselves. So any argument 'that absolves bad men of responsibility for wickedness would also deprive good men of responsibility for virtue'.

MAKING THE RIGHT DECISION

Discussing what a man needs to *do* to produce good results, Aristotle says that of any action we undertake we need to ensure that we have got it right in relation to: (i) the *time* at which we are acting; (ii) the *issues* on which we are acting; (iii) the *people* with whom we are engaging; (iv) the *reasons* why we are acting; and (v) the *methods* of action we employ. But what does Aristotle mean by 'right'? He provides a useful check-list. Is what we are doing, in the eyes of all the parties involved: (a) just (spanning meanings from 'legal' to 'fair'); (b) advantageous; (c) honourable, reputable; and (d) fitting, appropriate, especially in relation to motive?

Waffle about 'ethics', 'values' and 'best practice' could learn a thing or two from this hard-headed analysis.

ARISTOTLE ON THE SOUL

Pythagoras, in the sixth century BC, argued that from the moment of conception the foetus was body and soul with every innate human capacity intact. This was in contrast to Empedocles, who thought the foetus became fully human only at birth (as did the highly influential Stoics much later). Yet most ancient doctors, observing the physical development of the foetus in the womb, concluded that it *gradually* became human. A thirty-six, forty or fifty-day period for this development was popular, females developing later than males.

Aristotle enriched the debate by wondering what it was that made the embryo human. Here his concept of the soul (*psukhê*) was crucial. Unlike Plato, he did not see it as separate, let alone separable, from the body. He saw it as a set of (non-physical) 'faculties' that were necessary for a body to function (a sort of cybernetic information system). Humans needed four: nutrition, movement, perception/sensation, and reason. He concluded that each faculty came *in the womb*, and at a *different* stage of pregnancy. The embryo was, to start with, purely nutritional, like a carrot. Then it developed movement and perception/sensation, like an animal. Finally, it developed reason and became human – after forty days in the case of a male, ninety in the case of a female.

GETTING TO GRIPS WITH GRAMMAR

We are regularly told that if we do not know our grammar we cannot write our own language. That cuts out anyone producing literature before the fourth century BC, so bye-bye Homer, Sappho, Aeschylus... Aristotle was a major player in embarking on analysis of language. He defined particle (which also includes preposition), 'name' (noun, pronoun, adjective and probably adverb), conjunction and verb (distinguishing present and past tenses). He also talked of vowels, consonants, syllables, inflections (the changing endings of a word), subject and predicate, and even 'utterances' – a sentence or group of words producing a collective meaning (here he adds significantly 'there can be an utterance without verbs'). By the second century BC, eight parts of speech had been defined: noun (which included adjectives), pronoun, verb, adverb, article, participle, preposition and conjunction. Nouns were divided by their inflections into cases – nominative, vocative, accusative, genitive, dative; and into number – singular, plural and (in Greek only) dual. Phew! Greeks could start writing proper at last!

ON SEX MANIACS' EYES... AND OTHER PRESS-ING MATTERS

Aristotle was so famous that many books were falsely attributed to him. The pseudo-Aristotelian *Problems* are a good example. In question-and-answer format, they fearlessly confront the burning issues of the day. Book 1, dealing with medicine, asks (among much else), 'Why is the year unhealthy in which there is a large supply of small, toad-like frogs?' Book 3 tackles drink ('Why does everything appear to the very drunk to be going round in circles?'); book 4 deals with sex ('Why is it that bare feet are not good for sexual intercourse?', 'Why do male sex maniacs' eyes and buttocks sink inwards?'); and book 5 looks at fatigue ('Why is it difficult to walk up a steep hill?'). Book 33 dwells on nasal matters ('Why is sneezing between midnight and midday not a good thing?').

The answers take the form 'Is it because...?', and fill anything from one line to several pages. They rarely seem enlightening. But that is not the point: these questions, for all their genial lunacy, demonstrate an endless curiosity about the world, valuable in itself, that Greeks thought could be answered simply by bringing the mind to bear. It's the process that counts.

XII

322–229 BC

TIMELINE

323–283 BC	Egypt under Ptolemy I
317–307 BC	Demetrius (I) from Phalerum rules Athens; exiled 307 BC
307 BC	Demetrius II rules Athens
282 BC	Dynasty of Attalus, founded by Philetaerus in Pergamum
280 BC	Migrating Celts attack Greece and Asia Minor
c. 280 BC	The Alexandrian Museum and Library begun
	Rise of the Aetolian League of cities in central Greece
	Rise of the Achaean League of cities in the Peloponnese
277 BC	Antigonus II Gonatas ('knee-cap') succeeds Demetrius as king of Macedon
270 BC	Death of Epicurus

267 BC	Ptolemy's failed attempt to 'free' Greece
241–197 BC	Attalus I king of Pergamum carves out a small empire
239 BC	Antigonus II Gonatas dies; replaced by son Demetrius
231 BC	Attalus I defeats the Celts
229–179 BC	Philip V of Macedon takes over on death of Demetrius
226 BC	Earthquake on Rhodes

AFTER ALEXANDER:
THE EMPIRE DIVIDED

After Alexander's death, the Macedonians split up his 'empire' among themselves and – true Greeks – began fighting each other for sovereignty over all of it. By 260 BC, after a period of impossibly complex in-fighting, the empire had been carved up into three major and one small dynasty, all run by absolutist monarchs:

- **Egypt**, run by Ptolemy; the richest and most stable of the kingdoms, and ruler of the sea;
- **Asia Minor to central Asia**, the gigantic empire of Seleucus, followed by his son Antiochus;
- **Pergamum** on the west coast of Asia Minor under Philetaerus (282 BC), who carved out a small inland empire in Asia Minor after the death of Seleucus; this would become, by succession, the dynasty of Attalus (Attalids) in 241 BC;
- **Macedon**, under Antigonus II Gonatas from 277 BC, occupying almost all of northern and central Greece.

Given the mobility so typical of the relatively poverty-stricken Greek world, traders, craftsmen, athletes, ambassadors, philosophers and so on were keen to exploit the opportunities in the new Greek cities that sprang up abroad. For example, Greeks from about 200 cities settled by the Nile. Existing ancient cities such as Babylon were broadly left alone, but had no political or economic influence; some of them adopted Greek gymnasia and theatre culture. Arguably, this was *the* golden (but brief) period of Greek cultural influence, the language spoken from Egypt to India.

As for the Greek city-states, this was the turning point. From 322 BC onwards, the total independence of action they had once enjoyed (especially on foreign policy) was gone. Various rulers of Athens, imposed by Macedon, come and go: the philosopher Demetrius (I), Demetrius (II), and his son Antigonus II Gonatas, who succeeded him in Macedon in 277 BC.

Many Greek cities (largely with the exception of Sparta and Athens) united in leagues – the Achaean League (the Peloponnese) and Aetolian League (central Greece). These were military alliances but not led by a single *polis*; they are often cited as a model for federalism in eighteenth-century America.

The cities, however, still maintained some control over their *internal* administration, as they had had in the past. In Athens itself the structures of democracy stayed in place (Assembly, Steering Committee and so on), but were usually restricted to wealthier members, with the rich appointed to office and the final say lying with the Macedonian monarch.

Once a great and wealthy naval power, Athens slowly became more a city of culture and education. Philosophy flourished in Athens – Stoics and Epicureans, the study of logic, ethics and physics – as did culture: gymnasia, festivals and drama especially, with the formation of the

Artists of Dionysus. 'Communication skills' flourished (see pp. 192–3). But Athens became more and more dependent on sponsorship from wealthy Greeks and foreign powers, who acknowledged the importance of its past glory, to keep it from starvation and maintain its buildings.

Meanwhile, in Egypt Ptolemy I or II set up the West's first research centres: the Alexandrian Museum (in science) and the Alexandrian Library (in the humanities).

In 282 BC Philetaerus set himself up as king of Pergamum. In 280 BC Celts attacked Greece and were driven off in 277 BC. In 267 BC Ptolemy in alliance with Athens decided to weaken Macedonian power by taking on Antigonus Gonatas and declaring Greece 'free'. Their efforts failed, and in 263 BC Athens surrendered. The new puppet governor gave himself the right to veto everything. Any inter-state influence Athens had had was now gone. In 231 BC Attalus I, king of Pergamum (241–197 BC), defeated the Celts and set up a huge monument in celebration (now in Berlin). He begins to expand Pergamum's empire in Asia Minor.

In 239 BC Antigonus Gonatas of Macedon died, and his son (another Demetrius) succeeded as king; he died in 229 BC and was replaced by his nine-year-old son, Philip V. Once again, Athens made a break for freedom: it bribed the oligarchic Macedonian ruler to leave! For the next thirty years, Athens was relatively peaceful.

CONSTRUCTING THE PAST

Like Aristotle, the Athenian Demetrius (I) had connections with Macedon which account for his elevation in Athens. He was the first man to collect the fables of Aesop and to tie in the lists of Athenian archons (rulers) with the dates of the Olympic Games (Aristotle was honoured for doing the same with the Pythian Games). This required real research and was of high importance because it enabled Athenians to put dates to events in order to create an intelligible historical sequence (see below). This was all part of the gradual process of turning Athens into a living cultural museum, a place with little future but a magnificent past, where the elites of the Mediterranean would arrive to be educated and wonder at what had been achieved in Athens' 'golden age'.

Incidentally, Demetrius carried out a census in Athens, and counted 21,000 citizens, 10,000 metics and a barely credible 400,000 slaves! These included those working in mines, 'who dig as diligently as if they expect to bring up Pluto [god of the underworld] himself'. But the upheavals of the post-Alexander era had been severe, reducing many to slavery.

DOWN THE DRAIN

When Demetrius (I) was exiled in 307 BC, he ended up in Alexandria. It was he who persuaded Ptolemy of the virtue of starting his big research centres, the Alexandrian Museum and Library. Little good it did him in Athens. At his exile, many of the 360 bronze statues of him put up by the Athenians were melted down into chamber pots.

GREEK DATING SYSTEMS

The *marmor Parium* is a marble inscription from the island of Paros. It was composed in the middle of the third century BC, and its 'base' date, from which everything else was reckoned, was 'when Diognetus was archon' (by our reckoning, that is 264 BC). So the dates are expressed as 'x years before the archonship of Diognetus'. This system depended, of course, on the existence of chronological lists of priests/officials (see above). It is one of the three methods by which Greeks dated events:

(i) with reference to the year in which a priest or executive official (archon) was in power, as above;

(ii) with reference to the first Olympic Game, held (by our reckoning) in 776 BC. They were held thereafter every four years. This four-year period of time was called an 'Olympiad', and chronological lists of these were kept. So 'the first Olympiad' would indicate the period 776–772 BC, perhaps further sharpened up to the year with reference to (e.g.) an archon ('when Charops of Athens was in his first year as archon') or an Olympic victor ('when Dorieus from Rhodes won his second victory');

(iii) when there were no lists of archons/priests/Olympiads (etc.) available – i.e. before 776 BC – dates were roughly calculated by single generations, often a period of about forty years.

SYNCHRONIZING DATES

So much for the ancient Greek dating systems; but how were we able to synchronize their dates with our AD/BC system? There were four stages:

(i)   a number of Greeks synchronized their own histories, matching individual Athenian, Spartan, Argive (etc.) dating systems with Olympiads;

(ii) Eusebius, the fourth-century AD bishop of Caesarea, synchronized this system with the Abrahamic ('years after Abraham') and Roman ('years after foundation of Rome') dating systems;

(iii) The BC/AD system was invented in the sixth century AD by the Scythian monk Dionysius Exiguus (Denis the Small).

He calculated that 532 years had passed since the birth of Jesus, thereby establishing the principle of a system based on BC/AD. So all AD dates could now be worked out. For instance, since the Roman emperor Diocletian had come to power 248 years before AD 532, he came to power in 532 minus 248, or AD 284. The Anglo-Saxon historian Bede was one of the first historians to adopt the AD system in his *Ecclesiastical History of the English People* (AD 731).

(iv) In the early seventeenth century, the French Jesuit Denis Pétau (Dionysius Petavius) extended the system to the period BC. An example: by the AD system, Diocletian came to power in AD 284. By the Roman system, he came to power 1,037 years after the foundation of Rome. Therefore Rome was founded in 1037 minus 284, or 753 BC.

ART CONQUERS ALL

The great painter Protogenes was working on his masterpiece, *Ialysus, Founder of Rhodes*, using four coats of paint to help preserve it, but could not get the foam issuing from the jaws of a panting dog quite right. This was important: in the classical canon, art had to imitate nature as precisely as possible. Eventually he gave up and in his fury slapped the painting with a sponge – producing the effect he required! When Demetrius (II) was besieging Rhodes in 305 BC, Protogenes continued to work outside the city walls, telling Demetrius that he knew he (Demetrius) was besieging Rhodes, not the arts. Demetrius ensured he was protected, and apparently refused to set fire to Rhodes because it would have meant burning down the building in which *Ialysus* was stored – and thereby lost the chance of victory.

A COMMON TONGUE

On the whole, the new Macedonian kings, while remaining on top, were relaxed about local customs. The Ptolemies were happy to be seen as pharoahs, and built temples to the local gods. The Seleucid/ Antiochids married into Babylonian families and fostered their cults. What was remarkable was the spread of *koinê* ('common') Greek (see p. 336). The Indian king Asoka converted to Buddhism around 260 BC and near Kandahar (Afghanistan) put up rock-cut inscriptions in local languages and in Greek, in which he mentions trying to convert Greeks to Buddhism:

> In the past there were no Buddhist teachers but such officers
> were appointed by me thirteen years after my coronation.
> Now they work among all religions for the establishment
> of Buddha, for the promotion of Buddha, and for the welfare
> and happiness of all who are devoted to Buddha. They work
> among the Greeks...

In the third century BC, the Old Testament began to be translated into *koinê* Greek for Jews in Egypt (the Septuagint – the name, from the Latin word for 'seventy', refers to the number of Jewish scholars who were supposed to have done the work); and a Jew living in Alexandria in the second century BC called Ezekiel (no relation of the biblical Ezekiel) wrote in *koinê* Greek a five-act Greek-style tragedy of the story of Exodus (only 269 lines survive). But it is no surprise that Antiochus IV failed to turn Jerusalem into a Greek city and abolish Jewish customs in 167 BC, a move that led directly to the successful revolt against Antiochus led by Judas Maccabee.

LUVVIES ALL

The actors' union was called 'Artists of Dionysus', a worldwide union formed in the third century BC by 280 poets, technicians, musician and actors. Some replaced 'Artists' with 'Toadies'. This union lasted 500 years. Its last recorded title (under the emperor Aurelian) was, modestly, 'The Sacred Musical Travelling Aurelian Great World Guild of the Artists of Dionysus'. The actors demanded freedom of travel by land and sea, and freedom from taxation and arrest. At Delphi they got prior rights to consult the oracle and to hospitality, for them and their descendants. For performing in Samos, Polus from Aegina, a top luvvie, demanded public acclamation, rights of citizenship, access to the council for anything he wanted, a front seat at all games and a golden crown. *Plus ça change...* The Samians were only too happy to oblige and put up a huge inscription to this effect.

Not surprisingly, performers had a reputation for arrogance and bad behaviour. In the pseudo-Aristotelian *Problems* (see p. 312) the question is asked: 'Why are Artists of Dionysus mostly without principles?' The answer is that 'their profession does not encourage reason and wisdom, and most of their life is spent in either rank self-indulgence or poverty, conditions always productive of low moral standards'. They could get away with all this because theatrical and sporting shows were staged as festivals in honour of the gods (Dionysus and Heracles), whom the performers were serving.

TRIBAL NAMING RIGHTS

When one is in a position of no power, as Athens was, flattering gestures are needed to win friends and influence people. So Demetrius (II) was enthusiastically welcomed into Athens as 'liberator', and he and his father Antigonus were both given divine status (the idea was catching: see p. 302). Two new tribes named after them – Demetrias and Antigonis – were added to the existing ten, and their images were woven into Athena's robe (see p. 125) at the Panathenaea! This became something of a trend. When Athens got support against Macedon from Ptolemy (IV) in 224 BC, they created a thirteenth tribe – Ptolemais. The number rose to fourteen (with the addition of Attalid) in 200 BC, when Attalus, king of Pergamum, arrived to help the Athenians against the Macedonian king Philip V, who had ferociously ravaged Attica (see p. 341). In 196 BC, after the Romans had defeated Philip V, the Athenians cursed the whole Macedonian people, and abolished the Demetrias and Antigonis tribes, leaving twelve in all.

STOICS AND EPICUREANS

Two philosophies were developed in Athens in the late fourth and third centuries BC that were to have a powerful influence upon Roman and later thought, especially in the area of scientific theorizing.

Stoicism was the brainchild of Zeno, a Greek from Cyprus, who came to Athens in 313 BC. It acquired its name from the *stoa* (a long, pillared portico) in which he taught.

Epicurus invented Epicureanism. He was born on the island of Samos, and in 306 BC he bought a house in Athens with a garden which became the headquarters of Epicureanism (when ancient writers talk about 'the garden', this is the philosophy they mean).

These philosophies shared two principles, based on Socrates' belief that the best way to live must be connected with the natural order of the cosmos. First, they were both ethical – they showed adherents what the good life was and, at the practical level, how to lead it. And second, they were 'holistic' – their views about the good life derived from their beliefs about the material construction and workings of the universe. No longer could 'scientific' speculation about the nature of the universe be divorced from its consequences for human existence.

Further, over time, they pointed to a change in direction: away from the intensely political concerns of the elites of the classical democratic *polis* to the more personal concerns of individuals battling with the problems of everyday life in a world of monarchs.

GOD'S BREATH IN US ALL

Knowing nothing about monkeys playing with typewriters and producing the complete works of Shakespeare, Stoics argued that a universe as beneficial as ours was about as likely to emerge at random as an infinitely large collection of alphabetic letters, tipped randomly on the ground, would spell out the *Annals* of Ennius (a Roman epic poet).

Stoics held that the universe was all matter, or stuff. This stuff was infused with a sort of heavenly fire or breath (*pneuma*) (think of the stuff as wire, and *pneuma* as electricity). This *pneuma* was the equivalent of the laws of nature – the reason why the universe was as it was, the reason why the universe was intelligible: effectively, *logos* ('reason') was the Stoic god. And this god was in us, because our soul was the part of us that shared in the divine *pneuma*. The more we could lead rational lives, then, the closer to the divine and therefore the happier we would be. But what was a rational life? Largely, keeping a firm grip on the only things we *could* control – our thoughts and emotions, to ensure they did not lead us astray; but also, because *all* humans had this divine *pneuma* inside them, doing good works in the world.

ATOMS TO ATOMS...

Epicureanism was named after its inventor Epicurus (Greek: *Epikouros*). Born in 306 BC, he was an atomist (see p. 209), and reasoned that, since everything must be made up of atoms – man, his soul, even the gods – then at death we and our souls dissolve into the great atom pool in the sky. The cosmos, in other words, was not like a perfectly functioning, eternal machine, but had emerged randomly and was constantly changing. Further, since gods were simply atoms, they had no interest in controlling or judging human life. Death, therefore, was nothing to be worried about. In such a world, Epicurus reasoned, absence of physical and mental pain (*ataraxia*, 'disassociation from worry') was the key to happiness. So one had to (among much else) remove desire for anything that caused anxiety, especially anything that had no limits, such as wealth or status, because these could never be satisfied. This philosophy could easily be construed as a search for private pleasure, without any commitment to the greater good ('we must free ourselves from the prison of affairs and politics,' says one source), and regularly was. Hence our 'epicurean'.

THE STONE CITY

Alexandria was founded by Alexander in 331 BC, after he had expelled the Persians from Egypt. It was originally an Egyptian village named

Rhakotis. Alexander had with him at the time an architect and town-planner called Dinocrates. Dressed like Hercules in a lion skin to catch Alexander's attention, he laid out plans for a city four times larger than Athens. It was to be built entirely of stone – an amazing expense. But why not? Since wealth was in agriculture, and the Nile made Egypt easily the most fertile land of the ancient world, the place was fabulously rich and had a gigantic labour force. Alexandria's difference from other cities was highlighted by the fact that it was often called Alexandria *by* Egypt rather than *in* Egypt, as if it were a private, gated enclave for Macedonians and Greeks alone.

THE JEWEL OF THE NILE

Ptolemy I made Alexandria the capital of his kingdom and turned it into the major seaport of the eastern Mediterranean. In time it would become the second largest Mediterranean city after Rome, with half a million inhabitants (third in the whole ancient world after Rome and Constantinople). It had a good harbour and was close to the Nile. Commercially, it could not be bettered. Outside the harbour, Ptolemy had constructed the Pharos lighthouse, 470 feet (143 metres) high – one of the seven wonders of the world – to guide in shipping. Many Greeks came to settle in Alexandria and became to a certain extent Egyptianized. They accepted Egyptian traditions, including mummification and the custom of brother–sister marriage in the ruling family, and they built temples to the old Egyptian gods.

LOOKING AFTER NUMBER ONE

The Ptolemies had no one's interests at heart but their own. Almost everything in daily use was made in royal factories or under royal licence, all profits to the king. A vast bureaucracy was put in place to ensure the tax came in. The Ptolemies held monopolies in the major Egyptian products such as olive oil, paper supplies (papyrus) and exotic perfumes, and exported grain (millions of tons a year), drugs, glassware, gold, silver and faience. Iron, tin, copper, horses, timber and elephants featured prominently among the imports. Workers who did not channel supplies through Alexandria (where the king would tax it) faced the death penalty. Banking was another state monopoly, and loans attracted interest rates of 24 per cent, double that in force anywhere else. And most of the money wound up in the king's and his ministers' pockets, to spend as they pleased – largely on the royal palace, their fleet and vast mercenary army. One minister was even able to pay for an army out of private funds.

TROUBLE IN THE CITY

By the second century BC, Alexandria held some 300,000 people, mainly Macedonians, Greeks, Egyptians and Jews, and was the largest city in the Mediterranean. Teeming with traders, soldiers, businessmen, bureaucrats, agents, craftsmen and slaves, and ruled by a royal court steeped in luxury, it was more like the vast Near Eastern cities of Nineveh and Babylon centuries earlier than a modest democratic Greek city-state. But it was not a harmonious city, and over time Alexandria became more and more subject to disturbances. Labourers skived off work and sabotaged harvests, or wrecked dykes and irrigation canals. Petty pilfering and strikes were common.

CELTIC TIGERS

Around 281 BC bands of migrating Celts (*Galatai* in Greek: the term 'Gauls' is misleading) invaded the Balkans. Some attacked Macedon, nearly reaching Delphi, while others were welcomed into Asia Minor by the Greek king of Bithynia Nicomedes, who wanted their help to expand his kingdom. These he settled in central Asia Minor, calling it Galatia. They terrorized the region, demanding Celt-geld from the locals, until Attalus of Pergamum sorted them out (see below). From then on they made a good living hiring themselves out as mercenaries to the Ptolemies and Attalids. Galatia became a client state of Rome in 64 BC.

A LIVER TRANSFER

It was said that the soldiers of Attalus I, king of Pergamum, were terrified at the prospect of taking on the Celts in 232 BC. But after the pre-battle sacrifice, the priest was able to announce that the words 'Victory for the King' had appeared on the animal's liver. The troops, greatly heartened, fought and won a great victory. It later emerged that Attalus had written the words backwards on his own hand in ink, and while examining the victim had imprinted them on the liver.

HAIRY SIEVES

The historian Diodorus, writing in the first century BC, describes the Celts as tall, well muscled, white of skin, with blond hair, whose colour they sharpened by washing it in lime-water. Further:

> Some of them shave their beards, but others let it grow a
> little; and the nobles shave their cheeks, but they let the

moustache grow until it covers the mouth. Consequently, when they are eating, their moustaches become entangled in the food, and when they are drinking, the beverage passes, as it were, through a kind of a strainer.

WHEN A PTOLEMY PUTS THE BOAT OUT...

A celebration by Ptolemy II in the 270s BC gives some idea of what a Ptolemy could do if he put his mind to it (and many did). A pavilion for guests, 75 feet (23 metres) high, with a canopy in fetching scarlet-and-white, contained 130 couches in a circle, flowers everywhere and a portico outside for a stroll, which might also take in Ptolemy's Royal Zoo. Alongside the displays of wealth – 400 cartloads of silver plate, 20 of gold and 800 of spices – there were 57,600 infantry, 23,200 horse, 2,000 bulls covered in gold, 2,400 dogs, 150 men carrying exotic trees with birds in them, and 120 boys carrying saffron on gold platters. Satyrs with gilt ivy leaves on their torches, Dionysiac revellers with gold crowns, figures dressed as Victory with gold wings, and the tallest actors in town helped the show along, together with a variety of exotic animals: huge elephants, goats, hartebeest, camels, ostriches, peacocks, a large white bear, three bear cubs, fourteen leopards, sixteen cheetahs, a giraffe and an Ethiopian rhinoceros. A gold mixing-bowl holding 150 gallons was on display, together with a wine-skin stitched together out of leopard pelts carrying 30,000 gallons of wine, which it dribbled out over the length of the route, and a vast float with fountains gushing milk and wine. There was also a cart-borne golden phallus nearly 200 feet long, draped with gold ribbons and bows and tipped with a star 9 feet round. Athenaeus' description runs to over fifteen pages (see p. 363).

THE THINK-TANK ON THE NILE

Greeks were a competitive lot, and Macedonians particularly so: they felt they needed to prove their Greekness to a disbelieving world. When Ptolemy took over Egypt, he was prompted by Demetrius to turn Alexandria into an intellectual centre to rival Athens itself. But there was something else. Egypt was a land of wonder, hugely admired by ancients Greeks for its vast monuments such as the pyramids and for its age-old tradition of wisdom and love of learning. So Ptolemy would rival the Egyptians as well, and decided to use their fabulous wealth to make Alexandria the greatest cultural and scientific centre in the world.

To do so, Ptolemy I or II (we do not know for sure) built the Alexandrian Museum in the early third century BC, the world's first scientific research institute, and the Library, the finest collection of ancient Greek texts (490,000 of them) ever gathered in one place. Then, wielding their cheque-books, the Ptolemies persuaded the finest minds of their day from all over the Mediterranean to work in Alexandria. Great thinkers, always appreciative of those who will pay them to ruminate, flooded in. Among the star intellectuals were Euclid, Archimedes, Apollonius of Perga, Aristarchus of Samos and Eratosthenes (see below).

THE ROUGH ROAD TO GEOMETRY

In his *Elements* (*c.* 300 BC), starting from a few simple axioms that were obvious to everyone, Euclid deduced, link by link, proof by proof, every proposition in his geometry. Ever since, proving propositions from basic axioms has been the business of mathematics. Not that it was easy: when one of the Ptolemies told Euclid to make it easier, he famously replied that there was no royal road to geometry.

THE GREATEST MATHEMATICIAN?

From Euclid's 'school' emerged Archimedes (287–212 BC), the greatest mathematician of antiquity, and Apollonius from Perga (see below). Archimedes studied at the Alexandrian Museum from about 260 BC, before returning to his native Syracuse in Sicily to continue his work. To glance at a few of his achievements: his masterly mathematical proofs at times anticipated integral calculus; he invented by himself and developed to incredible elaboration the science of hydrostatics (the pressure and equilibrium of liquids at rest); he was the first man to work out accurately the value of pi; and he was the first to come up with the formula for measuring the volume of a sphere. Arguably, no other mathematician has ever made so many advances.

YOU (ST)REEKER!

Archimedes had a problem. He had been asked by a king to confirm whether the crown he had been given was solid gold. Let us assume Archimedes knew how much (to put it in our terms) a cubic inch of gold should weigh. Calculate the volume of the crown (how many cubic inches), weigh it, and see if it matched what it *should* weigh. If it did not, some other substance of different density had been added to it.

But how was he to discover the volume of a gold crown? He could melt it down and pour it into a measuring device. Probably unwise. He mulled over the problem in the public baths. Rather than a single huge Roman-style bath, these were individual hip-baths, in which you sat while a slave poured water over you. As Archimedes stood up and sat down, stood up and sat down (one may guess), he noticed that he spilled different volumes of water over the edge of the hip-bath, depending on how much of his bottom he sank into it. Eureka!

1 Place a cake tin on a large frying pan.

2 Fill the cake tin with water to the brim.

3 Gently lower the crown into the cake tin (no splashing).

4 The volume of water spilling out into the frying pan equals the volume of the crown.

5 Pour the water into a measuring device.

Hence the excited nude sprint home. And the answer? The goldsmith had cheated.

Incidentally, Archimedes shouted not *eureka* but *heurêka* (as in our 'heuristics'), which means 'I have found it!'

<ONI< <APER$

Apollonius from Perga, 'the great geometer', came to Alexandria around 240 BC to work in the mathematical school, and is famous for one outstanding treatise – the *Conics*, the geometry of the different cross-sections which can result from sawing at various angles through a cone (an area in which Archimedes worked too). When, in 1600, Kepler was wrestling with Copernicus' bold idea that the planets, including the earth, moved around the sun, he was able to fit each orbit to an ellipse – a conic section. Newton's gravitational theory showed that every simple celestial orbit had to be one or other of these conic sections.

BLUE-SKY THINKER

Aristarchus from Samos, an astronomer (*c.* 310–230 BC), advanced the hypothesis that the sun and stars are stationary while the earth spins on its axis and orbits the sun. He was well ahead of his time – Nicolaus Copernicus was to make a similar claim in 1543, some 1,800 years later. Indeed, so innovative was Aristarchus' thinking that it was proposed to bring a charge of impiety against him. He also invented and put into practice a method of comparing the sizes and distances of the moon and the sun which revealed the unexpected vastness of the heavens.

BETA MALE

In 245 BC Ptolemy III summoned to Alexandria Eratosthenes, who was born in Cyrene in Libya and educated in Athens. His nickname was to be Beta, because he knew too much about everything to become Alpha in any of them!

He was the first man to measure accurately the size of the earth, calculating it at 24,662 miles (39,690 km) – an astonishingly good attempt, as the true value is 24,817 miles (39,939 km). 'The world was now grasped', as the Roman encyclopedist Pliny put it. In his three-volume *Geographika*, Eratosthenes was thus able to produce a world map (or what he knew of the world at the time). He named over 400 cities, linking them up with grids that enabled distances between them to be measured. He even divided the earth into five climate zones – two freezing zones around the poles, two temperate zones, and a zone encompassing the equator and the tropics!

THE <ORP$E <ORP$

The intellectual freedom of the Alexandrian Museum enabled doctors to dissect corpses for a while, an activity otherwise forbidden by religious taboos. They invented names for their discoveries, and some of them, such as epiglottis, retina and duodenum, are essentially the ones we use today.

Among the doctors, Herophilus (335–280 BC) was the first to recognize the connection between the heartbeat and the pulse. He distinguished between arteries and veins, and reinstated the brain as the seat of intelligence (Aristotle had said it was the heart, see Alcmaeon, p. 173).

Erasistratus (304–250 BC) realized that every organ in the body was 'plumbed' into the system by three sets of vessels (veins, arteries and nerves). He divided the latter into sensory nerves (carrying information from our senses) and motor nerves (carrying orders to our muscles). He also guessed at the capillary network connecting arteries and veins, and discovered some aspects of the circulation of blood.

Incidentally, 'hypochondria' is an English term, derived from the Greek *hupokhondrion*, 'abdomen', because the abdomen was thought to be the seat of melancholy.

TOY$'R'U$

In his treatise *Pneumatics*, Hero (AD 10–70) states that air is a material substance consisting, like all material substances, of particles in a vacuum. 'Like a pile of springy shavings', it can be (say) compressed, but it will always return to its original volume. So if a vacuum is created by suction, water will rise to fill it, even upwards! Burn a candle in an enclosed vessel over water, and the water level will rise to replace the air destroyed by the fire. He used these observations to explain siphons, pumps and much else. On the strength of this, he invented all sorts of gadgets – nothing more than toys, really – including a sort of steam-engine, a vending machine, a wind-powered organ, a force pump (used on fire engines), and a sort of mechanical puppet show, ten minutes long.

THE ALEXANDRIAN LIBRARY

For all its brilliance, the Alexandrian Museum was a relatively small department of the cultural institution. Most of the learned men supported by the Ptolemaic dynasty were poets and literary scholars in the arts faculty, the great Alexandrian Library. Of most importance for our texts was the work of the textual critics. Their aim was to rescue, preserve and make available in sound editions the whole of classical Greek literature. Indeed, all our texts of Greek literature descend ultimately from Alexandrian editions. If they got them wrong, we've got them wrong. The Ptolemies vigorously pursued this end by attempting to get a copy of every book in the world.

INTER–LIBRARY THEFTS

In the mid-third century BC, the bibliophile Ptolemy III contacted the library at Athens asking for their official copies of the manuscripts of Aeschylus, Sophocles and Euripides. The Athenians agreed to lend them, against a returnable deposit of fifteen talents (the cost of building about fifteen warships). Deciding this was a bargain, Ptolemy never returned them, though he did magnanimously send copies back in their place. Meanwhile, all books arriving in Alexandria were confiscated, and cheap copies made to return to the hapless owners. These tactics so swelled the Library that a second storehouse was needed.

THE SAVIOUR OF GREEK LITERATURE

To catalogue and classify books as they came into the Alexandrian Library was a big enough job by itself. One of its directors, Zenodotus, was the first man we know of to list books alphabetically; his successor Callimachus was the first to produce a detailed bibliography of all Greek literature – author, brief biography, works – each work with its own shelf number, a vital reference tool. Other Greek kings got the idea, and rival scholarly libraries sprang up in Antioch and Pergamum, poaching top directors. Without the Alexandrian Library's scholars, scouring the world for books and copying, preserving, restoring and distributing them – and the Romans, who fell in love with Greek literature and made it a centrepiece of their education – Greek literature would almost certainly have perished.

THE IMPORTANCE OF TALKING PROPER

The Greek language was expressed in many different dialects. But when Philip II's all-conquering Macedonian court adopted Attic Greek (the dialect of Athens) in the fourth century BC, Attic gradually became standard throughout the Greek-speaking world, in a simplified form called *koinê* ('common') Greek (the language of the New Testament). This caused problems for those whose first language was not Greek (for instance, all those people out in the East whom Alexander and his successors swamped in Greek language and culture). How could they be certain they were speaking and – much more important – writing it correctly? What were the educational implications? *Hellênismos*, a Greekness 'faultless in respect of rules and without careless usage', became a priority for them. The Greeks even had a word for 'speaking incorrectly' – *soloikos* (whence our 'solecism'), which was said to derive from the Athenian colonists of Soloi in Cilicia (southern Turkey) what had forgot how to talk proper.

THE COLOSSUS OF RHODES

One of the few places to resist takeover by the Macedonian kings was the island of Rhodes. It did, however, maintain friendly relations with that other great seafaring power, the Ptolemies. In 226 BC the island suffered a devastating earthquake, which also destroyed the gigantic Colossus of Rhodes, a bronze statue of the sun-god, 110 feet (33 metres) high, so huge that 'few people can make their arms meet round its thumb'. It had been built to celebrate Rhodes' defeat of Demetrius in 304 BC (see p. 320). No one knows where it was located – it certainly did not bestride the harbour, as is commonly said. Ptolemy III immediately offered to help out the island with a truly colossal donation:

> Three hundred talents of silver, a million artabas [1 artabas
> = 9 gallons/40 litres] of wheat, timber for the construction of
> 10 quinqueremes and 10 triremes, consisting of 40,000 cubits
> [1 cubit = c. 20 inches/50 cm] of squared pine planking, 1,000
> talents of bronze coinage, 3,000 talents of tow, 3,000 pieces
> of sail-cloth, 3,000 talents (of bronze?) for the repair of the
> Colossus, 100 architects with 350 workmen, and 14 talents
> every year for their wages, and in addition 12,000 artabas

of wheat for competitions and sacrifices, and 20,000 for the supplying of 10 triremes. Most of this he gave at once, as well as a third of the money promised.

The Rhodians declined the offer to repair the Colossus, however: they said it was forbidden by an oracle which said the statue had offended the sun-god; hence the earthquake. The remains lay there for 900 years. In AD 654 Arabs plundered Rhodes and sold the remains to a trader who (apparently) needed 900 camels to convey them to Syria. A further tale has it that the metal was subsequently converted into the cannon-balls with which the Ottoman sultan Suleiman the Magnificent battered Rhodes into submission in 1522. Yes, well... Incidentally, no ancient source says the statue straddled the hardbour. That was a medieval invention.

XIII

229–146 BC

TIMELINE

218 BC	Hannibal crosses the Alps, starting a sixteen-year war against the Romans
215 BC	Philip V of Macedon allies himself with Carthage
212–206 BC	First Macedonian War: Rome, Attalus I and Aetolian League against Macedon
202 BC	Rome defeats Carthage
200–197 BC	Second Macedonian War; Philip V defeated at Cynoscephalae
188 BC	Rome defeats Antiochus III and hands over Asia Minor to the Attalids
179 BC	Philip V dies, to be replaced by his son Perseus
171–168 BC	Third Macedonian War: Macedon's kingdom ended and becomes a Roman province
168 BC	Antiochus IV fails to take Egypt
155 BC	Athenian embassy in Rome

146 BC   Rome destroys Carthage and Corinth; Macedon
            under Roman control

MACEDON FALLS
TO ROME

In 218 BC Hannibal from Carthage in North Africa launched his attack on Italy, starting the Second Punic War. At first Rome suffered serious defeats, and in 215 BC Philip V, king of Macedon, allied himself to Carthage in an attempt to exploit the situation: by trying to take control of the rest of Greece and the Greek leagues and trying his luck in Illyria, where Rome had interests. But Rome, the Aetolian League and Attalus I of Pergamum took him on. Rome did not yet have permanent boots on the ground in Greece but put them there when necessary. This engagement – the First Macedonian War (212–206 BC) – ended in a stalemate 'peace'.

After finally defeating Carthage in 202 BC, the Romans decided to sort out Philip once and for all. Proclaiming themselves champions of Greek freedom and supported by Athens and Attalus I of Pergamum, the Romans declared war on Philip in 200 BC.

This Second Macedonian War (200–197 BC) saw Athens badly ravaged by Philip (see p. 323), but he was defeated at Cynoscephalae in 197 BC. This marked the end of the 'invincible' Macedonian phalanx and Macedonian control over other Greek states.

Philip and his son Perseus now turned to defending Macedon. In 188 BC Rome saw off Antiochus III's attempt to take over Greece and handed Asia Minor over to the Attalids. Philip died in 179 BC, and the Third Macedonian War (171–168 BC) saw Perseus beaten by the Romans at Pydna. That was the end of Alexander's independent Macedon. In 168 BC Antiochus IV, thinking he saw a chance to extend his power, tried to conquer the Ptolemies, but Rome brutally humiliated him. These events saw a resurgence in the fortunes of Athens, which was now firmly ensconced as an ally of Rome. Rome gave Athens control of some Greek islands, notably the major trading centre of Delos, further increasing Athens' revenues.

In 146 BC Rome destroyed Carthage; defeated the Achaean League of Greek cities, which had resisted Rome's move south from Macedon; and ravaged Corinth, as a warning to Greeks to accept their new Roman master – or else.

THE END OF MACEDON

After the Romans had wiped out the Macedonian army in the battles of 171–168 BC, King Perseus surrendered. Among the leading families of Macedonian court and society taken as hostages to Rome was Polybius, who was to become accepted into Roman society, an ambassador for Roman interests and an admiring historian of Rome. Around 300,000 Macedonian citizens were sold into slavery, cities and villages were destroyed, and land was divided up among retired Roman soldiers and allies. Macedon itself was separated up into four states, romantically labelled I, II, III and IV. Minimum contact was allowed between them (though, inevitably, they still squabbled). That was the end of Alexander the Great's kingdom as a force in the world.

THE FIRST 'ROYAL FAMILY'

Antiochus III, heir to Seleucus' vast eastern kingdom and encouraged by the exiled Hannibal, decided to take on Rome, together with the Aetolian League of Greek cities. Foolish move. In 188 BC he was defeated, and Rome handed over Asia Minor to the Attalids, then under the kingship of Eumenes II. This caused the dynasty to rethink its operation completely. Abandoning any pretence to absolutist monarchism, it turned itself into a domestic, family-loving institution, touring the country waving to loyal subjects and devolving power away from the centre to big cities such as Ephesus, Pergamum and Sardis. It also, uniquely, abandoned all reference to the royal household on its coinage – no portraits, no reference to 'kings'. The Attalids were not stupid: they knew that real power now resided with Rome.

SLOW LEARNER

In 168 BC Antiochus IV decided to renew battle against the Ptolemies in Egypt, and had some success. Keen to build on it, he was met by a Roman commission led by Popillius Laenas. Popillius refused Antiochus' hand, and instead placed in it orders from the Roman senate to retreat. Antiochus said he would consult on the matter, but Popillius drew a circle round him in the sand and told him not to step out of it till he had given his reply. Antiochus thought for a bit, replied 'I shall do what the Senate thinks right', and withdrew his army. Only then did Popillius return his handshake. To such humiliation were the successors of Alexander the Great now submitted.

SCANDALIZING ROME

Athens, feeling supremely confident of Roman favour, had foolishly sacked the nearby village of Oropus without Roman consent. The Romans were not impressed and imposed a fine of 500 talents. In 155 BC Athens sent a delegation of three philosophers to Rome to plead for a reduction to 100 talents: a Stoic, an Aristotelian and the sceptic philosopher Carneades. During his stay in Rome, Carneades gave two lectures on the topic of justice, arguing on the first day for its importance, and on the second day refuting that argument. Among the audience was Cato the Elder, who stood for all the 'good old Roman virtues'. He was appalled at this clever-dickery and demanded the philosophers be sent back to Greece before they corrupted the Roman youth. But they did win the reduction in the fine.

Carneades was opposed to dogma (especially Stoicism) and was characterized as a 'probabilist'. What this meant in practice was that the wise man would form opinions by deciding what was the most probable outcome of any action, but always in the knowledge that he might be wrong. His judgement was certainly wrong on this occasion, but his lecture left its mark: here was a new way of thinking about the world for the Romans to digest.

GREECE CAPTIVATES ROME

Whatever Cato the Elder might have thought about it, Rome was now at the centre not just of a political but also of a cultural empire. The result, as the poet Horace said, was that:

Captured Greece took captive its savage victor and
Brought culture to unsophisticated Latium.

Virtually all Roman literature found its roots in Greek. By the first century BC Greek literature and Greek-inspired Roman literature were a central feature of the Roman cultural and educational scene. Elite Romans like Caesar and Cicero went to Greece to get educated in the real thing; the first emperor, Augustus (31 BC–AD 14), went out of his way to present a cultivated, Greek side to his otherwise all-Roman image. Educated Greeks went the other way, flocking to Rome to make their fortunes in the education and culture business.

ARTY SPOILS OF WAR

Romans began to help themselves liberally to Greek art. When Marcellus, fighting the Carthaginians in the Second Punic War, sacked Syracuse in 211 BC (so Plutarch tells us):

> He returned with the majority of the finest dedications [statues, etc., dedicated to the gods] in Syracuse to provide a spectacle for his triumph and adorn the city. For before this time, Romans did not possess, let alone were even aware of, such magnificent and exquisite work, nor did they appreciate art of grace and subtlety; it was all barbarian arms and bloody spoils of war, crowned with the memorials and trophies of military triumphs. [Some did not approve of this development] because the Roman people had been used only to fighting or farming and had no experience of the indolent life of luxury. But Marcellus stuffed them full of leisured, fancy chat about art and artists, so they spent their days showing off their sophisticated critical skills.

Aemilius Paullus returned from his conquests in Greece in 167 BC with

'statues, paintings and colossal images, carried on 250 chariots, for the appreciation of which a whole day was barely sufficient'.

SEVEN WONDERS OF THE WORLD

Wishing to get a solid grip on the world around them (especially their classical past), Greeks were great compilers of lists, whether it was plays that had won prizes at festivals, champions at Olympia, or the world's greatest sights (and sites). About 140 BC Antipater, a Greek from Sidon, composed a poem celebrating the seven wonders of the world. He names the walls of Babylon, the hanging gardens of Babylon, the statue of Zeus at Olympia, the Colossus in Rhodes, the pyramids, the tomb of Mausolus in Halicarnassus (modern Bodrum), and the temple of Artemis (Diana) in Ephesus. The lighthouse of Pharos at Alexandria was another popular candidate. It is notable that no Roman monument ever featured in the list; and it has recently been argued that the gardens of Babylon were in fact in Nineveh.

XIV

146–27 BC

TIMELINE

133 BC	Attalus III bequeaths Pergamum to Rome
89 BC	Mithradates' attack on the Roman East
86 BC	Sulla loots Athens
62 BC	Pompey conquers the Greek East: Antiochus' kingdom ended
49–30 BC	Rome's civil wars: Caesar against Pompey (49–46 BC), Octavian/Augustus against Marc Antony and Cleopatra (32–31 BC)
30 BC	Augustus takes over Ptolemaic Egypt; Ptolemy's kingdom ended
27 BC	Southern Greece becomes the Roman province of Achaea

THE END OF ALEXANDER'S EMPIRE

M acedon was now a full Roman province, and Rome gave its governor the power to extend that control southwards. In just over 100 years, the whole of what had once been Alexander's Macedonian empire – but which at his death had been taken over and run by Greek kings for nearly 300 years – would become Roman:

- In 133 BC Attalus III, well aware of Roman military might and seeing the way the wind was blowing, actually *bequeathed* Pergamum to Rome.
- In 62 BC the Roman general Pompey the Great returned after taking out Mithradates, king of Pontus, and went on to conquer the eastern kingdoms of Antiochus/Seleucus and bring them under Roman control.
- In 30 BC Caesar's heir Octavian, soon to become the first Roman emperor Augustus, defeated Marc Antony and his lover Cleopatra (the last of the Ptolemies) and made Egypt a Roman province.

- In 27 BC southern Greece was turned into the Roman province of Achaea.

ATTALID REALPOLITIK

The Attalids had long been sensitive to the power of Rome. In the following private letter (*c.* 160 BC), discussing his plans for keeping the Celts at bay (see p. 328), the earlier Attalid king Eumenes II indicates as much:

> To go ahead without consulting the Romans seemed to involve considerable danger. If we were successful, the result would be jealousy, displeasure and hostile suspicion, but if we failed, certain destruction. For it was likely that the Romans would not stir a finger but would look on with satisfaction, since we had undertaken such a great project without consulting *them*. But now should we suffer any reverse – may heaven forbid – we would get help because we had acted in everything with their assent... I have therefore decided to send messengers continually to Rome...

No surprise, then, that in 133 BC Attalus III decided to bequeath his empire in Asia Minor to the Romans.

HEAVENLY TOYS

In 1900 a group of Greek sponge divers off the island of Antikythera, south of the Peloponnese, brought up out of a wreck a lump of corroded, encrusted brass in a box. It broke into three pieces, and other bits fell off. It was clear that it was a geared machine of some sort, but serious work began on it only fifty years later. When it had been x-rayed and cleaned, it was found to have Greek inscriptions on it. It turned out to be a mechanical device for predicting a range of celestial phenomena – lunar and solar eclipses, planetary movements and so on – based on then current astronomical theories, probably dating to around 100 BC. It is a unique find, but Cicero mentions two machines of this sort built by Archimedes. Here he describes what happened when one of them was moved:

> In fact, when this sphere or planetarium was moved, we observed the moon distanced the sun as many degrees by a turn of the wheel in the machine, as she does in so many days in the heavens. From which it resulted, that the progress of the sun was marked as in the heavens, and that the moon touched the point where she is obscured by the earth's shadow at the instant the sun appears above the horizon.

So there may well have been a culture of producing cunning devices of this sort, perhaps originating in Alexandria (see p. 334). But they never progressed beyond being brilliantly clever toys.

ATHENS' LAST BREAK FOR FREEDOM

Mithradates, king of Pontus (in northern Asia Minor, a kingdom established by Alexander), had long wanted to drive the Romans out of Asia Minor. In 89 BC he incited a revolt against the Romans there, and Athens, sensing a return to the glory days of independence, sent a deputation to Mithradates, who persuaded the Athenians to break with Rome (see p. 342). It was another disastrous decision. The Roman general Sulla dealt with Mithradates for the time being, and in 86 BC entered, burned and looted Athens. True to form, in 85 BC Athens hailed Sulla as 'liberator' and reverted to Roman control under a pro-Roman oligarchy of a few wealthy Greek families. Virtually no decrees of its Assembly or Steering Committee are heard of for some twenty years.

MISSED TREASURES

Sulla looted happily away in Athens (and Epidaurus, Olympia and Delphi), but at least preserved the library of Aristotle and brought it to Rome, where the Greek grammarian Tyrannio (an ex-slave), who helped Cicero with his library, took charge of it. But Sulla did miss one hoard. In their assault on Piraeus in 86 BC the Romans had burnt down a warehouse. Assuming nothing was inside it, Sulla ignored it. In 1959 excavators found five superb bronze statues in the rubble (including two of Artemis, one of Apollo and one of Athena). The many excavated caches of coins buried for safe-keeping at this time indicate the fear felt among the Athenians at the prospect of Roman looting and reprisals.

ATHENS GETS THE ROMAN TREATMENT

Because of its status and reputation, Athens had long been favoured with benefactions from foreign rulers, as if it was as important to be represented there as it was at shrines like Olympia and Delphi. The Attalids (who modelled their culture on that of Athens) had been especially generous in financing impressive public buildings, and Antiochus IV, the Ptolemies and Mithradates had all chipped in. Now it was the Romans' turn. Pompey, Julius Caesar and Augustus gave gifts in cash or buildings and, when necessary, grain, as Athens always needed imports to feed its population. Roman streets, Roman brick and Roman buildings appeared there – a market-place, a temple inaugurating a cult of Augustus, and so on. Thirteen altars to Augustus could be found in the lower city, and statues of important Romans could be found everywhere. That is why visitors to Athens today find so much of it 'romanized'.

ROME'S CIVIL WARS

Sulla had dealt with Mithradates only for the moment, and Mithradates continued to cause trouble. In 66 BC Pompey the Great went out east to finish him off and, while he was about it, also to end the reign of Antiochus XIII, the king of Alexander's eastern empire. Roman civil wars followed: first between Pompey and Caesar (49–46 BC); then between Caesar's heir Octavian (later Augustus) with Marc Antony against Caesar's assassins Brutus and Cassius (42 BC); and finally, after a split, between Octavian, now ruler of the Roman West, and Antony and the last Ptolemy, Cleopatra, rulers of the Roman East (32–31 BC). This saw the end of the Ptolemaic dynasty and Rome's final major triumph over the heirs of Alexander the Great.

BATTLEGROUND GREECE

Greece came out badly from the Roman civil wars, largely because Pompey, through his conquests in the East, and later Antony, through his leadership over the Roman East, had their major bases there. So Greece saw much of the fighting, especially at Philippi (42 BC) and Actium (31 BC). In 45 BC Servius Sulpicius wrote to console his friend, the Roman statesman Cicero, on the death of his daughter Tullia by reflecting on the transience of things:

> I want to mention to you a circumstance which gave me
> no common consolation, on the chance of its also proving
> capable of diminishing your sorrow. On my voyage from
> Asia, as I was sailing from Aegina towards Megara, I began
> to survey the localities that were on every side of me. Behind
> me was Aegina, in front Megara, on my right Piraeus, on my
> left Corinth: towns which at one time were most flourishing,
> but now lay before my eyes in ruin and decay.

In 31 BC, when Antony's camp in Greece ran out of mules to bring in grain, Greek citizens were forced to carry sacks of their own grain 100 miles over the mountains to feed Antony's troops.

THE CRADLE OF CIVILIZATION

In 48 BC, after Athens had backed yet another loser in Pompey, Julius Caesar received its surrender and asked: 'How often will the glory of your ancestors prevent you from self-destruction?' Clearly Caesar reckoned that the Athenians were assuming, like Achilles in Shakespeare's *Troilus and Cressida*, that they could successfully rely on their (past) 'virtue' to 'seek remuneration for the thing it *was*'. This was a sound judgement. There always seemed to be someone who would bail the Athenians out. In 59 BC Cicero explained why. Athens, he said, was 'where men think that humanity, learning, religion... rights and laws were born, and from where they were spread all over the world'. No wonder the Romans and many others wanted to visit, look and learn there.

FIGHTING FOR PUPILS

Schools did not exist so much as individual professors, to whom new students attached themselves with extraordinary fanaticism. In Athens, for example, students kept watch at the harbour Piraeus to waylay incoming freshers. Since captains of these ships were frequently paid by a professor to deliver their cargo to him and no one else, landings would often take place at secret locations by night. Libanius (AD 314–93), who was eventually to become a professor at Antioch, tells of the stories he heard as a youth about 'the fighting between schools that took place in the heart of Athens: I had heard of the cudgels, knives and stones they used, the wounds, the court-actions, and the deeds of derring-do that students performed to raise the prestige of their professors'; and he admits to looking forward to joining in.

FADING GLORIES

Politically, the Greek world on the mainland and in Asia Minor was now under the generally light touch of the Roman empire. The cities paid Roman taxes and were obliged to allow troops to be stationed there as needed, but otherwise they ran their own internal affairs, with the assent of the Roman provincial governor. Athens remained an important philosophical centre, though it never again climbed the cultural and intellectual heights of its glory years in the fifth and fourth centuries BC; but its past stood it in good stead, and its thoroughly deserved educational reputation – notably for teaching the skills of persuasive speaking – ensured that it was a revered destination and could hold its head high in the Roman world. The emperor Hadrian (AD 117–38) in particular was a passionate Graecophile. His benefactions transformed Athens' skyline and can be found all over the Greek East.

FROM POETRY TO HISTORY

Theirs may have been a civilization in eclipse, but Greeks did not stop writing and thinking. A brief tour of some of the highlights would include:

The Greek Anthology is a collection of some 3,700 poems spread over 1,500 years, including epigrams, erotica, epitaphs, pederastica, satires, riddles and much more. It presents the whole conspectus, from the brilliance of great poets like Meleager and Palladas to the purest doggerel.

Sextus Empiricus (*c.* AD 160–210) wrote the definitive work on a type of sceptic philosophy which denied that firm knowledge about anything was possible: we should suspend judgement about the truth or falsehood of any proposition (compare Carneades, p. 344).

Christian thinkers engaged intensively with Greek philosophers (especially Plato), while **Greek scholars** wrote extensive and learned commentaries on, for example, Aristotle.

Novelists churned out adventure stories of virtue rewarded (e.g. Longus' *Daphnis and Chloe*, written in Lesbos, second century AD).

Pausanias (second century AD) wrote a highly detailed guidebook based on his extensive travels around central Greece and the Peloponnese. It went into very great detail. At one stage he reports coming across a small building consisting of oak columns and roof; the locals told him it was a memorial, but they had no idea to whom!

The most distinguished **scientist** was Claudius Ptolemy (second century AD), who lived in Alexandria (note 'Claudius': it was common for Greeks who were Roman citizens to adopt a Roman name). His three major works, highly influential on later Islamic and European science, were: the *Almagest*, a comprehensive survey of astronomy (*Almagest* is Arabic, coined on the Greek title *hê* ('the', Arabic *al*) *megistê* ('greatest') *suntaxis*, '[mathematical] treatise'); *Geographia*, building on Eratosthenes (see p. 333); and *Tetrabiblos* ('four books') on astrology.

The doctor **Galen** (AD 129– *c.* 216), working mostly in Rome, may have written in the region of 500 treatises. His surviving dogmatic, pugnacious and hugely influential works in Greek, together with those translated into Latin and Arabic (perhaps about a third of his total writings), make up about a *quarter* of all surviving ancient Greek literature! He covered anatomy, physiology, neurology (very good on stress), pathology and pharmacology, as well as philosophy and logic and the meaning of words (he points out that the Greek word for 'ostrich' suggests it is a cross between a sparrow and a camel). He thought playing catch was the best of all gymnastic exercises.

Lucian, a Syrian (second century AD), is one of the world's funniest satirists.

Historians, some writing in Latin, worked away as diligently as ever. We have major work surviving by Dionysius from Halicarnassus (first century BC; Rome to the First Punic War); Strabo (first century BC, from Pontus; worked in Rome, general encyclopedia of the ancient world); Diodorus (first century BC, from Sicily; from early Greece and Troy to Julius Caesar); Josephus (first century AD, worked in Rome; histories of the Jews), Plutarch (first and second centuries AD, born and worked in Chaeronea; essayist and biographer of famous Greeks and Romans); Appian from Alexandria (second century AD; Roman civil wars); Arrian (second century AD, born in Nicomedia; life of Alexander the Great); and Cassius Dio (third century AD, born in Nicaea; from Aeneas to AD 229). These all bear witness to a flourishing historical tradition.

Most influential of all, the **New Testament**, composed in *koinê* Greek by Jews between (roughly) AD 60–150, gave the world the stories of Jesus in the four gospels 'proving' he was the Messiah; the story of the early church in Acts of the Apostles; twenty-one 'letters' to churches by St Paul offering advice and instruction; and Revelation, prophecies and advice to seven churches in Asia Minor.

ROME'S ABSORPTION OF GREEK CULTURE

The other side of the coin was Greek influence on Rome, now the ruler of an empire of some 50 million people, stretching from Britain to Syria, and from the Rhine–Danube to North Africa and Egypt. The Romans had been in cultural contact with the Greeks from the third century BC, and in the second century BC had begun to take serious interest in their teaching of rhetoric, the key to success in a world dominated by the ability to persuade face to face in political and legal debating chambers.

Aware that Greeks were far ahead of them in numerous areas – architecture, medicine, astronomy, political theory, philosophy, literature, art – Romans began to work towards a version of Greek culture adapted to the Roman world. Some Roman generals were (surprisingly) happy for sculptors to depict them as nude as any Greek hero. Cicero and Varro were highly influential on the rhetorical, grammatical and philosophical side (hence Greek *philosophos*, Latin *philosophus*, English 'philosopher'; Greek *rhêtor*, Latin *orator*, and so on); Pliny the Elder on science and technology; Vitruvius on architecture; Celsus on medicine; and so on. Major poets such as Virgil, Lucretius, Catullus, Horace and Ovid all acknowledged their Greek indebtedness, while producing work that was unquestionably Roman. The result of all this was that the Romans preserved in Latin much Greek learning that would otherwise have been lost to us.

Paradoxically, Athens did not have a public (but non-lending) library till the second century AD ('Open from the first hour to the sixth', says an inscription). Rome's first public library was Julius Caesar's idea and constructed in 39 BC.

WESTERN ROOTS

Since Latin became the language of the church, and the church – founded in the Greek East with its New Testament composed in Greek – was the main medium of education, a powerful Graeco-Roman-Christian synthesis laid deep the West's cultural, intellectual and educational foundations. The Latin and Greek languages were also to have a profound influence on English, at root a Germanic language which was hugely enriched by Latin-based French after 1066 and by the import of Greek vocabulary during the classical revival from the fourteenth century.

Of all the major art forms, only ancient music left no impact on the West. Ironically, 'music' derives from ancient Greek *mousikê*, the product of the nine *Mousai* (Muses), goddesses of culture and memory. As the Greeks understood, you cannot have one without the other.

EPILOGUE

THE SURVIVAL OF GREEK LITERATURE

Virtually all of what we know about the ancient Greeks (and Romans) derives from works they wrote that have survived down the millennia. But how? And why? This epilogue looks at some of the answers. It is worth saying here: we have no original autograph manuscripts of anything. Everything that survives is a copy of a copy of a copy...

PAPYRUS SCROLLS

Papyrus, origin of our 'paper', was made from the stem of the papyrus plant, the main source of which was Egypt. The outer rind was first stripped off, and the sticky fibrous inner pith cut lengthwise into thin strips. These were laid side by side, and others laid across them at right angles; they were then hammered flat to form a sheet of paper, dried out and polished. The sheets were then united to form a scroll, which was between 10 and 22 feet (*c.* 3–7 metres) long; the maximum was twenty sheets to a scroll. It was an expensive operation.

These were the earliest form of 'book', and there was a flourishing trade in them in ancient Athens. But papyrus, being a vegetable, did not last long except in very dry conditions. Anything written on a papyrus scroll would not last down the generations unless it was continually copied and recopied by hand. Literature which became part of a school syllabus, for example, stood a good chance of survival, but most has been lost even so.

FROM BOOK TO VELLUM

In the first century AD Romans invented the book (called a *codex*), which was clearly far easier to use than a lengthy scroll that required constant rolling and unrolling. Anything that was not copied into book format did not survive in manuscript form (but see below). From the fourth century AD animal skins (vellum or parchment) became the 'paper' of choice. (The word 'parchment' apparently derives from 'Pergamum', where the Attalids started to use it in the third century BC.) Vellum lasts a very long time indeed. Anything not transferred to vellum did not survive in manuscript form either. By now education was in the hands of the church, which still understood the importance of pagan education, but modified it to suit Christian values. That also affected the choice of pagan literature allowed to survive. Poets like Archilochus (see p. 84) would obviously not find favour.

Vellum is reusable. The existing text can be scraped off and overwritten with another one. The result is a 'palimpsest', from the Greek *palimpsêstos*, 'scraped again'. Pagan texts were regularly overwritten in this way with Christian ones. Infra-red technology is now used to bring the original text to light.

THE GREEK HERITAGE IN PERIL

In the eleventh century AD Turkish peoples, converting to Islam, started moving west into Asia Minor. It slowly became clear that they would represent a serious threat to Greek libraries, the most important of which were in Constantinople (this was once the Greek city of Byzantium, rebuilt and renamed after the Roman emperor Constantine, and renamed Istanbul after the Turks eventually took it on 29 May 1453). So to preserve their Greek heritage, scholars and dealers set about getting hold of Greek manuscripts and bringing them to the West, across the Adriatic into Italy in particular. Because the collapse of the Roman empire in the West in the fifth century AD had left Europe essentially a Greek-free zone, this was one of the events that heralded the Greek revival in Western Europe (the renaissance, or rebirth, of classical culture).

Every Greek manuscript that survived all these changes into the fifteenth century, when Gutenberg invented movable type and mechanical printing, is available to us today.

THE ART OF EDITING

All writing was originally INCAPITALSWITHNOPUNCTUATION NOREALLYANDNOGAPSBETWEENTHEWORDSWELL IASKYOUTRICKYORWHAT. The smallest subdivision was the paragraph – a line in the margin. Scholars working in the Alexandrian Library, who were committed to preserving the classics, had to invent the art of editing (see p. 335). The Alexandrian editions of Greek texts, published with the authority of the Library behind them, became the original sources for virtually all later copies and were circulated throughout the ancient world. All our manuscripts of classical works are based on these editions. If these editors got them wrong... Happily for us, where pre-Alexandrian papyrus fragments of these works emerge from the desert, they mostly agree with our texts. Minuscule writing and full punctuation were developed from the sixth century AD. The Greek alphabet is the source of our own (via Latin) and of the Russian Cyrillic alphabet, named after St Cyril who invented it (ninth century AD).

THE TREASURE OF GIOVANNI AURISPA

In 1421 the young Sicilian manuscript dealer Giovanni Aurispa was on his way to Constantinople, looking to save the classics of ancient Greek literature from the Turks and bring them back to Italy. His friend Francesco Filelfo said in a letter to him, 'You're dedicated to dealing in books. I'd prefer you to be dedicated to reading them.' When, in 1423, Aurispa arrived back in Venice from his searches in the great libraries of Constantinople, he brought with him a treasure trove of no fewer than 238 manuscripts. They featured the great names of classical Greek literature – Aeschylus, Sophocles, Plato and many more.

To give two examples of the full picture: we have 190 manuscripts of Homer's *Iliad*, all written at some time from the tenth century AD onwards, and 457 papyri, some little more than fragments, going back to the third century BC, on which our modern printed texts are based. Of the tragedians, our modern texts of Euripides are based on 276 manuscripts and 54 papyri. All are kept in libraries in the West.

ATHENAEUS' GOLD-MINE

One of the most remarkable manuscripts that Aurispa brought back with him was Athenaeus' *Experts at Dinner* (*Deipnosophistai*). In about AD 200 Athenaeus, a rhetorician and grammarian, composed a lunatic, but wonderful, fifteen-book account of a dinner given over several days by a wealthy book-collector, Larensius, for twenty-four professors who sat round the table discussing everything under the sun. They bang away, unfolding their thoughts on a vast range of topics suitable for raising at any ancient (or modern) symposium – but particularly, food, drink and sex, interspersed with comments on music, songs, dances, games, luxury and discussions of literature, history and abstruse points of grammar.

The importance of Athenaeus' work is not only that it gives us the word *pornographos* ('one who depicts prostitutes') and a vast range of other information, but also that all his professors support their various theories about the questions in hand with quotations from Greek literature. As a result, some 1,250 authors are quoted together with around 10,000 lines of verse, some of it whole poems – and much of it survives in no other source.

So Athenaeus is a literary gold-mine. For example, no manuscripts of the great poetess Sappho survive – all that we have of her derives from fragments retrieved from the desert, or quotations in authors who did survive. Athenaeus is a major contributor in the latter category.

THE PATRON SAINT OF THE INTERNET

Another source of much otherwise lost information is the ancient encyclopedia. Bishop of Seville (AD 600–36), Isidore died before his *Etymologies*, an encyclopedia of all human knowledge in twenty books, was published. Written in simple Latin, it was all a man needed in order to have access to everything he wanted to know about the world but never dared ask, from the twenty-eight types of common noun to the names of women's outer garments: all information, sacred and secular, was there for the taking, in one handy volume. Across the West for

1,000 years, it was the standard work of reference for the Middle Ages, second only to the Bible, and one of the earliest printed books (1472). It was lifted from sources almost entirely at second or third hand, none of it checked, and much of it unconditional eyewash. No wonder the Vatican has made Isidore patron saint of the internet.

OXYRHYNCHUS: BURIED GEMS IN THE DESERT

If authors do not survive through a manuscript tradition or quotation in authors that do survive, they may survive in papyri dug up from the desert. Here is the story of one such papyrus dump and some of its finds.

In 1896/7 mounds near el-Behnesa in Egypt (ancient Oxyrhynchus) were chosen for exploration by a British team led by Bernard Grenfell and Arthur Hunt, two young Oxford graduates. They were after papyrus texts, which survive best under desert conditions, and on 11 January 1897 they dug up the Gospel according to St Thomas. The mounds – ancient rubbish tips – turned out to be rich beyond their wildest dreams: the world of Greeks in Egypt from the Ptolemies to the Romans revealed in all its glory and mundanity. When their dig ended in 1907, they had uncovered half a million pieces and scraps, which were all boxed up and dispatched to universities for decipherment and analysis. To date, they fill more than seventy volumes of the journal devoted to their publication; at least forty more are planned. The problem is that expert papyrologists are very thin on the ground: who knows what wonders lie in those boxes, still waiting to be deciphered? A couple of hitherto unknown poems by Sappho have recently emerged.

OXYRHYNCHUS: RUBBISH FINDS

When government offices in Egypt wanted a clear-out, they piled old accounts, tax returns, census material, etc. into wicker baskets and dumped them out in the desert. Citizens followed suit with their rubbish, and since papyrus was expensive, they used both sides to write on – a shopping list on one side, perhaps, a letter on the other. All this and more was revealed by the Oxyrhynchus finds: high poetry, vulgar farce, sales, loans, wills, contracts, tax returns, government orders, private letters, shopping lists, gospels and household accounts. They tell of a world distant from that of the Alexandrian Museum and Library, let alone Ptolemy's court.

OXYRHYNCHUS: THE WORKERS

Papyri from Oxyrhynchus give some idea of the range of occupations available in Egypt. In one single city block, eighteen properties are listed. The residents include two fishermen, one vegetable seller, and a man who worked in the cloakroom of the baths; a builder, a carpenter and a baker; a linen weaver, a dyer and an embroiderer. A rich commercial landscape emerges. Elsewhere one finds millers, butchers and fishmongers; masons, carpenters, plasterers and painters; potters and basket-weavers; goldsmiths and silversmiths; sailors and shipbuilders; barbers, hairdressers and undertakers; schoolteachers, lawyers and stenographers; donkey-drivers and mouse-catchers; prostitutes, athletes and entertainers.

OXYRHYNCHUS: IMPERIAL VISIT

The Roman emperor was soon to arrive in the town. Lavish preparations were made and harassed governors ('not once but many times have I sent you written notice...') ordered up meat, wine, bread, and bedding for troops and the imperial residence. Once arrived, the emperor would pass judgement on important local issues: one involved a pig-breeder who could not get the fodder he required.

OXYRHYNCHUS: OFFICIALDOM

There was serious money in being an official, since the efficient functioning of the state depended on writing. Roman Egypt was divided for administrative purposes into counties, regions and villages. Orders came from the top down; information and taxes from the bottom up. At every stage, paperwork was required. When there was a nationwide census, county officials would have to process about a million returns. When a minor official held court in a large town, he received 1,806 written petitions in two and a half days.

The system often broke under the strain. Here the Roman governor sent a letter to all owners of property, ordering them to re-register within six months because the property archive for the whole of Egypt had become out of date; here an archive building collapsed, taking many of its precious documents with it. The archive-keepers were held responsible and charged for its repair. For thirty-five years they fought the case.

OXYRHYNCHUS: SCRAMBLING FOR JOBS

It was common to scramble for lucrative jobs in Egypt through letters of introduction to powerful men. One addressed to the wealthy landowner Zenon read:

The bearer of this letter is well known to me. He wants employment in one department or another. Please get to know him and introduce him to all the right people, for his and my sake. He really is worthy of special treatment.

The army was equally attractive. A young man Aeschines, fuming that his mistress had abandoned him, decided to go on a voyage to forget it all. A friend suggested he joins Ptolemy's army:

If you really mean to emigrate, Ptolemy is the world's best paymaster. He's amusing, got taste, likes the ladies, is very courteous, knows who his friends are (and his enemies). If you are ready to put on your military gear, and courageous enough to plant both feet firmly on the ground and repel an enemy attack, Egypt is the place for you.

BLUFFER'S GUIDES

Another way in which ancient texts might survive is through summaries, or 'epitomes'. Around AD 855 – the date is uncertain – the 45-year-old Photius, soon to undergo his first stint as Patriarch of Constantinople, was invited to join a potentially dangerous diplomatic mission to the Arabs. Before he left, his brother Tarasius asked him to make a summary of all the books he had read. The result was Photius' famous *Bibliothêka* (Greek for 'library'): a bluffer's guide to no fewer than 280 books by a very large number of authors, ranging from classical Greek through Hellenistic and Roman imperial literature to the Byzantine period itself.

The importance of Photius' collection lies in the fact that about half of the books summarized are now lost: of the thirty-three historians Photius summarizes, twenty do not otherwise survive. Theology – given the domination of Christianity – takes up 43 per cent of the collection, but history, especially fabulous oriental history, Attic orators such as Lysias and Isocrates, and novelists such as Lucian frequently command his attention. Notable absentees are Plato, Aristotle, Stoics, Epicureans and *all* poets. Perhaps he was trying to tell us something – or perhaps they were too well known to require a review (he tells us he omitted 'works in common circulation').

The whole thing is a rag-bag, unsystematic in arrangement and content, with summaries running from half a page – for all nine books of Herodotus! – to over twenty pages for other works. The reason for this, as Photius tells us in the dedicatory letter to his brother, is that the pieces were arranged 'in the order in which our memory recalled each of them' and were, almost incredibly, composed from memory (he talks of the 'difficulty of achieving accurate recollection'). What giants they were then!

EMENDING THE TEXT

A scholar dealing with a manuscript or (even more acutely) a papyrus fragment encounters serious problems: straightening it out, mending it, ensuring it does not fall apart under examination, dating it from the style of the handwriting, decipherment (with all the problems of poor handwriting, odd conventions of spelling, plain bad spelling, holes caused by bookworm, blotches in the papyrus), transliteration into printable form, translation (if it is translatable), saying what the text is all about, determining authorship, emending the text where it makes no sense, and so on. Here is an illustration of just one sort of problem. The scribe of the fourteenth-century manuscript of Euripides that we call 'L' was copying out Euripides' *Hêraklês Mainomenos* ('Heracles Going Mad'). Heracles in a fit of madness has slaughtered his children and fallen asleep, and now he wakes up. His father Amphitryon is in attendance. It all starts sanely enough (*HM*, line 1,111):

HERACLES: Father, why are you weeping and veiling your eyes, retreating far from your dear son?

AMPHITRYON: My son! Still mine, for all the evil you have done!

HERACLES: What dreadful thing have I done to make you weep?

So far, then, pretty crisp stuff. The scribe was now faced with a reply by Amphitryon made up of the following run of letters:

AKANTHEÔNTISEIPATHOIKATASTENOI

This stumped him completely. It was all Greek as far as he was concerned. Well, there it was: his job was to split this line up into words. It was not his fault if they made no sense. Perhaps Euripides had gone briefly mad too – we all have our off days. This is how he did it (I add modern conventions of punctuation and the sound 'h' in Greek):

akantheôn tis, eipath', [h]oi katastenoi

This says: 'Of-the-spines [a-certain] one, say [all of you], whither may-it-groan' – an unimpressive reply to the question 'What dreadful thing have I done to make you weep?' He should have divided the letters up as follows:

[h]a k'an theôn tis, ei pathoi, katastenoi

This rather more appropriate answer means: 'Such things as one of-the-gods, if he-were-to-suffer [them], would-groan-at.'

Nevertheless, a word of praise for the hapless scribe. First, he did not quietly 'disappear' the line. Second, he did not attempt to emend the text. Had he done so, he may well have botched it beyond recovery. He copied out what he saw and moved on. Good for him.

ENDPIECE

In the famous chorus from his *Antigone* (see p. 185), Sophocles hymns the extraordinary imagination and inventiveness of man in mastering the natural world – navigation, agriculture, hunting, domestication, medicine – and in constructing a social one. Seemingly all-resourceful, death alone he cannot escape. But for all his admirable brilliance, the challenge of good or evil remains obstinately unresolved.

The chorus is printed here to clarify the steps in the argument. The Greek for 'fill one with awe' is one word – *deina*. It covers a range of meanings: 'fearful, dangerous, strange, wonderful, awesome, powerful, clever'.

Many things fill one with awe, but none more so than man!
He crosses the grey seas in winter storms, holding his course
    through the surges that open up the depths around him;
he wears away the immortal and inexhaustible Earth, the

highest of the gods, as his ploughs turn the soil with oxen,
  back and forth, year on year;

he captures the flocks of simple birds and the tribes of savage
  beasts and the watery brood of the sea, catching them in his
  woven nets – man, the skilful;

with his contrivances he overcomes the beasts of the country
  that roam the hills, and tames the long-maned horse with
  the yoke, and the tireless mountain bull;

he has taught himself speech, and thought quick as the wind,
  and the spirit that makes laws for cities, and shelter from
  frosts on inhospitable hills and sharp arrows of the rain
– all-resourceful man;

he meets nothing in the future without resource;

only from Hades shall he procure no refuge, yet he has plotted
  escape from desperate illnesses.

Ingenious above all expectation is his power of skilled
  invention; and with it he moves on, now to wickedness,
  now to nobility;

respecting the laws of the land and the oaths which the gods
  have sworn to uphold, he rises high in the city;

outcast from the city is he who, recklessly daring, devotes
  himself to evil.

(Sophocles, *Antigone*, 332–71)

That's the Greeks for you.

READING LIST

Alston, R., Hall, E. and Proffitt, L. (eds), *Reading Ancient Slavery* (Bloomsbury, 2011)

Austin, M. M., *The Hellenistic World from Alexander to the Roman Conquest* (Cambridge, 1981)

Barnes, J., *Aristotle* (Oxford, 1982)

Barnes, J., *The Presocratic Philosophers* (Routledge, 1982)

Barnes, J., *Early Greek Philosophy* (Penguin, 1987)

Beale, A., *Greek Athletics and the Olympics* (Cambridge, 2011)

Beard, M., *The Parthenon* (Profile, 2002)

Boardman, J., Griffin, J. and Murray, O. (eds), *The Oxford History of the Classical World* (Oxford, 1986)

Bradley, K. and Cartledge, P. (eds), *The Cambridge History of Ancient Slavery*, vol. 1: 'The Ancient Mediterranean World' (Cambridge, 2011)

Braund, D. and Wilkins, J. (eds) *Athenaeus and his World* (Exeter, 2000)

Brunschwig, J. and Lloyd, G. E. R. (eds), *Greek Thought: A Guide to Classical Knowledge* (Harvard, 2000)

Buxton, R., *The Complete World of Greek Mythology* (Thames and Hudson, 2004)

Camp, J. M., *The Archaeology of Athens* (Yale, 2001)

Cartledge, P., *Agesilaos and the Crisis of Sparta* (Bloomsbury, 1987)

Cartledge, P., *Ancient Greece: A History in Eleven Cities* (Oxford, 2009)

Cartledge, P., *Ancient Greece: A Very Short Introduction* (Oxford, 2011)

Cartledge, P., *After Thermopylae* (Oxford, 2013)

Chadwick, J., *Linear B and Related Scripts* (British Museum, 1987)

Chadwick, J., *The Mycenaean World* (Cambridge, 1976)

Clark, S. R. L., *Ancient Mediterranean Philosophy* (Bloomsbury, 2013)

Cline, E. H. (ed.), *The Bronze Age Aegean: c. 3000–100 BC* (Oxford, 2010)

Crouch, D. P., *Water Management in Greek Cities* (Oxford, 1993)

Davidson, J., *Courtesans and Fishcakes* (Harper Collins, 1997)

Deger-Jalkotzy, S. and Lemos, I. S. (eds), *Ancient Greece: From the Mycenaean Palaces to the Age of Homer* (Edinburgh, 2006)

Dowden, K., *The Uses of Greek Mythology* (Routledge, 1992)

Feeney, D., *Caesar's Calendar* (California, 2007)

Finley, M. I. and Pleket, H. W., *The Olympian Games: The First Thousand Years* (Chatto and Windus, 1976)

Finley, M. I. (ed.), *The Legacy of Greece* (Oxford, 1984)

Freeman, C., *Egypt, Greece and Rome* ([3rd edn] Oxford, 2014)

French, R., *Ancient Natural History* (Routledge, 1994)

Frost, F., 'Sausage and meat preservation in antiquity', *Greek, Roman and Byzantine Studies*, 40 (1999)

Garland, R., *The Piraeus* (Bloomsbury, 1987)

Garland, R., *Introducing New Gods* (Duckworth, 1992)

Gaskin, J., *The Traveller's Guide to Classical Philosophy* (Thames and Hudson, 2011)

Gere, C., *The Tomb of Agamemnon* (Profile, 2006)

Gere, C., *Knossos and the Prophets of Modernism* (Chicago, 2009)

Green, P., *Alexander to Actium* (Thames and Hudson, 1990)

Habicht, C., tr. D. L. Schneider, *Athens from Alexander to Antony* (Harvard, 1997)

Hall, J. M., *A History of the Archaic Greek World* (Blackwell, 2007)

Hanson, V. D. (ed.), *Hoplites: The Classical Greek Battle Experience* (Routledge, 1991)

Harding, P., *Androtion and the* Atthis (Oxford, 1994)

Harris, W. V., *Dreams and Experience in Classical Antiquity* (Harvard, 2009)

Joint Association of Classical Teachers, *The World of Athens* (Cambridge [2nd edn, rev. R. Osborne], 2008)

Jones, D. E. H., 'The Museum of Alexandria', *Smithsonian Magazine* (vol. 2, no. 9 [1971] and vol. 2, no. 10 [1972])

Jones, P., *The Intelligent Person's Guide to Classics* (Bloomsbury, 1999)

Jones, P., *Homer*: The Iliad, tr. E. V. Rieu, revised and with new introduction (Penguin, 2003)

Jones, P., *Vote for Caesar* (Orion, 2008)

Krentz, P., *The Battle of Marathon* (Yale, 2010)

Lane Fox, R., *The Classical World* (Penguin, 2005)

Lapatin, K., *Mysteries of the Snake Goddess* (New York, 2002)

Leroi, A. M., *The Lagoon: How Aristotle Invented Science* (Bloomsbury, 2014)

Lloyd, G. E. R., *The Revolutions of Wisdom* (California, 1987)

Murray, O., *Early Greece* (Fontana [2nd edn], 1993)

Naerebout, F. G. and Singor, H. W., *Antiquity: Greeks and Romans in Context* (Wiley-Blackwell, 2014)

Neils, J., *Ancient Greece* (British Museum, 2008)

Osborne, R. and Hornblower, S. (eds), *Ritual, Finance and Politics* (Oxford, 1994)

Osborne, R., *Greece in the Making: 1200–479 BC* (Routledge, 1996)

Osborne, R. (ed.), *Classical Greece* (Oxford, 2000)

Osborne, R. [see under 'Joint Association of Classical Teachers', above]

Osborne, R. (ed.), *Athenian Democracy* (London Association of Classical Teachers [LACTOR 5], 2014)

Parsons, P., *City of the Sharp-nosed Fish: Greek Lives in Roman Egypt* (Weidenfeld and Nicolson, 2007)

Pomeroy, S., Burstein, S., Donlan, W. and Roberts, J., *Ancient Greece* (Oxford, 1999)

Reden, S. von, *Money in Classical Antiquity* (Cambridge, 2010)

Rhodes, P. J., *A History of the Classical Greek World, 478–323 BC* (Blackwell, 2006)

Rood, T., *The Sea! The Sea! The Shout of the Ten Thousand in the Modern Imagination* (Duckworth, 2004)

Salmon, J. B., *Wealthy Corinth: A History of the City to 338 BC* (Oxford, 1984)

Scott, M., *From Democrats to Kings* (Icon, 2009)

Scott, M., *Delphi: A History of the Center of the World* (Princeton, 2014)

Sedley, D., *Creationism and its Critics in Antiquity* (California, 2007)

Shelmerdine, C. W. (ed.), *The Cambridge Companion to the Aegean Bronze Age* (Cambridge, 2008)

Shipley, G. and Salmon, J. (eds), *Human Landscapes in Classical Antiquity* (Routledge, 1996)

Smith, M. L., *Olympics in Athens 1896* (Profile, 2004)

Spivey, N., *Understanding Greek Sculpture* (Thames and Hudson, 1996)

Stoneman, R., *Land of Lost Gods* (Hutchinson, 1987)

Stoneman, R., *The Greek Alexander Romance* (Penguin, 1991)

Stoneman, R., *Athens: A Traveller's History* (Phoenix, 2004)

Stoneman, R., *Alexander the Great: A Life in Legend* (Yale, 2007)

Thonemann, P. (ed.), *Attalid Asia Minor: Money, International Relations, and the State* (Oxford, 2013)

Walbank, F. W., *The Hellenistic World* (Fontana, 1992)

Waterfield, R., *Athens: A History* (Macmillan, 2004)

Waterfield, R., *Taken at the Flood: The Roman Conquest of Greece* (Oxford, 2014)

West, M.L. (tr.) *Hesiod: Theogony, Works and Days* (Oxford, 1988)

West, M. L. (tr.), *Greek Lyric Poetry* (Oxford, 1993)

West, M. L., *Hellenica*, vol. 3 (Oxford, 2013)

Worthington, I., *Philip II of Macedonia* (Yale, 2008)

INDEX

Achaean League, 316, 342
Achilles, 45, 59–66, 296, 354
Actium, battle of, 353
actors, 186–7, 198, 220
  see also Artists of Dionysus
Aegeus, King, 16–17
Aegispotami, 232, 245–6
Aemillius Paullus, 346
Aeneas, 45
Aeschines, 251, 282–3
Aeschylus, 52, 138, 168–9, 335, 363
  Oresteia, 179–80, 187
  Persians, 142, 168, 187
Aesop's fables, 127–7, 317
Aethra, 16
Aetolian League, 316, 341
Agamemnon, 51–22, 59
  and Aeschylus' *Oresteia*, 179–80
  the 'face of', 67–8
Agesilaus, king of Sparta, 83, 257, 259, 271
Agis, king of Sparta, 83
agriculture, 12, 63, 80, 147–8, 158
Akrotiri, 9
Alaksandu, king of Wilusa, 25–6, 54
Alcibiades, 231–2, 235–7, 239, 245–7, 251
Alcmaeon, 173–4
Alcmaeonids, 104, 111–12, 124, 138–9
  curse of, 92–3, 135
Alcmena, 38
Alexander the Great, 281–2, 284–5, 295–307
  and Aristotle, 299–300, 307–8
  his death, 297, 303–4, 315
  destruction of Thebes, 289
  and Diogenes, 286
  divinity of, 302
  employment of mercenaries, 249
  and founding of Alexandria, 325–6
  legends of, 305–6
  his tomb, 304–5

Alexandria, founding of, 325–7
Alexandrian Museum and Library, 317–18, 330–1, 334–6, 366
alphabets, 35, 363
amnesties, 247
Amphipolis, 282
Anacreon, 137
Anaxagoras, 171
Anchialus, 298
animal intelligence, 128–9
Antigonus II Gonatas, king of Macedon, 315–17, 323
Antikythera, 350
Antioch, 336, 355
Antiochus I, King, 315
Antiochus III, King, 343
Antiochus IV, King, 321–2, 342–3, 349, 352–3
Antipater, 285, 306, 346
Apelles, 299
Aphrodite, 12, 36, 41, 45, 51, 107, 290
  and sacred prostitutes, 102–3
Apollo, 12, 42, 64, 66, 298, 352
  temple at Delphi, 90, 112, 218
Apollodorus, 292
Apollonius of Perga, 330–2
Appian, 357
Archelaus, king of Macedon, 275–6
Archestratus, 218
Archilochus, and erotic poetry, 78, 84–6, 98, 361
Archimedes, 330–2, 351
Areopagus, 91, 170, 180
Arginusae, 244
Argos, 58, 159
Aridane, 17–19, 45
Aristagoras, 141
Aristarchus of Samos, 330, 333
Aristides 'the Just', 169–70
Aristogeiton, 137
Ariston, 287
Aristophanes, 196, 220–3
  Clouds, 187, 221, 226–7, 251
  Lysistrata, 240–1
  Men from Archanae, 220–1

Aristotle, 307–12, 317–18
  Alexander the Great and, 299–300
  and athletes, 133
and biology, 308–9
  commentaries on, 356
  and definition of art, 208
  doctrine of the mean, 308
  and four-element theory, 172
  and grammar, 311–12
  his library, 352
  and marriage, 241–2
  and mercenaries, 249
  and the name 'Greeks', 79
  and Plato, 261–2, 264
  pseudo-Aristotelian works, 312, 322
  and rhetoric, 193
  and seat of intelligence, 334
  and size of the state, 70
  and slavery, 151–2
  and the soul, 310–11
  and Thales, 96
  and tyrants, 93, 100
  and virtue, 309–10
*arkhôn*s, 28–9
Arrian, 302–4, 358
Artaphrenes, 141
Artaxerxes, king of Persia, 232, 246, 248, 257
Artemidorus of Ephesus, 153
Artemis, 42, 352
  temple at Ephesus, 299, 346
Artemisia, of Halicarnassus, 163–4
Artemisium, 146, 162
Artists of Dionysus, 317, 322
Aryans, 68
Asoka, King, 321
Assurbanipal, king of Assyria, 298
astronomy, 332–3, 351
Athena, 46, 51, 135, 147, 180
  birth of, 42, 44
  and Odysseus, 52, 61, 66
  her robe, 323
  temples, altars and statues, 91, 111, 125, 163, 206–7, 352

Athenaeus, 363–4
Athenian Assembly
  appointment of officials, 190–1
  democratization of, 104,
    139–40, 149, 171, 188–90
  and execution of *stratēgoi*,
    244–5
  and legal system, 176–7
  and ostracism, 157
  rates of pay, 247
  and state religion, 160
Athens
  and Alcmaeonid curse, 92–3,
    135
  brothels, 107
  building on Acropolis, 111
  census results, 318
  classes of citizens, 104–5, 171
  declining power, 316–17
  defeated by Sparta, 104, 112,
    138–9
  defensive walls, 146, 150, 184,
    246, 257
  and Delian League, 146–7, 170
  development of democracy, 79,
    103–5, 111–12, 139–40, 147,
    149–50, 170–1, 188–93, 205
  dramatic festivals, 112, 125,
    167–9, 196
  early history, 45–6
  end of democracy, 307
  legal system, 170–1, 176–9,
    188–9
  and myths, 16–17
  the name, 46
  naming of tribes, 323
  naval power, 145–7, 149–50,
    157–60
  and oligarchies, 232, 246–7
  and Olympic Games, 40
  outbreak of plague, 184, 204–5
  public library, 359
  and revolt of Mytilene, 215–16
  romanization of, 352–6
  rule of law, 91–2, 105–6
  sacked by Persians, 146, 163,
    165
  schools, 355
  subjection to Rome, 342, 344,
    351–2
  taxation, 216–18
  water supplies, 107–8, 136
athletes, 114–17, 133
  and sex, 117
Atlantis, legend of, 9, 263–4

atomic theory, 208–9, 325
Atossa, queen of Persia, 168
Attalus I, king of Pergamum,
  315, 317, 323, 328, 341
Attalus III, king of Pergamum,
  349–50
Augeas, king of Elis, 38
Augustus, Emperor, 345, 349,
  352–3
Aurispa, Giovanni, 363

Babylon, 295, 297, 316, 327, 346
Bacon, Francis, 173
Bactria, 297
bankers, 260–1
barbarians, differentiated from
  Greeks, 94
Barnes, Jonathan, 307
Bede, 320
Bendis, cult of, 150
Bessus, 295, 297
Blegen, Carl, 11
boar's tusk helmets, 54
boxing, 37, 39, 115, 119, 166
brain, as seat of intelligence,
  173, 334
Brasida, 184
bronze, 7, 22, 27–8, 54
Brookes, William Penny, 274
brothels, 107
Brutus and Cassius, 353
Buddhism, 305, 321
bull-leaping, 10, 15
Butler, Samuel, 58
Byzantium, 78, 136, 283, 362
  see also Constantinople

Callimachus, 336
Calvert, Frank, 67
Candace, queen of Egypt, 306
Cape Gelidonya shipwreck, 22
Cape Matapan, 248
Carneades, 344
Carthage, 235, 341–2
Carystus, 146
Cassius Dio, 358
Cato the Elder, 344
Catullus, 359
Cecrops, 45–6
Celsus, 359
Celts, 317, 328–9, 350
Cephisodoros (slave-owner),
  152–3
ceramics, 24
Chabrias (athlete), 291

Chadwick, John, 12
Chaeronea, battle of, 279, 284–5
chariot-races, 37–9, 115, 124–5
Charmis, 39
child-bearing, 241–3
Chios, 58
chorus, in Greek drama, 187, 220
Churchill, Winston, 281
Cicero, 345, 351–2, 354, 358
Cimon, 146–7
Claudius Ptolemy, 356–7
clay tablets, 7, 11–15, 25, 27
Cleis, 99
Cleisthenes, 112, 139, 149, 193,
  307
Cleitus, 296, 302–3
Cleombrotus, 269
Cleomenes, King, 112, 139, 141
Cleon, 177, 215, 222–5
Cleopatra, 295, 349, 353
Clepsydra (prostitute), 289
Cnidus, 290
coinage, 78, 97–7
  Attic 'owls', 112
Colophon, 58, 132
Colossus of Rhodes, 337–8, 346
comedy, *see* drama
Conon, 245, 287
Constantinople, 326, 362–3
  see also Byzantium
contraception, 135, 243
Copernicus, Nicolaus, 332–3
copper, 5, 7, 22–3
Corcyra, 100, 183–4, 214
Corinth, 78, 100–1, 163, 184, 246,
  248, 291, 342
  sacred prostitutes, 102–3
Corinth Canal, 101–2
Cos, 290
Cotswold Olympics, 274
Coubertin, Baron Pierre de, 156,
  273–4
couriers, Persian, 154
Crannon, battle of, 306
Cratinus, 138
criminals, and punishments,
  212, 266
Critias, 195, 251, 247
Croesus, King, 106, 111, 113,
  120, 122–3, 299
Cunaxa, battle of, 248
Cupid and Psyche, 305
Cyclopses, 18, 41, 52, 61, 65
Cylon, 78, 91–3, 124
Cynics, 286–7

Cynoscephalae, battle of, 341
Cyrene, 248, 333
Cyrus I, king of Persia, 111, 113, 122–3, 153–4
Cyrus II, king of Persia, 232, 248, 257

Daedalus, 15–16
Darius, king of Persia, 113, 142, 145, 154–5, 158, 168
Darius III, king of Persia, 295, 296
dating systems, 318–20
Datis, general, 155
Decamnichus (assassin), 275–6
Decelea, 231
Delian League, 146–7, 170, 206
Delos, 342
Delphic oracle, 78, 89–91, 112, 138, 211, 298
    Artists of Dionysus and, 322
    King Croesus and, 122–3
    and *mania*, 161
    and Persian wars, 159–60
    Theagenes of Thasos and, 167
demes (villages), 139, 149
Demeter, 41, 85, 238
Demetrius (I), king of Macedon, 316–18, 330
Demetrius (II), king of Macedon, 316, 320–1, 323
Democritus, 195
Demodocus, 58
Demosthenes, 260, 279, 282–4, 287–8
Deucalion, 46
dialectic method, 211
Diem, Carl, 275
Dieneces, 83
dikasts, 177–8, 251, 292
dildoes, 241
Dinocrates, 326
Diocletian, Emperor, 320
Diodorus, 94, 328, 357
Diodotus, 215–16
Diogenes, 133, 286–7
Dionysia, 112, 125, 167–8, 179, 220
Dionysius of Halicarnassus, 357
Dionysius I of Syracuse, 82, 249
Dionysius II of Syracuse, 265
Dionysus, 12, 42, 45, 112, 125–6, 167, 322
Dionysus Exiguus, 320
doctors, 213–14, 334

see also medicine
donkey, diligent, 208
Dordona, oracle, at, 298
Dover, Robert, 274
Dracon, 91–2
drama, 167–9, 186–7, 203
    audiences, 198, 220
    festivals, 112, 125, 167–9, 196
    see also actors; chorus
dreams, 153
drinking habits, Persian, 154
Droysen, J. G., 295

earth, estimate of size, 333
eclipses, 95, 172, 195, 351
Egesta, 231, 235
Elatea, 284
elephants, 300, 327, 329
Eleusinian mysteries, 237–8
Empedocles, 153, 172, 174, 310
Ennius, 324
Epaminondas, 258, 269–71
Ephesus, 131, 153, 343
    temple of Artemis, 299, 346
Ephialtes, 147, 162, 170–1, 176
Epicureans, 316, 323–5
Epicurus, 323, 325
Epimetheus, 44
Episthenes (male lover), 285
epitomies, 368–9
Erasistratus, 334
Eratosthenes, 330, 333
etymology, 264
Euboea, 79, 183
Euclid, 330–1
Eumenes II, King, 343, 350
eunomia (good order), 82
Eupalinos' tunnel, 126–7
Euripides, 169, 196–8, 226, 276, 280
    Bacchae, 126, 187, 280
    Héraklês Mainomenos, 370–1
    manuscripts of, 335, 363, 370–1
    Medea, 196–8
Eurotas, river, 82
Eurybiades, general, 146, 163
Eusebius, bishop of Caesarea, 319
Evans, Sir Arthur, 5–6, 11, 18–20
exégétai (secular experts), 160
Ezekiel (tragedian), 321

Fates, the, 45
Filelfo, Francesco, 363
fire, 23–4

gifted to man, 43
First Macedonian War, 341
fish, 218–19
frescoes
    Minoan, 9, 17–19, 24
    Mycenaean, 18, 26
Freud, Sigmund, 204

Galatia, 328
Galen, 357
Garrett, Robert, 274
Gaugamela, battle of, 296
geometry, 330–1
gerousia (hereditary 'kings'), 83
Giants, 41
Gilgamesh, epic of, 65
Gilliéron, Émile, and his son, 19–20
Gladstone, William Ewart, 67
Gnathaena (prostitute), 289
gods
    birth of, 41–2
    existence and nature of, 194–6
    Homer and, 65–6, 132, 195
    and Linear B, 12, 28
    Xenophanes and, 132
Gospel of Thomas, 365
Graea, 79
grammar, 311–12
Granicus, battle of, 296, 303
Greek Anthology, 356
Greek language, 28, 316, 321, 336–7, 358–9
Greek literature, 335–6, 345, 356–8
    survival of, 360–72
Greeks (the name), 2, 79
Gylippus, 239

Hadrian, Emperor, 173, 355
Halicarnassus, 119, 163, 346, 3
57
Hannibal, 341, 343
Harmodius, 137
Hector, 59–60, 62–3, 66
Helen of Troy, 49, 51, 62, 67
helots, 79–81, 83, 170, 225–6
Hera, 41–2, 51, 126
Heracles, 38–9, 45, 77, 322
Heraclitus of Ephesus, 131–2
Hermes, statues defaced, 237
Hero, 334–5
Herodotus
    and Aesop, 127
    and beliefs, 132

compared with Thucydides,
  187–8
and Eupalinos' tunnel, 126
first historian, 113, 119–22
and freedom, 112
and the Greeks, 1
and King Croesus, 113, 120,
  122–4
and Persian wars, 36, 141–2,
  159, 163, 165
and Persians, 154
Photius' epitome, 369
and Pisistratus, 134–5
and Trojan War, 56, 120
Herophilus, 334
Herostratus, 299
Hesiod, 33–4, 40–5, 62, 65, 70–4,
  96, 104
and women, 73–4
hetairas, 290
Hieron of Syracuse, 116
Hipparchus, 112, 137–8
Hippias, 112, 137–8, 141, 155
Hippocrates, 173–6, 243
Hippodameia, 38
Hisarlik, 6, 24–6
excavation of, 67
and Trojan War, 53–4, 57
history, Greek idea of, 45–6, 50
Hittites, 7, 25, 54, 57
Homer, 49–66
Alexander the Great and, 296
and emergence of poleis, 69
and fighting in phalanxes, 87
and gods, 65–6, 132, 195
and homosexuality, 61–2
and honour, 62–3
identity of, 58
manuscripts of, 363
and oral poetry, 56–8
recitations of, 125
and similes, 63–4
and slavery, 151
translations of, 305
use of flashbacks and reminiscences, 203
and women, 62
and writing, 33
Homeridae, 58
homosexuality, 36, 61–2, 81,
  253–4, 284–5
see also pederasty
hoplites, 78, 87–9, 155, 183
Horace, 359
hubris, 287

humans, origins of, 42–4
humours, theory of, 174–6, 243
hypochondria, 334
Hysiae, Spartans capture, 234
hysteria, 243

infanticide, 244
interest-bearing loans, 97
Ionian revolt, 113, 141–2, 145
Iphigeneia, 52, 180
Isagoras, 112, 138–9
Isidas, described by Plutarch, 271
Isocrates, 287–8, 369
Isthmian Games, 111, 113
Ithaca, 58

Jason and the Golden Fleece, 45
Jerusalem, 322
Josephus, 357
Judas Maccabee, 322
Julius Caesar, 345, 352–4, 359

kebabs, 21–2
Keftiu, 10
Kepler, Johannes, 332
klepsydra (water-clock), 178–9
Knossos, 5–6, 10–11, 17, 19–20,
  54
krypteia, 83

Lamachus, 235, 239
Lamia, 306
Lampascus, 138, 245
Lampon (prophet), 171
Lang, Andrew, 64
Laocoon, 52
Laurium silver mines, 146, 152,
  157–8
League of Corinth, 280, 285,
  288–9
leitourgia (liturgy) system,
  216–18
Lenaea, 167
Leonidas, 146, 162
Leontiscus, the 'finger-breaker',
  115
Lesbos, 78, 98, 356
Leucippus, 95
Leuctra, battle of, 248, 258, 269
Libanius, 355
libraries, public, 359
Linear A, 6, 9, 11, 21
Linear B, 6, 10–12, 21, 26, 28, 35
  and Homeric language, 55, 64
  and oinops ('wine-dark'), 64

and record-keeping, 7, 56
Longus, 356
Louis, Spyridon, 274–5
Lucian, 195, 273, 357, 369
Lucretius, 359
Lycurgus, 77, 82–3
Lysander, 232, 245–6
Lysias, 151, 369

Macedon
Persian conquest of, 155
rise of, 279–81
Roman defeat of, 341–3
subjection to Rome, 349
Macedonian army, 281
Magna Graecia, 77–8
Magnesia, 169
Mantinea, battle of, 258, 271
Marathon, battle of, 145, 155–6,
  158
Marc Antony, 349, 353–4
Marcellus, 345
Mardonius, 146, 155, 165–6
marmor Parium, 318
marriage, ages at, 241–2
mathematics, 331–2
see also geometry
Mausoleum of Halicarnassus, 346
Maximus of Tyre, 118
medicine, 173–6, 213–14, 357
Megacles (I), arkhôn, 91–3, 124
Megacles (II), arkhôn, 112
Megacles (III), arkhôn, 135
Meleager, 356
Melos, 231, 233–4
Memnon, King, 45
mercenaries, 97, 159, 248–50
Messenia, 77, 79–80, 82, 88, 258
metal-working, 24
metics, 150–1, 318
migration, 77–8, 86
Miletus, 113, 141, 241
milk, 74
Miltiades, 145–6, 155
Minoan Crete
economy and record-keeping,
  12–13, 21
and eruption of Thera, 8–9
excavation and restoration, 11,
  18–20
gods, 12
Greek conquest of, 6, 10, 12
language, 11–12, 21
myths, 15–17
palaces, 17–18, 54

taxation, 13–14
textiles, 14–15
Minos, King, 5, 11, 15–17, 19, 45
Minotaur, 16–17, 19
Mithridates, king of Pontus, 349, 351–3
Mnesiphilus, 148
monkeys, 9, 20
More, Sir Thomas, 264–5
Morrison, Professor John, 164–5
Mount Athos peninsula, 158–9
Mount Ossa, 289
Mount Pentelikon, 208
mummification, 326
music, ancient, 359
Mycenae, 12, 18, 26, 54
  excavation of, 67
Mycenaean Greece
  conquest of Crete, 6, 10, 12
  conquest of Hisarlik, 24–6
  decline of, 26–7
  palaces, 17–18, 54
  shipwrecks, 22–3
Myrtilos, 38, 179
myth, nature of, 130–1
Mytilene, 184, 215–16

Napoleon Bonaparte, 299
Naxos, 17, 141, 146
Neaera (prostitute), 291
Nemean Games, 111, 113
Nero, Emperor, 102
New Testament, 336, 358–9
Newton, Isaac, 332
Nicias, 184, 224–5, 231, 235–7, 239
Nicomedes, king of Bithynia, 328
Nineveh, 327, 346

Odysseus, 49–52, 60–1, 65–6, 92
Oedipus, 90
Oinomaus, king of Pisa, 38
Old Testament, 321
olives and olive oil, 78, 82, 125, 135–6
  and contraception, 135, 243
Olympia, 37–8, 272–3, 282, 346
Olympiads (four-year periods), 319
Olympias, 165, 288
Olympias (trireme), 165
Olympic Games, 33–4, 37–40, 111, 113–19
  Alcmaeon and, 124
  and dating systems, 318–19

Diogenes and, 286
earliest winners, 39–40
marathon-running, 156–7
and the modern era, 273–5
and nudity, 39, 117–18
prizes, 113–14
victory poems, 102
Xenophanes and, 133
oral poetry, 56–8
Orestes, 52, 180
Oropus, Athenians sack, 344
Orsippus of Megara, 39
ostracism, 157, 169–70
ostrich eggshells, 9, 23
Ovid, 359
Oxyrhynchus, 365–8

palaces
  Minoan, 17–18, 54
  Mycenaean, 17–18, 54
palimpsest, 361
Palladas, 356
Panathenaic Games, 111–12, 124–5, 207, 291, 323
Pandora, 44
pankration, 37, 115–16, 118–19, 166
pan-scales, 22–3
Panthoidas, king of Sparta, 83
papyri, 327, 360–3, 365–6, 369
Paralus (trireme), 245–6
parchment, 361
Paris (Alexandros), 51, 53
Parmenides, 134
Paros, 78, 85, 318
Parrhasius, 272
Parthenon, building of, 183, 205–8
Pasion, 151, 261
Pasiphae, 15–16
patents, 134
Pausanias, king of Sparta, 247
Pausanias (assassin), 288
Pausanias (travel writer), 206, 273, 356
pederasty, 81, 118, 253–4
Pelopidas, general, 260
Peloponnesian League, 80
Pelops, 38
perfumes, 13, 23–4, 327
Pergamum, 315, 317, 336, 343, 349
Periander, tyrant of Ambracia, 254

Periander, tyrant of Corinth, 78, 100–1
Pericles, 147, 150, 168, 171, 223
  and building of Parthenon, 183, 205–6
  Funeral Speech, 200–2
  and Peloponnesian war, 183–4, 199–200
  and power of persuasion, 191–2
  prosecution of, 191
perioikoi ('neighbours'), 80–1
Persepolis, 297
Perseus, king of Macedon, 342
Persian empire, 153–4
  Alexander the Great's invasion, 295–304
Pétau, Denis, 320
Phaestos, 5, 10
Phalerum, 145
phalloi, 126, 329
Phano (prostitute), 291
Pharos lighthouse, 326, 346
Pheidippides, 156
Pherecydes, 36
Philetaerus, king of Pergamum, 315, 317
Philip II, king of Macedon, 83, 189, 279–85, 301, 336
  assassination of, 288, 295
Philip V, king of Macedon, 317, 323, 341–2
Philippi, battle of, 353
Phillidas, 260
philoi ('friends'), 74
philosophy
  beginnings of philosophy, 94–6, 131–2, 134
  causes and meanings, 171–2
  four-element and humour theories, 172–6
  see also Cynics; Epicureans; sophists; Stoics
Phocaea, 78
Phocians, 162, 282
Phoenician script, 35
Phormio, 261
Photius, patriarch, 368–9
Phryne (*hetaira*), 290
Phrynichus, 142, 164, 168
Phrynion, 291
pigs, 72
Pindar, 102, 289
Piraeus, 97, 145, 149–50, 165, 199, 246–7, 352, 355

Pisistratus, 111–12, 125, 134–6
Plataea, battle of, 146, 165–6
Plataea, Theban assault on, 184,
    198–9
Plato, 261–9
    and Aristotle, 307, 311
    and Athenian diet, 219
    and athletes, 133
    and Atlantis, 9, 263–4
    cave analogy, 262–3
    Christian thinkers and, 356
    and definition of man, 286
    and democracy, 82, 266–7
    and Diogenes, 286
    and education, 265, 268–9
    and etymology, 264
    and *eunomia*, 82
    and the Greeks, 1
    and homosexuality in the
        military, 285
    manuscripts of, 363
    and punishments, 266
    and size of the state, 69–70,
        265–6
    and Socrates, 211, 251–3,
        261–2, 264
    and sophists, 148, 194
    and the theatre, 198
    theory of Forms, 262
    and utopias, 264–6, 287
Pliny, 299, 333, 358
Plutarch
    and animal intelligence, 128
    and causes and meanings,
        171–2
    and death of Alcibiades, 246–7
    and the Delphic oracle, 161
    and Demosthenes' cowardice,
        284
    description of Isidas, 271
    and diligent donkey, 208
    and homosexuality, 81, 285
    and the theatre, 198
    and Themistocles, 148–9
    and tourism at Delphi, 273
poetry, and early literature, 36
poleis
    defence of, 78, 81, 87, 147–8
    emergence of, 28, 57, 69–70,
        78–9
    numbers and size of, 69–70
    and rule of tyrants, 78, 91, 93
    and state religion, 66, 160
Polus (actor), 322
Polybius, 342

Polycrates of Samos, 126
Pompey the Great, 349, 352–4
Popillius Laenas, 343
pornographos, 364
Poseidon, 15-16, 41, 46, 65, 125
Potidaea, 184
pottery
    Athenian black-figure, 111,
        129–30
    Corinthian, 111, 129
    and pederasty, 254
    styles of, 8, 24
Praxiteles, 290
Priam, King, 51, 53, 59, 62–3
    'Priam's treasure', 67–8
priests, role of, 40
Prodicus, 195
Prometheus, 42–6
prophêtai (interpreters), 90
proskunêsis (obeisance), 302
prostitutes, 289–91
    sacred, 102–3
    see also brothels
Protagoras, 194–5, 262
Protogenes, 320–1
Proto-Indo-European, 34–5
psephology, 178
Ptolemy I, 304–5, 317, 326, 330
Ptolemy II, 317, 329–30
Ptolemy III, 333, 335, 337
Ptolemy IV, 323
Pushkin Museum, 68
Pydna, battle of, 342
Pylos, 11, 14, 26–7, 58, 223
Pythagoras, 310
Pythia, 90, 161
Pythian Games, 111, 113, 133,
    291, 318

Quintus Curtius, 297

religion, nature of Greek, 66
retail trade, invention of, 123–4
retsina, 22
rhetoric, 192–3, 287–8, 358
Rhodes, siege of, 320–1
    see also Colossus of Rhodes
Roman literature, 336, 345
Rome, founding of, 320
Roxane, princess, 297, 301

sacrifice, 43, 66, 90
    human, 27
St Augustine, 107
St Cyril, 363

St Isidore of Seville, 364–5
St Mark, 305
St Paul, 103, 358
Salamis, battle of, 146, 158,
    162–5, 168, 170
Samos, 126–7, 184, 200, 240,
    322–3
Sappho, 78–9, 98–100, 364–5
Sardis, 113, 123–4, 142, 154, 343
sausages, 72
Schliemann, Heinrich, 54, 67–8
sculpture, 118, 272, 358
seal-stones, 9–11, 15, 24, 26
Second Macedonian War, 341
Second Punic War, 341, 345
Seleucus, 315, 343, 349
Selinus, 235
Semele, 126
Servius Sulpicius, 353
Seven Wonders of the World,
    346
Sextus Empiricus, 356
sheep, and wool production,
    14–15
shipwrecks, Mycenaean, 22–3
Simonides, 137–8, 162
Siphnos, 157
Siwah, oracle at, 296, 298–9, 304
slaves, 151–3, 178, 318
Smyrna, 39, 58
snake goddess, chryselephan-
    tine, 20
Socrates, 210–12
    and Alcibiades, 237
    and Aristophanes' *Clouds*, 221,
        226–7
    and Athenian Assembly, 244
    and Diogenes, 286
    and sophists, 148
    and Stoics and Epicureans, 324
    trial and execution, 232, 250–3
    Xenophon and, 248
Sogdia, 297
solecism, 337
Solon, 79, 92, 103–7, 123, 139,
    148, 171, 176
sophists, 148–9, 193–5, 197, 207,
    209–11, 262, 283
Sophocles, 169, 238
    Antigone, 185–6, 371–2
    manuscripts of, 335, 363
    Oedipus Turannos, 202–4
soul (*psukhê*), 310–11
Sparta, 79–84
    and brevity of speech, 83–4

defeat of Athens, 104, 112,
  138–9
emergence of, 69, 77, 79–80
fear of helot revolt, 225–6
food, 82
gerousia, 259
and Messenia, 77, 79–80, 88
and Olympic Games, 39–40
order and discipline in, 82–3
population collapse, 270
professional army, 80–1
women in, 81, 84
Spartiates, 80–1, 83, 166, 184,
  223–4, 259, 269
Sphacteria, 184, 223–4
Stephanus, 291–2
Stoics, 311, 316, 323–5, 344
Strabo, 357
stratêgoi
  condemned to death, 191
  election of, 105, 140
sukophantai, 105–6
Suleiman the Magnificent,
  Sultan, 338
Sulla, general, 352–3
summakhia ('fighting together'),
  258
sundials, 172
supplication, 92
Susa, 154, 168, 297
swastikas, 16, 68
swearing, 223
Sybaris, 134
symposia, 137–8, 280, 302, 364
Syracuse, 39, 77, 231, 239, 345

Tarsus, 298
terebinth, 23
Thales of Miletus, 78, 96, 131
Thasos, 147, 166–7, 170
Theagenes, 166–7
Thebes, 12, 26–7, 39, 159, 246,
  257–8, 260, 269–71
  destruction of, 289
  the 'Sacred Band', 284–5
Themistocles, 145–9, 157, 160,
  162–4, 169
Theophrastus, 220
Thera (Santorini), eruption of,
  6, 8–9, 263
Thermopylae, 83, 146, 162–3,
  183

Theseus, 16–18
Thessaly, 39, 183, 282, 289
Thetis, 45, 50, 59–60
Thibron, 248
Third Macedonian War, 342
Thrace, Persian conquest of, 155
Thrasyllus, 150
Thucydides, 171
Thucydides (historian)
  admiration for Pericles, 192,
    202, 205
  and battle of Syracuse, 239–40
  and capture of Hysiae, 234
  and child-bearing, 242
  and Cleon, 223–5
  compared with Herodotus,
    187–8
  description of the plague,
    204–5
  and expedition to Sicily, 235–7
  and Melian debate, 233–4
  and naked athletes, 39
  and Peloponnesian war, 184,
    198–9, 214–16, 233–7,
    239–40, 246
  and revolt of Mytilene, 215–16
  and Themistocles, 149
timê (honour), 62–3
Tiryns, 12, 26, 54
Titans, 41
tourism, 273
tragedy, *see* drama
treason, 108, 238
triremes, 78, 97–8, 146, 160, 183,
  217, 219, 224
  and revolt of Mytilene, 215–16
  and *The Times* debate, 164–5
Troezen, 16–17
Trojan War, 45, 50–8, 65, 120,
  296
Troy, excavation of, 67
Tullia (Cicero's daughter), 354
Tyrannio, 352
tyrants, 78, 91, 93, 100–1
Tyrtaeus, 78, 88

Uluburun shipwreck, 22–3

Varro, 358
Ventris, Michael, 12
Virgil, 52, 359
Vitruvius, 359

Waugh, Evelyn, 19
Wenlock Olympic Games, 274
Williams, Gardner, 274
Wilusa, 25–6, 53, 57
women
  and Aristophanes' *Lysistrata*,
    240–1
  and child-bearing, 242–3
  creation of, 44
  in Herodotus' histories, 120
  Hesiod and, 73–4
  Homer and, 62
  marriage and property, 241–2,
    244
  poets, 99
  Spartan, 81, 84
writing tablets, 23

Xenophanes, 132–3
Xenophon, 98, 232, 245, 248–50,
  285
  Anabasis, 249–50
Xenophon of Corinth, 102
Xerxes, king of Persia, 145–6,
  158–9, 163–5, 168

Zeno, 323
Zenodotus, 336
Zenon (landowner), 367
Zeus
  averter of flies, 39
  and birth of Dionysus, 126
  and creation of woman, 44
  emerges as top god, 34, 41–2,
    66
  god of supplication, 92
  and justice, 44–5
  Olympian Zeus, 37–9, 112
  statue at Olympia, 346
  tricked by Prometheus, 43
  and Trojan War, 50–1
  and the weather, 195–6
Zeus Ammon, oracle of, 296,
  298–9
Zeuxis, 272, 280
Zopyrus, 210

A NOTE ON THE AUTHOR

Peter Jones was educated at Cambridge University and taught Classics at Cambridge and at Newcastle University, before retiring in 1997. He has written a regular column, 'Ancient & Modern', in the *Spectator* for many years and is the author of various books on the Classics, including the bestselling *Learn Latin* and *Learn Ancient Greek*, as well as *Reading Virgil's* Aeneid *I and II*, *Vote for Caesar* and *Veni Vidi Vici*.